Five Laterals

and

a Trombone

CAL, STANFORD, AND THE WILDEST ENDING IN COLLEGE FOOTBALL HISTORY

Five Laterals

and

a Trombone

CAL, STANFORD, AND THE WILDEST ENDING IN COLLEGE FOOTBALL HISTORY

Tyler Bridges

TRIUMPH
BOOKS

Library of Congress has catalogued the previous edition as follows:

Names: Bridges, Tyler, author.

Title: Five laterals and a trombone: Cal, Stanford, and the wildest ending in college football history / Tyler Bridges.

Description: Chicago, Illinois: Triumph Books, [2022] | Includes bibliographical references.

Identifiers: LCCN 2022022489 (print) | LCCN 2022022490 (ebook) | ISBN 9781637271155 (hardcover) | ISBN 9781637271179 (epub)

Subjects: LCSH: California Golden Bears (Football team)—History. | Stanford Cardinal (Football team)—History. | University of California, Berkeley—Football—History. | Stanford University—Football—History. | Sports rivalries—California. | BISAC: SPORTS & RECREATION / Football | HISTORY / United States / State & Local / West (AK, CA, CO, HI, ID, MT, NV, UT, WY)

Classification: LCC GV958.U518 B75 2022 (print) | LCC GV958.U518 (ebook) | DDC 796.3309794—dc23/eng/20220624

LC record available at https://lccn.loc.gov/2022022489

LC ebook record available at https://lccn.loc.gov/2022022490

This book is available in quantity at special discounts for your group or organization. For further information, contact:

Triumph Books LLC
814 North Franklin Street
Chicago, Illinois 60610
(312) 337-0747
www.triumphbooks.com

Printed in U.S.A.
ISBN: 978-1-63727-480-4
Design by Nord Compo
Cover design by Preston Pisellini

To the 80,000 or so fans, players, band members, journalists, university employees, and others at the 1982 Big Game at Cal's Memorial Stadium.

And to my late father Richard, a 1953 graduate of Stanford's law school, and to my daughter Luciana, who is scheduled to graduate from Stanford in 2025.

CONTENTS

FOREWORD

As far back as I can remember, I liked to throw things. When I was a kid, I threw dirt clods and snowballs at telephone poles and cars. I graduated to throwing baseballs and footballs and shooting basketballs. However, as Tyler Bridges relates in Chapter Three, I didn't get to throw the ball much in ninth grade in Pullman, Washington, because our team ran the single-wing offense. I've often wondered what would have happened if we hadn't moved to Granada Hills when my dad Jack was hired to be the head coach at Cal State Northridge. Jack Neumeier, my new coach at Granada Hills High School, ran an innovative offense that threw the ball on nearly every down. I was in heaven.

When I was a senior, I narrowed my choices to Stanford, USC, and San Jose State, where my dad then served as the head coach. I decided against USC, however, because they were Tailback U. From when my dad coached at Washington State, I had always wanted to play in the Pac-10. That gave Stanford an edge. But how could I say no to my dad at San Jose State? I idolized him, and he was my best friend. But my mom Jan intervened. She said I should go to Stanford because they offered such strong academics. My Stanford degree would help me whether or not I played professional sports, she said. Rod Dowhower, who had just replaced Bill Walsh as the head coach, said I could run Bill's West Coast offense at Stanford. Jim Fassel, the offensive coordinator, was the closer. He said that Stanford was Quarterback U with all the great quarterbacks in recent years—Jim Plunkett, who won the Heisman, Mike Boryla, Guy Benjamin, Steve Dils, and Turk Schonert.

The thing I remember about Stanford is that students were as important as the athletes. Football interested the student body, but it wasn't the most important thing. The university really did make you be a part of the student body. I majored in economics and gained some of the tools and skills that helped me later with the restaurants and car dealerships that I now own.

At a lot of schools, the athletes get isolated by having their own living and eating facilities. That didn't happen at Stanford. I enjoyed playing football—and baseball during my freshman and sophomore years—but I also enjoyed being a student. It was nice to have the crossover. That's part of what's great about the Stanford experience. You could play high-level football but also have the high-level experience of going to school there and being around quality people. I still look back at the guys I went to school with—and it's amazing the success they've had.

The only disappointment was we didn't have the success we wanted to have on the field, though we won a lot of big games. The problem was we didn't play with a lot of consistency. Still, there were a lot of good football players, including running backs Mike Dotterer and Vincent White and several guys who made their mark in the NFL: tight end Chris Dressel, linebacker Garin Veris, linebacker Dave Wyman, and wide receiver Emile Harry. I still have good buddies that I was teammates with—Dennis Engel, Rob Moore, Ken Orvick, Don Lonsinger, Mike Tolliver, and Kenny Margerum are just a few of them.

Paul Wiggin, the head coach, was a good man who really cared about his players. Besides Fassel, several of our assistant coaches went on to become head coaches in the NFL: Denny Green, George Seifert, and Ray Handley. I was especially close with Fassel since he was the offensive coordinator. I give him a lot of credit for my success because of the techniques and discipline he taught me, including the precise steps to take while dropping back. Getting your footwork right is really important.

Tyler's book, of course, focuses on the 1982 Big Game. First, let me say that Cal versus Stanford is one of the great all-time rivalries in college football. It's played every year, there are lots of traditions associated with it, and the two schools are only 40 miles apart.

I haven't been able back to make it to the Bay Area for a Big Game in a long time. But even now, when I run into friends from Cal, I jokingly call them "Dirty Golden Bears." Of course, they have a few choice names for me. Old traditions die hard! Jokes aside, it's always been a respectful rivalry.

At the beginning of the season, we always circled that game on the schedule and wanted to win it and the Axe. We knew that winning the 1982 Big Game wouldn't be easy for us, of course. Gale Gilbert was on his way to becoming a top quarterback, and John Tuggle was a tough runner. I was most concerned with their defense, especially Rich Stachowski, Gary Plummer, and Reggie Camp on their front line. Ron Rivera at linebacker was their leading tackler, someone you had to pay attention to on every down. He was especially strong against the run, but he could also rush the passer and drop into coverage.

Winning the Big Game meant something extra in 1982 because if we won, we'd go to the Hall of Fame Bowl. Back then, no matter what bowl you went to, it meant something because there were so few of them. Plus, if we lost, it would be my last collegiate game.

It was a typical hard-fought Big Game. Late in the contest, it looked like we were going to lose. We faced fourth and 17 on our own 13-yard line, were down by two points, and had only 53 seconds left. The odds were clearly not in our favor at that point. But I received great protection and was able to complete a pass to Emile that kept the drive alive. We kept the chains moving, and then Mark Harmon kicked what we thought was the game-winning field goal. We were so excited. We had beaten our big rival, and it also meant I'd get to extend my college career and play with my buddies one more time in the bowl game.

And then one historic play took it all away from us. We couldn't believe it. We were stunned. Within a three-minute span, my teammates and I went from reaching the highest of highs to plunging to the lowest of lows. I never went through an emotional roller coaster like that in my entire career at Stanford or with the Denver Broncos. Still, time does heal wounds and provide perspective. I've been fortunate enough to play in more Super Bowls than most. I guess it all evens out.

*—**John Elway** graduated from Stanford in 1983 as the NCAA career leader in completions and he was second in total offense and third in touchdown passes. The No. 1 pick in the 1983 NFL Draft, he went on to play 16 years for the Denver Broncos. After three losses in the Super Bowl, Elway capped his career by winning the NFL title in his final two seasons and was inducted into the Pro Football Hall of Fame in 2004. Elway served as the Broncos' general manager for a decade, during which they won Super Bowl 50 against the Carolina Panthers.*

FOREWORD

Along with my family, football has been at the center of my life. My introduction to the game came when I was in second grade at Fort Meade, Maryland. My father Eugenio, a career Army officer, was stationed there. It was just pee-wee football, but I took to it. Over time, as my father was transferred to new bases, my three brothers, all terrific athletes, were my best friends and my best teammates. And I could always count on the support of my mother Dolores.

Life can be funny. As Tyler Bridges writes in Chapter Seven, when I was a senior at Seaside High School near Carmel, California, I almost decided to go to Stanford. But I made the right choice in the end. Cal was the perfect place for me. I liked being a student-athlete, playing for a high quality football program but being able to mix with the student body and have good conversations with professors.

I'll never forget what professor Harry Edwards, a noted civil rights activist and sociologist who often worked with athletes, told me. "Don't let football be your identity," he said. "Let football be the vehicle to move forward in life."

Roger Theder was the head coach when I came to Cal. I had a great deal of respect for him and was upset when he was fired after my sophomore year. Joe Kapp was hired to replace him. Coach Kapp was a big name, of course. He had a Hispanic background, just like me. My mom's older brothers had played football against him in Salinas when they were growing up. Coach Kapp always stressed the importance of graduating from Cal. I did that in four years and majored in social science.

I had a great group of teammates at Cal, especially on defense. In 1982, the front line consisted of Rich Stachowski, Gary Plummer, and Reggie

Camp. The linebacking corps may have been the strongest unit on the team: Eddie Walsh, Chris Hampton, Tim Lucas, Rich Dixon, and Paul Najarian.

Our defensive backfield consisted of John Sullivan, Ahmad Anderson, Kevin Moen, Fred Williams, Gregg Beagle, Jimmy Stewart, Clemont Williams, and Richard Rodgers. Richard, who handled the ball twice on The Play, has been one of my coaches with the Carolina Panthers and again with the Washington Commanders. He's a special guy.

We started off well during the 1982 season and were 6–4 heading into that year's Big Game against Stanford. Tyler does a great job of telling the story of that day, so I won't say much here. It was a big deal playing against John Elway, who at the time was considered perhaps the greatest college quarterback ever. (A quick digression: I intercepted John in 1987 in my first start as a strongside linebacker for the Chicago Bears. I dropped into the flat and sloughed into the hole. He never saw me. I still have the ball.)

I'll never forget the scene in the locker room after our amazing victory in the 1982 Big Game. It was a total team effort. You've never seen such a joyous group of guys. And we could hear the huge crowd outside yelling their support for us. Afterward, I walked with my mom and dad on Bancroft Avenue along fraternity row to where they had parked. All the students were whooping it up. I laugh as I think about it today: my dad went into the SAE house, told them I was his son, and came out with two beers—one for me, the other for him!

I had a good senior year in 1983. I'll never forget that after the last home game that year Coach Kapp pulled me into the equipment room. He brought out a bottle of tequila and poured each of us a shot. It was his way of letting me know how much he appreciated me.

I can thank Cal for so many things. The most important was meeting Stephanie Tamayo, a point guard on the women's basketball team. We met in August 1983 when I was a senior, and we clicked right away. She's been with me every step of the way since then.

Stephanie insisted that I go into coaching after my playing career ended in Chicago and I had spent several years working for a local TV station. I've really enjoyed being back in football. Coaching has given me the chance to compete on the playing field and to try to impart life lessons off of it, as Coach Kapp; Ron Lynn, the defensive coordinator at Cal; and other coaches did for me. I've tried to be a leader of men in good times and bad times, and I've tried to instill a sense of family on the team.

I always tell my players there are three things they can control: your attitude, your preparation, and your effort. If you want something, you've got to go get it. They're not going to send a limo.

Along the way, I've had coaches and players who were part of all the big-name college football rivalries. I think all of them pale in comparison to the one between Stanford and Cal. The two schools are among the best academic institutions in the country, they run quality athletic programs, and they are separated by only 40 miles.

To us at Cal, it was good versus evil. It was the Jedi versus the Empire. It was the public school kids versus the private school kids. And a hell of a trophy was at stake every year. We played for the Axe.

But there is a mutual respect among players at each school. You knew how hard it was to get into the other institution. It's not a bitter rivalry. It's almost like playing against your brothers. You want to beat them badly. But you can be friendly afterward.

Over the years, I've seen some great last-minute heroics: guys laying out for catches or making interceptions or blocked kicks. The Play is as iconic as it gets. It still means a lot, and it goes back to what Joe Kapp said: "The Bear will not quit, the Bear will not die." Or as Yogi Berra said: "It ain't over till it's over."

—Ron Rivera graduated from Cal in 1984 after having led the Bears in tackles during his sophomore, junior, and senior seasons. Drafted in the second round by Chicago, he played linebacker for the Chicago Bears for nine years. He served as an assistant coach for the Chicago Bears, Philadelphia Eagles, and San Diego Chargers before being named head coach of the Carolina Panthers. They lost Super Bowl 50 to the Denver Broncos. Rivera has been the head coach of the Washington Commanders since 2020.

CHAPTER 1

THE 1980 BIG GAME— THE PRELUDE

Stanford quarterback John Elway made his distinctive pigeon-toed walk back to the line of scrimmage and put his hands under the center. It was November 22, 1980. More than 78,000 fans crammed into Cal's Memorial Stadium in Berkeley were watching a hard-fought battle between two storied universities separated only by 40 miles and the San Francisco Bay. The Cal Bears led by a touchdown, but their lead was not safe. Elway, only a sophomore, was already establishing a reputation for engineering game-winning drives. He had brought Stanford to Cal's 6-yard line with only 1:15 left in the game. But now it was fourth down. Could Elway produce the score? The packed stadium sensed that the game had come down to this one play.

The excited crowd couldn't know then that what they were watching was a dress rehearsal for an even more dramatic ending to the Cal–Stanford game two years later in 1982.

First things first, however. The 1980 match marked the 83rd edition of the oldest football rivalry west of the Mississippi. Both schools were top ranked, but with distinct origins. Founded in 1868, the University of California at Berkeley was California's first land-grant university, a public institution. Leland Stanford Junior University opened its doors 23 years later in 1891, founded by grief-stricken parents and named after their only son, who died of typhoid fever at age 15. The boy's father, Leland Stanford Sr., made a fortune as a railroad tycoon and went on to be elected governor of California and then as a senator. Leland Sr. and his wife Jane Stanford created the university on land that had been a family farm adjoining the town of Palo Alto. Stanford was a private university.

Students at the two schools decided to play their first football game in 1892, just a year after Stanford opened. The organizer from Stanford was the manager of the football team, an undergraduate named Herbert Hoover, who would become president of the United States. He and the Cal manager printed 10,000 tickets for a match to be held in San Francisco. But when 20,000 fans showed up, Hoover and his Cal counterpart were left scrambling to collect admissions. That was one problem. Another was that no one brought a football. A man who owned a sporting goods store galloped off by horse to find one, delaying the start of the game for an hour.

College football was still in its infancy. In 1892, a touchdown counted for four points. Given the sport's roots in rugby, a field goal put five points on the board. Teams tried to bludgeon each other with mass formations and gang tackling. Stanford won the inaugural game 14–10. By 1900, the rivalry had become so passionate that it became known as the Big Game. That year, tragedy struck when a roof adjoining the field collapsed, and 22 fans died. It remains the deadliest accident in United States sporting history.

The rivalry paused after 1905 when the two schools stopped playing football but resumed in 1919. In the following decades, the Big Game was the biggest athletic event in the Bay Area, with the winner claiming rights to a trophy known as the Axe. Traditionally, each school held a bonfire rally before the Big Game, which was played in late November. Last-minute victories and upsets became the norm.

Cal's teams were known as the Golden Bears, a nod to the grizzly bear being a symbol of the state of California. The official mascot was a costumed bear with a perpetual smile named Oski. The identity of the students who wore the Oski suit was kept secret.

Stanford's athletic teams were known for decades as the Indians, and a member of the Yurok tribe, Timm Williams, danced on the football field during the pregame and halftime shows of the Stanford band. But in 1972, after vehement protests from Native American students that the mascot was demeaning and reinforced racial stereotypes, Stanford's president scrapped the Indians in favor of the Cardinals, a reference to the school's vivid red colors. The new mascot didn't excite anybody, however. Students put the question to a vote in 1975. The winner? The "Robber Barons," an irreverent reference to how critics said Leland Stanford Sr. earned his fortune. The students' choice didn't sit well with the university's administration, of course. So Stanford remained the Cardinals until 1981 when Stanford president Donald Kennedy decreed that the mascot would be Cardinal—singular.

Over the years, the two schools developed distinct personalities. Cal gained a reputation as one of the country's finest public universities while Stanford became known as one of the top private institutions. Although students from the two schools didn't exactly hate each other, there was no love lost between the two sides either. Stanford students mocked their Cal counterparts as "weenies." In turn, Cal students disparaged Stanford as the home of the privileged and the spoiled.

Undergrads at each school tried to top the other with collegiate hijinks, especially as the Big Game approached. One year, Cal students released blue-and-gold dyed mice in the Stanford library. Stanford students reciprocated with red-and-white ones at Cal. Attempts to steal the Axe from their foe were a regular occurrence.

Their rivalry was especially intense on the playing field, with bragging rights for the year at stake at each Big Game. In college football, the winning of bragging rights can energize an entire school—its alumni, its administration, its faculty, and, of course, its students. That was less true at Stanford and Cal because academics mattered more than prowess on the football field.

Sometimes, non-academic activities mattered the most, especially in Berkeley. The Free Speech Movement began at Cal in 1964 as students agitated for a greater say in university affairs at a time when civil rights and anti-Vietnam War protests were beginning to transform college campuses. Cal became one of the leading anti-war campuses in the United States. This produced a backlash. Ronald Reagan ran for governor of California in 1966 on a promise to bring law and order to UC Berkeley. Reagan railed against the "beatniks, radicals, and filthy speech advocates" who had turned California's flagship university into a "rallying point of communists and a center of sexual misconduct." In 1969, Governor Reagan sent 2,200 National Guard troops to uproot students and activists who were trying to transform a university-owned lot near the campus into "People's Park."

Stanford students also marched for civil rights and for ending the war and occupied an academic building on campus where research was conducted for the Department of Defense. On more than one occasion, the police launched tear gas to disperse protesting students.

During the 1960s, ironically, the Cal marching band kept its traditional military-style uniforms and spirit songs, while the Stanford band underwent a dramatic transformation. By 1970, Stanford's band was regularly challenging convention—and creating controversy. In 1975, the band adopted the tree as its unofficial mascot. From then on, a student wearing a green, leafy costume would prance and cavort during the band's performances.

By 1980, Cal retained its counter-culture tradition. But it also had a thriving Greek system. At Stanford, students were becoming more and more focused on engineering and computer science, with Stanford and Palo Alto beginning to emerge as the heart of what would become known as Silicon Valley. Steve Wozniak and Steven Jobs were developing the first personal computers after founding the Apple Computer Company in a garage only 10 miles from the Stanford campus in 1976. The pioneering Hewlett-Packard Corporation, whose headquarters were located only a mile from Stanford, had been founded by two Stanford grads decades earlier, and its current CEO was a Stanford alum.

While the two universities reflected and reinforced larger changes in society, the annual Big Game was a constant, a contest surrounded by its own unique traditions that both sides celebrated each year.

In 1979, Cal had won the Big Game in thrilling fashion. Ahead 21–14 in the final minute of play, the Bears stopped Stanford on fourth and goal at the 1-yard line. Stanford's quarterback was Turk Schonert, a senior who led the NCAA in passing that year. Elway, a freshman, played sparingly. Cal's triumph that year gave it 33 Big Game victories to 39 for Stanford with 10 ties.

In 1980, Cal came into the 83ʳᵈ Big Game as heavy underdogs. The
Bears had stumbled and fumbled throughout the season, defeating only
the two woeful Oregon schools. The low point had come when USC wal-
loped Cal 60–7. The Bears' 2–8 record left head coach Roger Theder's job
in jeopardy heading into the Bears' season finale against Stanford. Following
an injury to the first stringer, a freshman redshirt walk-on named J Torchio
was now his starting quarterback. Stanford was favored by 15 points.

Stanford entered the 1980 Big Game with a 6–4 record behind its
rookie head coach, Paul Wiggin, and sophomore Elway in his first year as
a starter. Elway had already burst onto the national college football scene
in Stanford's fourth game of the season, on the road against highly ranked
Oklahoma, when Stanford whipped the Sooners 31–14 behind a phenomenal
Elway performance. Now, if Stanford could wrap up its season by winning
the Big Game, the team would be invited to the Peach Bowl.

Just before the game began, Cal rooters mocked their rival's chances
by taking aim at a favorite target, the Stanford band. Cal rooters launched
peaches at the Stanford bandsmen during their pregame show on the field.
Anticipating this greeting, the band brought along members of Stanford's
lacrosse team to catch the projectiles with their sticks and hurl the peaches
back into Cal's rooting section.

The Bears took the opening kickoff and marched for a quick touchdown.
Stanford matched it. Cal scored two more touchdowns—one after Elway
was stripped of the ball on his own 5-yard line—to take a 21–7 lead heading into the fourth quarter. Stanford fought back. Running back Vincent
White scored two touchdowns to tie the game 21–21. With 4:56 left in the
game, Theder called a timeout with his offense on the field. It was fourth
and 2 for Cal on its own 45-yard line. Should the Bears go for it in the
hopes that they could make a first down and then score a touchdown or
kick a game-winning field goal? The stakes were high. If they failed and
turned over the ball, Elway would need only 20 yards to put Stanford in
field-goal range. Or he might even orchestrate the team's third touchdown
that quarter. But if Cal punted, Elway also was easily capable of marching

Stanford downfield to the winning score. Theder decided to punt. It was a beauty that the Bears downed on the Stanford 5-yard line.

Backed up against their own end zone, Stanford called for a run by White to give Elway more room to throw the ball on subsequent downs. But Elway's handoff was thin, meaning he didn't put the ball squarely into White's midsection as he began to run toward the line. Instead, Elway placed the ball on White's hip, just out of his grasp. As White ran forward, the ball fell to the ground, and a Cal defensive lineman jumped on it at the Stanford 3-yard line. Elway, who had landed on his hands and knees while trying to recover the ball, dropped his helmet to the turf in frustration. Now it was first and goal for Cal.

Cal had a golden chance to score a touchdown and win the game behind Torchio, the unheralded quarterback. He had a notable Cal pedigree. His father had starred for the Bears in the 1950s and in one Big Game had even run back an interception for a touchdown. Torchio had additional ties to the program, having served as a ballboy for Cal in the 1970s while growing up in nearby Moraga. Now he was in a position to engineer a victory over Stanford.

Throughout the game, Torchio noticed that Stanford's right defensive end was aggressively charging to the center of the line on handoffs up the middle, trying to make the tackle. Torchio told coaches on the sideline that this created an opportunity for him to fake a handoff to the right side, pivot in the opposite direction, and carry the ball around the left end, a play known as a naked bootleg. Torchio would be "naked" because he would not have any blockers. Success depended on the Stanford defenders on the left side of the quarterback buying a Cal run to the other side.

Before Torchio headed back onto the field, Cal offensive coordinator Al Saunders gave him a final instruction: don't tell any of your teammates about your plan to run the naked bootleg except the halfback to make sure he doesn't try to grab the ball away from the quarterback. By keeping the call from them, Saunders said, the offensive linemen would fully sell the fake to the defense. Torchio needed only three yards to score.

The plan developed just as they had planned it. Torchio took the hike, and the linemen blocked to the right to clear a path for the halfback running in that direction. But the quarterback kept the ball. Fooled, the Stanford defenders started toward the middle. Torchio raced around the left side and was tackled only after he crossed the goal line. Cal now led 28–21.

The game wasn't over—by a long shot. Elway had four minutes, an eternity in football time, to tie or win the game. But the Bears quickly put Stanford's offense in a hole. Facing third and 13, Elway bought more time by scrambling for a first down. Then he hit White with a beautifully thrown pass down the left sideline. White was knocked out of bounds at the Cal 4-yard line. Stanford fans stood expectantly, confident that Elway was about to deliver a touchdown. "Maybe it's not our time," thought Ron Coccimiglio, the Bears senior free safety.

On first and goal, Elway rolled right but, after seeing no one open, deliberately threw the ball out of the end zone. On second down, White ran up the middle and was stopped two yards short of the goal line.

Facing third and goal from the 2-yard line, Cal defensive coordinator Gunther Cunningham expected Elway to run a bootleg by rolling to either the left or right with the support of at least one lineman. A bootleg would give Elway the option to throw the ball or use his quickness to dart into the end zone. To stop the bootleg, Cunningham decided to gamble by blitzing Elway from both sides. Cunningham's call was risky. Cal would be leaving an open lane to the end zone if Stanford ran up the middle, where the Bears would have fewer players.

Cal sent in its blitz scheme from the sideline with a series of hand signals. Steve Cacciari, the strongside linebacker, announced the call to his teammates in their huddle. As they broke, Cacciari took his position just behind the Bears defensive linemen.

On this crucial third-and-goal play, Stanford went with a handoff to White running up the middle. It seemed like the perfect call. But Cacciari shot forward before a Stanford lineman could block him and met White head-on two yards into the backfield. The collision knocked White backward two steps, but, with his powerful legs churning, he stayed on his feet. White bounced left, hoping he could find a path to the end zone. But cornerback Fred Williams tackled him for a four-yard loss. It was now fourth and goal at the 6-yard line, and Stanford needed a touchdown to stay in the game.

The next play would decide the 83rd Big Game. Cunningham decided to gamble once again. This time he was betting that Elway would roll to his right to have the option to pass or run it in. But this time, only one Bears defender would blitz Elway. He was a sophomore safety named Kevin Moen who played only when Cal had five defensive backs on the field. Moen was not fast but was fundamentally sound; coaches could count on him to execute his assignment correctly. His job would be to race in from Elway's right. Moen knew a running back would try to block him, so he would have to stay outside the running back's right hip to contain the quarterback inside.

Elway and Moen already shared some history. They had played against each other the year before in the 1979 North–South Shrine All-Star Game at the fabled Rose Bowl stadium. The contest pitted the best high school graduates from north Los Angeles County against those from the south. On one play, Elway threw a pass just over Moen's outstretched arm for a touchdown, and Elway's team won that contest. He was one up on Moen. Not that either one of them was thinking about this before the climactic play of the 1980 Big Game. It was a big moment, not a time for reflection.

Cacciari, seeing the defensive play call from the sideline, announced it to his teammates: "Nickel. Man. Storm." This meant Cal would play a nickel defense with five defensive backs and man-to-man coverage. "Storm" meant that Moen, the strong safety, would blitz.

Stanford's fullbacks shuttled in the call for each play. On fourth down, it was Jeff Haile's turn. A senior who had played sparingly during his career, Haile had started that day because the two fullbacks ahead of him were injured. He had acquitted himself well, gaining 58 yards on both runs and catches. Now Haile relayed the call to Elway: 78 Double Cross.

Seventy-Eight Double Cross aimed to confuse Cal's defense by using movement. At the snap, Stanford's offensive linemen would immediately shift right, and Elway would roll that way. Haile, behind Elway and to his right, would be responsible for any blitzing Cal players storming in from that side.

Andre Tyler, the left end, would run a crossing route to the right side. Ken Margerum, the right end, would cross to the left. Chris Dressel, the tight end, would run straight ahead into the end zone. Tyler was the primary receiver. He typically got open when he ran a shallow cross. The defender covering him usually couldn't keep up because he had to dodge his own teammates in the middle of the field. As soon as he heard Elway make the call in the huddle, Tyler was confident they would score, just as they had several times that season with the 78 Double Cross.

The Cal players appeared to recognize the formation. "Watch Tyler! Watch Tyler!" a defender yelled. But could they stop it? Elway took the snap, rolled right, and the three receivers ran their routes into the end zone. Cal, it turned out, had the perfect answer. Moen raced across the line of scrimmage. That surprised Elway as he rolled to his right. The blitz also surprised Haile. He tried to chop block Moen by diving at his legs, but he missed. Moen kept coming. Elway, backpedaling, wasn't able to quickly plant and throw the ball. All three receivers were finding open space in the end zone. Elway tried outrunning Moen to his right, but the Cal defender had sealed off that angle. Elway stopped, backed up a step, but Moen remained undeterred, locked on his target: a white jersey with a big red No. 7. Falling backward, with Moen in his face, Elway managed only a wobbly pass. It hit the turf short of Tyler, who was open in the right corner of the end zone. Elway's incomplete fourth-down pass meant Cal had won the 83rd Big Game and would maintain possession of the fabled Axe. Moen's teammates mobbed him when he reached the sideline.

No one knew it then, but John Elway and Kevin Moen would meet again on the same field in two years in the 1982 Big Game. Both were fated to play pivotal roles in the wildest finish ever to a college football game.

• CHAPTER 2 •

THE AXE

Gary Cartwright was growing concerned. He was sitting in the office of the sports information director at Harmon Gym on Cal's campus. The date was November 17, 1981, only four days before that year's Big Game. Cartwright, whose business card identified him as a freelance writer, had just interviewed the Cal official for *Inside Sports* magazine on the Cal–Stanford football rivalry, the oldest west of the Mississippi River. Now Cartwright and his photographer needed photos of the Axe, the prize held by Cal because the Bears had won the previous year's Big Game. But Cal officials were taking a long time to produce the trophy. Was something wrong?

Cartwright had reason to worry. He was actually Bob Moog, a 25-year-old Stanford grad whose real job was marketing a cure for arthritis derived from Green Lipped Mussels imported from New Zealand. He wasn't a freelance writer, and he wasn't writing a piece for the magazine. Instead, Moog was part of an elaborate Stanford trick to steal the Axe on the Berkeley campus just before the 1981 Big Game. To sound legit, Moog was using the name of a Texas-based sportswriter, figuring Cal officials would not call *Inside Sports* to confirm the assignment. Moog had spent the night before at a Sheraton hotel next to San Francisco International Airport, claiming he had just arrived in town, to seem even more legitimate.

In all, 18 Stanford students and recent alums were part of the scheme. It ultimately depended on Cal making the Axe available. The minutes ticked by in the office at Harmon Gym. Moog wondered again: *Was something wrong? Will we pull this off?* Moog became nervous. *Had his cover been blown? Could this result in an arrest?*

For decades, the Stanford Axe had been subjected to trickery, thievery, competition, celebration, and bloodlust by both sides. The object consisted of a gleaming 14-inch blade and a wooden handle that had been deliberately shortened years before. A plaque below the blade read:

THE STANFORD AXE

FORGED MARCH 1899

CAPTURED BY CALIFORNIA, APRIL 15, 1899

RECAPTURED BY STANFORD, APRIL 3, 1930

TO BE AWARDED ANNUALLY TO THE WINNER OF THE "BIG GAME"

Underneath the inscription were six bronze panels that listed the outcome of each year's game. The last one read:

1980 Cal, Stanford 21–14

The axe and the plaque were mounted on a rectangular piece of red cedar that measured three-feet by two-feet. In all, it weighed a hefty 75 pounds.

The Axe had quite a history. Its origins could be traced to the Axe yell, dreamed up by two Stanford students in 1896 as a way of antagonizing students at Cal, the more established university across the bay. The yell went like this:

Give 'em the Axe, the Axe, the Axe!

Give 'em the Axe, the Axe, the Axe!

Give 'em the Axe, give 'em the Axe, give 'em the Axe!

Where?

Right in the neck, the neck, the neck!

Right in the neck, the neck, the neck!

Right in the neck, right in the neck, right in the neck!

There!

Stanford's yell wasn't particularly creative—in fact, it mimicked the rhythm of the chorus of an Athenian comedy, "The Frogs," from some 2,000 years earlier—but it got under the skin of Cal students, and that's what mattered most.

In 1899, Stanford and Cal were scheduled to play an important three-game baseball series. Cal won the first game. Looking to inspire his team,

Stanford yell leader Billy Erb and several classmates forked over $4.50 to buy an axe. They painted most of it red and attached a four-foot wooden handle.

Erb brought out the axe at a huge Stanford bonfire rally two nights before the ballgame. Theatrically sharpening it on a grindstone, he then lopped off the head of a straw man dressed in blue and gold representing Cal. The crowd yelled and hollered its approval.

Two days later at the ballgame, played in San Francisco, Erb brandished the blade menacingly in front of Cal rooters as he led Stanford students in the Axe yell. If the Axe was supposed to inspire the Stanford team, it fell short of producing the necessary magic. Cal won the game. Stanford rooters slunk from the ball grounds. "Embittered by the disaster, they would gladly have made a ceremony out of taking the old Axe out to the Bay and dumping it in, had they thought about it," a 1930 book, *The Stanford Axe*, reported.

Three Stanford students left the ballpark with the totem only to be confronted by a horde of Cal students wanting to claim a souvenir of their victory. "Give me that axe!" one of them yelled. Suddenly, the Axe became valuable again to the Stanford crowd. A melee ensued. First, Cal had it, then Stanford grabbed it back. Another melee. Cal students got it back and sawed off the handle at a butcher shop to make it less conspicuous. With police assisting Stanford students in searching for the trophy, the Cal rooters hid it in one student's overcoat, and he took it on a ferry across the bay to Berkeley. Success! Hundreds of students attended a rally two days later to celebrate the brazen theft.

Several days later, some 30 Stanford men invaded a fraternity house in Berkeley but couldn't find the Axe. Afterward, officials of both schools sought to lower the temperature. *The Daily Californian* newspaper called for the Cal students to return the Axe. They refused to do so. And for the next three decades, the trophy remained in Cal's possession, locked in a bank vault, emerging into sunlight only at the annual Axe rally where Cal students flaunted it to the everlasting ire of Stanford.

That in turn prompted a group of Stanford students—21 in all—to design an intricate plan in 1930 to steal it back. The appointed moment came after an Axe rally at the Greek Theatre on the Berkeley campus, as Cal was returning the trophy to the bank vault. Five Stanford students hopped onto the running boards of the armored car, pretending to be guards. When the vehicle arrived at the bank, other Stanford students impersonating news photographers asked for a picture, calling out, "Let's have a good shot at the Axe!" Just as the Cal student holding the Axe exited the car, flash powder temporarily blinded him. That's when the Stanford students pounced and grabbed it. Another Stanford student tossed a tear gas cannister to disorient the Cal side, while another conspirator sped off with the Axe. The plan was a complete success. Back at Stanford, the students paraded the war booty around the campus and were hailed as conquering heroes, honored in the coming days with special dinners and dances. The "Immortal 21," they were called.

Three years later, both schools agreed to settle custody disputes on the football field. The winner of each year's Big Game would keep the Axe for the next 12 months. In the case of a tie, it would remain with the previous year's victor.

That didn't end the hijinks, of course. One school or the other would steal it every few years. In 1960, two Cal students even took the Axe from a group of other Cal students who had filched it from its supposedly secure hiding place on campus. The Cal students returned it the day after that year's Big Game, which the Bears won.

In 1964, Stanford students stole Cal's Victory Cannon—which was fired after every Bears touchdown—and Cal retaliated by pinching a Stanford banner, a bronze bell, and 17,000 cards held up by students in the stands to spell out words and symbols in tightly coordinated fashion during halftime shows. Stanford students upped the ante by stealing Cal's halftime cards. The two schools finally negotiated a truce called the Treaty at Castle Lanes, named after a local bowling alley where they met. But when the two sides went to exchange their booty, Stanford students tried to hold onto Cal's cannon. A Cal student pulled a gun. Thankfully, no one was hurt, and order was quickly restored.

A year later, in 1965, far from Cal and Stanford, a senior at Lawrenceville School in New Jersey named John Welborne reprogrammed the high school's bell system to shorten classes by five minutes and cancel that day's chapel session. The prank threw the school's administrators into a tizzy. But it was only a warm-up for an even bigger caper Welborne would attempt as a Cal student. Like other freshmen, he learned about the Big Game and the Axe. Unlike the other newcomers, however, he immediately began thinking about snatching the trophy. He raised the idea with a couple of upperclassmen. "We've tried and couldn't do it," they told Welborne. "Kid, you'll never be able to do it. It's impossible."

Hearing that only emboldened Welborne. Like a mad scientist, he didn't like being told that he couldn't do something.

Welborne began hitching rides to the Stanford campus and casing the Axe, which was locked in a steel case with a bulletproof glass window mounted on a wall at Tresidder Memorial Student Union. In the meantime, Welborne became vice chairman of Cal's Rally Committee, which offered rah-rah students a chance to organize both the card stunts during halftime shows and the bonfire rally held annually at Berkeley's Greek Theatre the night before the Big Game.

Rally Committee members invariably organized pranks as well. One night, Welborne and several others broke into a storage closet at Stanford Stadium and stole the cards that Stanford students were supposed to exhibit at halftime at one 1966 game. Another night, he climbed in a window at Stanford's athletic department during Big Game Week and painted the head coach's toilet seat blue and gold.

Welborne was only getting started, however. As a 19-year-old humanities major with a self-taught understanding of electronics, he turned his attention back to the Axe and was emboldened when he saw a newspaper photo of Stanford students removing it from the open glass case at Tresidder Union. This inadvertently gave him the missing pieces for his plan—the photo showed how the case opened and the type of alarm that protected it. Welborne had the newspaper enlarge the photo so he could study it in detail. "I had to figure out how they got the Axe in so I could get it out," he explained later.

Welborne made more trips to Stanford to study the movements of the Stanford Police Department—it was located 150 feet behind Tresidder, attached to the university firehouse—and to take pictures of Tresidder's exterior and of the Axe case. He could have been a cat burglar planning a million-dollar robbery. In Welborne's eyes, of course, this potential prize was far more valuable.

On the night before he planned to execute the heist, Welborne hid in the bushes outside of Dinkelspiel Auditorium, a stone's throw from the student union, to time police patrols and learn who came and went into Tresidder before dawn to determine when few people would be around. He even went into the student union and carried out a dry run, stopping just short of the point when he would have triggered the Axe display case alarms.

Welborne's plan was set to go. He and a fraternity brother named Pat Gilligan each drove a car across the bay in the predawn 24 hours later. They stashed Welborne's borrowed vehicle in Menlo Park and drove the last several miles together onto the Stanford campus in Gilligan's 1967 Volkswagen Beetle. Gilligan would serve as the getaway driver.

In the meantime, he hid in the bushes outside, waiting for a signal, while Welborne walked briskly toward Tresidder. It was just before 6:00 AM on May 12, 1967. Dressed in black, Welborne slipped through a kitchen door of the student union—it was kept open for early morning workers—and made his way through the kitchen and the cafeteria to the Axe case. He was carrying only a flashlight, a pocket knife, a set of Allen wrenches, a pair of pliers, and a two-by-four piece of wood. That's all he needed. Welborne placed the two-by-four across the handles of the cafeteria's double doors—to keep from being surprised by anyone from the kitchen—and went to work.

Welborne undid one set of screws and a set of bolts, except for the final bolt. Wasting no time, Welborne next raised the heavy case cover with his left hand—the hinge was at the top—and used his right to signal Gilligan with two flashlight blinks to return to the parking lot to start the car. Now, 10 minutes into his caper, Welborne was about to carry out the final step, one that he calculated would sound the alarm. He removed the final bolt and loosened the hinged case. Welborne grabbed the trophy while holding open the case with the other. Welborne allowed himself a brief smile. The Axe, as he had suspected, was not attached to anything. A moment later, he took possession of it with both hands. He then turned around, pushed through a door to the plaza outside, and set out toward Gilligan and the parking lot 75 yards away. Welborne staggered as he ran. The 75-pound Axe and its wooden frame were bulky and heavy.

Welborne reached the parking lot but didn't see Gilligan. Panic momentarily added to the adrenaline already coursing through his body. Then Welborne saw his fraternity brother wheeling his Beetle toward him. "Just drive!" Welborne shouted as he jumped in. They shot forward even before Welborne could close his door.

The alarm triggered by the removal of the Axe was ringing in the dispatch room at the Stanford Firehouse, only 150 feet away from the back entrance of Tresidder. Police officers typically hung out in the kitchen next to the dispatch room, and the first officer who came racing out was named Luther Long. He rushed into Tresidder through the kitchen but then encountered a blocked door, thanks to Welborne's two-by-four. Long backtracked and ran through another entrance to reach the Axe case. He arrived two minutes after the alarm sounded, but by that time, Welborne and Gilligan in the Beetle had made a right turn, then a left, then another right and were racing in their comically underpowered getaway car behind the university lake on campus, on their way to Menlo Park with the Axe. There they wrapped the trophy in plain brown paper and placed it in the trunk of Welborne's car. Forty-five minutes later, he stashed it in a locker at the Oakland airport.

Stanford police quickly notified their counterparts in Berkeley. Welborne was an immediate suspect given his larcenous activities for the Rally Committee. At about noon, he was summoned to meet with three deans. Welborne was not only a good thief, but he was a proficient liar as well. Questioned on the Axe's whereabouts, he responded, "I'm flattered that you ask, but I can't help you." The three deans didn't press him, perhaps delighted they could honestly report to their Stanford counterparts that they could shed no light on the theft.

The *Palo Alto Times* published an article that afternoon accompanied by a photo of three students examining the empty case. "Who's got the Axe, hey?" read the photo caption.

Only two people knew—Welborne and Gilligan—and neither was talking. Actually, a third person knew because Welborne and Gilligan later that day picked up the Axe from the airport storage locker and took the trophy to Gilligan's parents' house in nearby Piedmont. Gilligan swore his mother to secrecy as the three of them stored the Axe in the Gilligan's attic.

The Stanford Daily reported four days later that "the apparent coolness of the thief, and the inability to come up with any leads has caused many Stanfordites to surmise that the theft was an inside job." The next day, Welborne made clear that it was a Cal job when he anonymously sent a photo to local newspapers showing the Axe being held up with Cal's Campanile tower serving as a notable backdrop. Welborne, the photographer, hid Gilligan's face behind the trophy. In another cheeky move, he had the Axe photographed leaning against a front window of the *Oakland Tribune*.

If anyone expected the thief to reappear quickly, they were mistaken. The Axe remained missing for months, amid constant speculation regarding its location. Welborne finally devised an appropriate plan for the Axe to make its reappearance. On the day before the 1967 Big Game, a parade in downtown Berkeley celebrating the game was about to begin when a car swung onto the parade route. It was a Volkswagen Beetle with a sunroof, license plates altered by masking tape, and a sign mounted on each side that read "Stanford Axe." At the wheel was a Cal student named Michael Drewes. Welborne and Gilligan, wearing pillowcases over their heads, held the Axe up through the sunroof as Drewes drove at about 10 miles an hour—fast enough to catch everyone by surprise but slow enough for parade-goers to glimpse the Axe and roar their approval. Take that, Stanford!

Drewes exited from the parade route and made the short drive to Memorial Stadium. Gilligan had alerted the head coach that a surprise might show up in the locker room after practice. "Men, these guys have brought something to show you," Coach Ray Willsey told his players. "This is the trophy we're playing for tomorrow! I know you can do it!" With the reverence accorded to a sacred object, the players passed it around the locker room before returning it to Welborne and Gilligan.

They then made the short drive to the site of that night's planned bonfire rally at the Greek Theatre next to the football stadium. Welborne was the rally's organizer. He and Gilligan carried the Axe aloft onto the stage during the final moments. The packed house exploded at the wondrous surprise. Afterward, by prearrangement, the two students walked offstage and placed the totem in the open trunk of a police car. Cal's chief of police returned the Axe to Stanford the following day just as the Big Game was beginning. Stanford, then called the Indians, was heavily favored, having defeated the Bears during their previous six contests. But Cal smacked around Stanford, winning 26–3, taking possession of the Axe legitimately once again.

The Axe hijinks continued, of course. In 1973, on the Tuesday morning before that year's Big Game, Cal head coach Mike White called with a request to the student union office, which oversaw custody of the Axe. White wanted to take the trophy with him that day to Ming's restaurant in Palo Alto for the weekly luncheon of the Northern California Football Writers Association. A wire service photographer wanted photos of the trophy, White explained, adding that two Cal football players would meet him at the office and accompany him with the Axe to Palo Alto. "I want the Axe waiting for me when I get there," White told a secretary.

But in the grand tradition of Axe heists, the coach was a fake. "White" was actually a law student at the University of San Francisco named Matt Conway. The football players who showed up minutes later, wearing Cal letter jackets? They were fake, too, of course. Both were Stanford students. One was a senior named Tim Conway—Matt's brother—while the other was a junior named David Suliteanu. They lived in the Theta Delta Chi fraternity on campus.

When Tim Conway and Suliteanu arrived at the student union office, they learned that the Axe wasn't there. It had been taken away several days earlier for safekeeping. But then "Coach White" called again. This time, he said he had been detained in Oakland and wouldn't have time to stop in

Berkeley to collect the Axe. He expressed anger that the Axe wasn't at the office and added, "Well, make sure they get it out."

A long wait ensued. During that time, someone from the university office could have called the athletic department and discovered that White hadn't requested the Axe. Or they could have figured out that Conway and Suliteanu weren't actually Cal football players. Instead, the head of the student union office agreed to get the Axe and called George Hendrickson, a senior majoring in criminology who oversaw security for it. Hendrickson agreed to take the totem to Ming's, with the help of three others. The four of them donned their Cal Rally Committee uniforms—blue pants, white shirts, blue-and-gold rally hats, and white cardigan sweaters with a C and a bear in the middle of the C. Hendrickson and his mates retrieved the Axe from its hiding place and brought it to the student union office. Conway and Suliteanu generously offered to take the Axe to Ming's. Hendrickson demurred. For security's sake, he and the three others would ferry the Axe in their own car. *Hmmm*, thought Conway and Suliteanu. That was not part of the plan. "Men of less dedication, intelligence, moral caliber and gall might have given up at this point," *The Stanford Daily* reported later. But these students, "made of stronger stuff," agreed on the spot to the change and figured they would improvise from there. Conway and Suliteanu gamed out various options as they led a two-car caravan to Palo Alto.

In the meantime, Matt Conway, having already impersonated Coach White, was down to his last dime at a pay phone nearby on the Cal campus. He used it to call the house phone just off the dining room at the Theta Delt house. A basketball player named Steve Shupe answered. Matt Conway talked fast, explaining what was happening and what was needed—some guys had to get to Ming's as soon as possible, without Stanford gear, and provide muscle. Shupe didn't know Matt Conway and didn't know whether to believe this wild story, but he pounded on some doors and roused several brothers. Dan Broderick, the fraternity president, offered his car, a Dodge Coronet. They piled into his vehicle and raced toward the restaurant, 10 minutes away, not sure what to expect.

Tim Conway and Suliteanu were dismayed when they pulled into the Ming's parking lot at 12:15 PM. They saw no fraternity brothers. They briefly discussed how the two of them could try to wrestle the Axe away from the four Cal students. The odds weren't good, but why not try? As they walked to the Cal car, however, Suliteanu and Conway spied what to them was a heaven-sent present—two of their fraternity brothers, acting nonchalantly nearby. Now Suliteanu and Conway had a fighting chance. They asked Hendrickson to have two of the Cal students go inside the restaurant and tell Coach White that they had arrived with the Axe.

Now the odds had improved. Hendrickson pulled the Axe from the back seat of his car. Conway, who had played frosh football at Stanford, asked if he could hold the prize. "I've got it!" he shouted a moment later and began to run toward the fraternity brothers as Suliteanu detained one of the Cal students by bear-hugging him. Still, Hendrickson and the others gave chase. One of them caught up to Conway, tackling him on the hood of a pink Cadillac. The Axe flew over the roof of the car—and ended up in the hands of another Cal student, James Atkinson. He began to run back to the Cal car when he was suddenly confronted by Shupe, the Stanford basketball player, who towered over him. The other Theta Chi brothers arrived moments later. Shupe grabbed the Axe from Atkinson and, with his fraternity brothers running interference, raced across the parking lot back to the Dodge Coronet. Broderick gunned the engine, and they arrived at the Theta Delt house minutes later. All the fraternity brothers were so excited that they gathered for a photo with the trophy. Conway and Suliteanu sat in front, beaming, still wearing their Cal lettermen jackets. The two then drove to Palo Alto and hid the Axe underneath the bed of Suliteanu's grandmother.

"A small band of desperate and unethical Stanfordians executed yesterday with unmatched dastardliness—and good timing—the pilferage of our Beloved Battle Axe from its rightful place at Cal," *The Daily Californian* editorialized the next day. "A more shocking deed is hard to envision…It will be up to all Californians to use guile and force, on and off the field, in order to return the valuable Axe to its rightful owners."

Someone at Ming's had recognized Shupe running with the Axe. So suspicion immediately fell upon the Theta Delt house, and the identity of the perpetrators quickly became known. Conway and Suliteanu issued a "non-negotiable" set of mischievous demands to Stanford's police chief—including admission to the Stanford graduate school of their choice, Thanksgiving dinner with Stanford's president, three press box tickets to Saturday's Big Game and "a fake I.D. for the one member of the 'Infamous 3' who is not yet 21." It took university officials and the thieves two days to devise a solution on how Stanford would return the Axe—the Indians' captains would carry it onto the field and hand it over during the pregame coin toss. For several moments, the Bears' captains refused to accept it before they relented and took possession. With that settled, the two schools battled on the field for the right to legitimately claim the Axe. Stanford went on to win the game 26–17, regaining the prize three hours later.

Asked why they had stolen it, Suliteanu and Conway said they had wanted to add to "the glory and the mystique" of the Axe. Asked if he had a follow-up in mind, Suliteanu replied, "We thought we might steal the Axe back from Stanford and give it to Cal. That would be really classy."

Eight years later, with Cal having won the previous year's Big Game, Moog, aka Gary Cartwright, the ersatz sports journalist, found himself waiting for Cal officials to bring out the Axe. That would trigger the latest intricate plan to filch it from them in broad daylight. The plan had been the brainchild of a recent Stanford alum named Mark Breier. Even before graduating in 1981, Breier had formed a company that specialized in hair-raising schemes. It was called Amazing Events, and it was hired by people who wanted to spice up their gatherings. At one soiree, a waiter and waitress deliberately bumbled, dropping glasses and spilling food while the host grew more and more upset—until his wife clued him in, *Candid Camera*-style. At another, "workers" showed up to chop down a tree prized by a home-owner, who grew increasingly exasperated when the workers kept insisting on felling it—before they clued him in on the prank. In yet another, a hefty Stanford track and field star grabbed a professor from his classroom and carried him upside down to a surprise birthday party. At a Silicon Valley party, a supposedly drunk waiter got in a fight with a caterer and smashed a painting that partygoers had been told was the host's most recent purchase, worth millions of dollars. The "masterpiece" had been painted by Breier and another student earlier that day.

In other words, Breier, a 22-year-old economics graduate, possessed just the mischievous mind to plan a theft of the Axe.

It began with Moog playing Cartwright. Then a fake photographer would insist on taking a photo with a Cal cheerleader and a Stanford Dollie, one of the women who normally performed dance routines with the Stanford band. For the photo, they would be playfully tugging at the Axe on a bridge over Strawberry Creek, just behind Cal's athletic department. Then a lovers' quarrel would erupt nearby. Breier expected the Cal students guarding the Axe to leave their posts to help break it up. At that instant, a Stanford hammer thrower named Shaun Pickering—who was big, fast, and strong and had been "jogging" in the area—would swoop in and grab the Axe. Another Stanford track and field star would run interference. Toting the Axe, Pickering was to race down a wooded pathway with several other Stanford students hanging back to block any Cal pursuers. Pickering would jump onto the back of a waiting motorbike, be driven several blocks, drop the Axe into an open trunk of a waiting car, and be whisked away in another vehicle. Meanwhile, the car with the Axe would make its getaway. Breier had spent weeks with the other conspirators nailing down the plans and discussing all the possible contingencies. The day before, they ran through a timed dry rehearsal.

All of it hinged, of course, on the arrival of the Axe. Having completed the "interview" for his fake article, Moog waited in the office of the sports information director, John McCasey. The minutes dragged on. Finally, McCasey reappeared. "Sorry, guys," he said. "The Axe is being refurbished. I can't get access to it today."

Moog, playing Cartwright, expressed his anger. But there was nothing else he could do. The Axe remained safe in Cal's hands that week, until Stanford won the 1981 Big Game four days later. Stanford would hold the Axe heading into the 1982 Big Game.

• CHAPTER 3 •

THE QUARTERBACK

In the late summer of 1979, Stanford's football team was practicing during early ball. In was so early in fact, Stanford didn't even have a kicker on the field yet when it came time to practice defending kickoff returns. Defensive backs coach George Seifert was determined to carry out the drill regardless. He called over the team's highly recruited freshman quarterback. "Hey, Elway," Seifert said, "I need you to throw the ball downfield for the kickoff."

John Elway was happy to comply. He had just arrived on campus and wanted to make a good impression as a team player. Seifert tossed a ball to Elway. He lined up at the 40-yard line, the kickoff spot, with five players to his right and five to his left. Everyone was ready. Elway cocked his arm and threw the ball half the length of the field to the 20-yard line. Another set of Stanford players returned the kick.

But Seifert was unhappy. Not with the return team but with Elway. "Goddamn it!" Seifert shouted. "Not like that!" He wanted Elway's kickoff throw to travel farther, but he didn't specify how far. Seifert tossed the ball back to Elway and walked away. Elway turned to offensive coordinator Jim Fassel with a sly smile. "Should I let it go?" Elway asked.

"Yeah, let it go," Fassel replied, with a sly smile of his own.

Elway lined up again just behind the 40-yard line, flanked by the 10 kickoff defenders. He took a couple of steps and uncorked a throw that sailed and sailed. The return man watched it fly over his head and over the practice field's back fence. In all, it traveled some 80 yards. Seifert's jaw dropped.

On another summer day in 1981 on that same practice field at Stanford, five quarterbacks, wearing shorts and T-shirts, were taking turns throwing passes to receivers. Four of them were NFL signal callers who had starred at Stanford over the preceding decade: Guy Benjamin, Steve Dils, Turk Schonert, and Jim Plunkett. All had rung up big numbers at Stanford, with Benjamin, Dils, and Schonert each leading the NCAA in passing in three consecutive seasons. Plunkett had outshone them all, winning the Heisman Trophy in 1970, leading Stanford to a Rose Bowl victory in the 1971 New Year's game, and going on to quarterback the Oakland Raiders to a Super Bowl championship in early 1981, for which he was voted the Super Bowl MVP. Now, months later, he and the three other pros were working on their throwing mechanics before their seasons began. The fifth quarterback on that idyllic summer afternoon was Stanford's current quarterback, Elway. He had been the starter during his sophomore year and was about to begin his junior season.

First one quarterback threw the ball on a designated route to a receiver, and then it was another's turn. But in time, the four pros began to joke about Elway and make fun of themselves. Their personalities allowed that since none of the four was a diva. Elway's passes hummed, they agreed. Theirs sometimes floated. Elway's passes almost always hit the receiver in the right spot. Theirs, they acknowledged ruefully, were sometimes overthrown or underthrown. Plunkett said with a laugh that he didn't want to follow the junior in the throwing order. Elway's accuracy and velocity were making him look bad. The other three pros agreed, teasing each other.

But behind the self-deprecatory laughter lurked a stunning truth: as great as these quarterbacks were, Elway was better.

He had arrived at Stanford in 1979 heralded as the best prep quarterback in the country. Ironically, he had originally wanted to be a running back. It was 1975. Elway was about to begin ninth grade in Pullman, Washington, where his dad Jack was an assistant coach at Washington State. John Elway's hero was Calvin Hill, a four-time Pro Bowler and Super Bowl champ with the Dallas Cowboys. Hill was a tough runner, and the Cowboys were establishing themselves as America's Team. It didn't matter to Elway that he was only 5'8" and 130 pounds, a midget compared to Hill. Elway liked being in the middle of the action in football. And at a young age, he dominated as a running back. When he was in sixth grade, playing that position for the

Little Grizzlies team in Missoula, Montana, his dad arrived late for his first game. Asking what he had missed, another father said, "Either every other kid is the worst football player I've ever seen, or your boy is the greatest."

Being a running back also held appeal for Elway because quarterback in the 1970s was not yet the glamour position it would become. Bob Griese threw only 11 passes when the Miami Dolphins won the 1973 Super Bowl behind a bruising runner, Larry Csonka, and a stout defense. Griese threw even fewer passes—seven—when the Dolphins repeated as champs in 1974. Csonka carried the ball 33 times for 145 yards and two touchdowns, and he was selected as the game's Most Valuable Player. In 1975, Terry Bradshaw threw only 14 passes when the Pittsburgh Steelers won the Super Bowl, while Franco Harris rumbled for 158 yards and a touchdown on 34 carries. He was chosen as the MVP. Young Elway had his heart set on being the team's featured back when his dad drove him to the first day of practice for Pullman High in 1975.

Elway had another reason for wanting to be a running back. Pullman High was coached by Ray Hobbs. It was common knowledge that Coach Hobbs believed that only bad things happened when your team threw the ball. For 20 years, Hobbs had employed the old single-wing offense in which the quarterback either handed off to the fullback, the tailback, the wingback, or he carried the ball himself. Playing under Hobbs, a quarterback might throw only four or five passes a game.

When Jack and John Elway arrived at Pullman High that first day, Jack told John to wait before getting out of the car. Jack wanted to talk to him first. The running back would take a lot more hits and was more likely to be injured, Jack said. John would have a better future at quarterback. The son took his father's advice to heart, and by the time he reached the practice field, he had decided to be a quarterback. But John didn't shine during his freshman year in high school, given the handcuffs that Hobbs placed on the signal-caller. John merited more attention for pouring in points on the basketball court—he led the frosh team to a 17–1 record—and for the way he swung the bat on the baseball field.

Then a fluke of history sent the entire Elway family down a different path. Washington State—where Jack was the offensive coordinator—was set to win its 1975 game against its archrival, the University of Washington. But late in the game, Washington State's quarterback threw an interception that Washington returned for a touchdown. A minute later, Washington's quarterback heaved a pass downfield into a crowd. A Washington State defender deflected it twice only for the ball to land in the hands of a Washington receiver who raced for the winning touchdown. The heartbreaking loss led to the resignation of Washington State's coaching staff, including Jack Elway. He thought he might become the new head honcho, but when he wasn't chosen, Jack was open to new offers.

One came shortly afterward when Cal State University, Northridge, asked him to become its head coach. Sam Winningham, the university's athletic director, had heard good things about Jack's offensive football acumen. And when they met, Winningham realized that Jack was fun and would obviously be a hit with the players. That was especially important because his two predecessors had alienated the team with a tough, old-school approach.

For Jack, Cal State Northridge was a step down in some ways. It played in Division II of the NCAA, a rung below Washington State and other big-name schools. Jack would also have to teach classes in addition to coaching the team. But the job would give him the chance to show his stuff as the head man.

Leaving cold and rainy Pullman would also have major implications for Jack's son. Cal State Northridge was in the northern part of Los Angeles County in the San Fernando Valley. There, John would have the chance to play quarterback at a different high school, one that threw the ball. Winningham suggested that Jack check out Granada Hills High School. The head coach, Jack Neumeier, had broken with the prevailing wisdom of a run-first offense. Neumeier liked to throw the ball. In fact, he liked to throw the football a lot, employing what became known as the "spread" offense. It called for four wideouts on each play, a single running back, with the quarterback receiving the snap in the shotgun formation. The receivers' patterns depended on how the defense lined up to stop them. "Me? I like to fly," Neumeier explained in a 1978 interview with the *Los Angeles Times*. "It's too slow to take the train."

It was a radical, new approach that was beginning to attract notice in college football after the success of Darrel "Mouse" Davis, the head coach at Portland State. Jack was so taken by Neumeier and his spread offense that he enrolled John at Granada Hills for 10th grade, even before he and his wife Jan found their new house.

The guys on the Granada Hills team heard that a new quarterback had transferred to the school, nicknamed the Highlanders. When the 16-year-old Elway showed up for his first practice at Northridge Park, his teammates were unimpressed. He was 5'11", 160 pounds, scrawny, and knock-kneed. His chest was so underdeveloped that it appeared to be concave. Elway looked like he'd be lucky to make fourth string.

But then he began to throw the ball. It reached the receivers in a hurry. After several games, Elway became the starting quarterback.

There were growing pains along the way for the sophomore high schooler. In his first start, Elway was about to be sent in when Neumeier discovered that his quarterback had lost his mouthguard, which all players had to wear. Elway's twin sister Jana saw that it had fallen onto the field, so she ran out and brought it to her brother. Elway had to sit out only the next series of plays.

During an organized seven-on-seven passing league before his junior year, Elway's Granada Hills teammates immediately noticed that something was different. For one thing, he had grown about two inches. For another, he threw the ball differently, having mastered a throwing technique that came from a coaching buddy of his father's named Mike Price. They were throwing the ball in the backyard of the Elway home in Northridge when Price suggested a change in Elway's throwing motion.

As Elway described it years later, standing up to demonstrate, "He told me, 'When you throw a football, you release it at the highest point. You act like you're throwing over a rope, like a rope bridge. You put a rope up as high as you can put it. Wherever your arm extends to, when the ball comes out, it comes out over that rope.' At that point in time, that's when I really started becoming a good thrower. That was the one good coaching point that I got. That was the thing that got me out of the baseball throw to the football throw. It was invaluable."

Now, as Elway's receivers were soon to discover, he was throwing heat-seeking missiles. That, combined with his ability to place the ball exactly where the receiver wanted it, took his game to a whole new level. Scott Marshall, who was one of Elway's favorite targets during his junior year, was struck at how when he would run an 18-yard out pattern—running 18 yards straight ahead, then cutting sharply toward the sideline—Elway would deliver the ball as though it were following a path on a taut rope, with no discernible arc. Marshall had never seen a quarterback do that before. Marshall, Chris Sutton, Paul Bergmann, and Paul Scheper—Elway's primary receivers—practiced for his passes by lining up 10 yards apart and throwing the ball as hard as they could at each other. In time, they could catch almost every throw from Elway. That is, almost every throw. Marshall missed an Elway pass one day. It hit his right thumb and popped it out of place momentarily. And it wasn't just his offensive teammates who were at risk. Nick Macias, a teammate who played linebacker for Granada Hills, suffered a dislocated thumb and a partially broken finger trying to intercept Elway's passes during practice.

Elway starred from the get-go during his junior season, leading Granada Hills to upsets over big-name rivals. That set the stage for a showdown against San Fernando Valley, a traditional power. Down 35–33 with less than two minutes to play, Elway led Granada Hills down the field. On San Fernando's 9-yard line with 25 seconds left, Neumeier called for a pass play from Elway to Sutton in the corner of the end zone. Touchdown! But wait. A holding penalty nullified the score. Elway had one more chance, but now he was backed up to the 24-yard line with 20 seconds remaining. Neumeier called the same play, and again Sutton caught a touchdown. This time the score stood. It was the first of Elway's fabled fourth-quarter comebacks. He went on to lead Granada Hills to the city semifinals before they were eliminated.

Disaster struck, however, during Elway's senior season. He was scrambling in the sixth game of the season, against San Fernando Valley. He turned up field, planted his leg to fake a defender, and his left knee popped. He had torn his meniscus. Showing his grittiness, he had his knee taped, and he remained in the game. Elway even threw a 51-yard touchdown pass after the injury. But his season was over. He needed surgery. Elway had completed 129-of-198 passes and 19 touchdowns. Both *Parade* magazine and *Football News* named him the nation's top prep quarterback.

Elway recovered in time to play baseball during his senior season at Granada Hills. Even with all his football accolades, Elway seemed to be just as good, if not better, on the diamond. As a junior, he had led Granada Hills to a city title in baseball and was chosen City Player of the Year. Elway played six positions for the Highlanders, but he mostly patrolled the outfield. His star shone even brighter as a senior, as he led Granada Hills to the championship game, which was played at Dodger Stadium. Few people gave them a chance that evening against Crenshaw High School, which featured Darryl Strawberry, who was about to be the No. 1 overall pick in the 1980 Major League Baseball Draft. Playing before 20,000 fans, Crenshaw took the lead. The game seemed all but over when Elway was called in to pitch. He snuffed out a Crenshaw rally over four-and-two-thirds innings, holding Strawberry hitless against him, and Granada Hills came from behind to win its second consecutive city 4-A school title.

That same day, the Kansas City Royals selected Elway in the 18th round of the baseball draft. He would have gone in the first or second round if he hadn't said repeatedly that he planned to attend college. Elway again was selected as the City Player of the Year in baseball, with a .491 batting average and a pitching record of four wins and two losses.

But his prep career wasn't quite over. Elway still had one more football game to play—the 28th annual Shrine Football Classic on July 21, 1979, held at the Rose Bowl. He was anxious beforehand since this would be the first game following his knee injury and long recovery. But Elway looked even better than before. He scrambled, connected on short-and-medium passes, and threw for four touchdowns, leading the prep All-Stars from northern Los Angeles County over the southern county All-Stars 35–15. He was clearly ready for college.

By then, he had chosen Stanford over 60 other suitors. The other finalists were Notre Dame, USC, Missouri, and San Jose. Elway ruled out Notre Dame after traveling there after a snowstorm and having head coach Dan Devine ignore him. Elway rejected USC because it was Tailback U. They made their name running the ball. Stanford, on the other hand, was

Quarterback U. In 1977 and 1978, Stanford quarterbacks led the NCAA in passing categories.

Stanford enjoyed another advantage over the other schools. Fassel, the quarterbacks coach, had a salesman's intuitive sense of how to close a deal. He understood he needed the support of Jan Elway, John's mother. She had been emphasizing to her son that he needed to obtain a good education because one freak injury could derail his football career. That gave Stanford an edge due to its strong academic reputation.

But Stanford's emphasis on the passing attack may have carried the most weight. "I like to throw," Elway said in February 1979 when he announced his decision. "I threw a lot in high school, and I want to be able to continue in college. Stanford's offense will permit me to do that."

The other suitor, San Jose State, wouldn't normally have been in the running. It played in a lesser conference, while Stanford played in the glamorous Pac-10. But San Jose State had one asset no other school could match—it had hired Jack Elway as its new coach in December 1978 after three winning seasons at Cal State Northridge.

As Jack frequently noted, he sat with the best prep quarterback at the breakfast table. Not only that, but the father and son were extraordinarily close. John would have gone to San Jose State if Jack had asked him. But Jack told Fassel and others that he wouldn't do that, that John should decide what was best for him. After John chose to go to Stanford, Jack joked to *Sports Illustrated*, "I tell people that my offer to John was $2,000 under the table, a new car, and a mortgage on the house. I said I would go so far as to have an affair with his mother. Still, he didn't go for it."

Shortly after Elway arrived at Stanford in the fall of 1979, two highly touted quarterbacks transferred to other schools. Still, that didn't mean Elway was the starter, even though Steve Dils who had led the NCAA in passing during the preceding year in his one year as a starter at Stanford, had graduated. Turk Schonert, a senior, was next in line. Schonert had plenty of ability, and he knew Stanford's complicated offense.

Elway's new teammates quickly saw that he was a special athlete. For Mike Dotterer, a halfback who had played on the losing side in the Shrine

All-Star Game, the revelation came just after arriving on campus for their freshman year. They both were staying at the home of a wealthy alum near Stanford that featured a swimming pool and a tennis court. Dotterer was a phenomenal athlete who would star in both football and baseball for Stanford. He grabbed a racket and challenged Elway to a tennis match. The quarterback was drinking a beer, holding the can in one hand, the racket in the other as they warmed up. After a while, Dotterer called out, "Okay, we're ready, John. Put the beer down."

"I'm going to play with it," Elway replied.

I'm going to kick his ass, Dotterer thought to himself.

Instead, Elway beat him. Dotterer stalked off the court.

One night, Elway and his buddies were playing Ping-Pong at Branner, an all-freshman dorm. Elway vanquished his friends, one by one. A crowd gathered, and someone went to find the dorm's Ping-Pong champ, who arrived with his own paddle. Elway smoked him.

His new teammates were learning that he hated to lose and had a knack to win—at anything. Stanford was full of budding Type A's, but no one had ever seen anyone as competitive as him.

One day at practice, Elway threw a screen pass to Darrin Nelson, a dual threat who had won headlines as the first running back in college to rush for more than 1,000 yards and catch more than 50 passes in one season. He would go on to be a first-round draft choice of the Minnesota Vikings. But when Elway threw the short pass, it was a rocket. Nelson didn't even try to catch it. He figured the ball would have broken at least one finger. The veteran player was trying to teach a lesson to the younger player: not every pass has to be a fireball. But Elway was pissed that Nelson hadn't tried to catch it. To him, it didn't matter that it was practice.

Elway's passes arrived so fast that his receivers at Stanford weren't prepared to catch them at first. Don Lonsinger dove for a 10-yard pass one day in practice after it had been slightly tipped. The ball tore off the skin on the top half of his right pinkie. Lonsinger could see the bone sticking out. He had to redshirt that year and was left with a permanently crooked finger—and a memorable story to tell for years.

At another practice Jim Clymer, a tight end, ran a 10-yard cross over the middle. He was a fraction of a second late positioning his hands for an Elway pass. The skin of the ball tore the skin off the top of his palm. Clymer was able to tape it up and keep playing, but thought: *Damn, now I'm playing with the big boys.*

Others who weren't quick enough or let one of his passes slip through their hands received what became known as "The Elway Cross"—a mark on their chests from the pointed end of the football. The welt would typically remain for a couple of weeks.

Elway even broke the pinkie of his girlfriend, Janet Buchan, after she exhorted him to put a little heat during a friendly game of catch.

Elway's competitive fire showed up in other ways.

A nose guard named Kevin Lamar made a swim move one day in practice that surprised the offensive lineman blocking him and left Lamar with a clear lane toward Elway. Defensive linemen weren't supposed to hit quarterbacks during practice—to lessen the chances of injury for the team's most important player. Lamar knew this. He didn't intentionally try to hit the quarterback. But as he jumped up to knock down Elway's pass, he and the offensive lineman crashed into the quarterback. Everyone went down in a pile. Lamar was excited. He had just made the play of the day. But the coaches yelled at him: "We don't touch the quarterback!"

Elway, however, didn't care. "Bring it on!" he told Lamar. "Bring it on any time you want!"

Elway's response helped explain another reason for his success. His all-consuming approach inspired his teammates to follow him. After seeing Elway encourage his competitive play, Lamar would have done anything for him. Other guys who played hard for him could recount similar stories. Besides, Elway had so much talent, his teammates hated to let him down.

Elway also didn't cause friction as some No. 1 recruits would have. When he arrived at Stanford, he wanted to wear No. 11, his number at Granada Hills. But it belonged to a defensive back named Rick Gervais. Elway didn't make a fuss and accepted number seven. And of course, he managed to do more than okay with that jersey.

Elway played sporadically during his freshman year in 1979 since he was still learning the offense. Plus, it wasn't easy unseating Schonert, who was garnering the top passing rating in the country. In the 1979 Big Game, however, Schonert couldn't deliver a victory. With Stanford trailing 21–14, the quarterback brought his team to the Cal 1-yard line with 40 seconds left. But on fourth down, Cal defensive back Ron Coccimiglio knocked down Schonert's pass.

In 1980, following Schonert's graduation, Elway, a sophomore, became the starting quarterback. He was now 6'4", 200 pounds. Not only did Elway throw harder than any other quarterback—and not only did he want to win more than any other player—he was quick, and his core strength made him difficult to bring down without a solid hit. As the Associated Press reported: "Watch the way the arm moves, though, with the rest of Elway's body when he throws the ball. Play it back in slow motion if you can. First, he sets his feet, cocks his hips, and opens up his shoulders by swinging his left arm. Then he snaps his right shoulder back, stretching powerful stomach and chest muscles across the bow of his body and catapults the ball forward with enormous force."

The full Elway package was on display when Stanford traveled to Oklahoma for its fourth game of the 1980 season. The Sooners had been a premier football team for years and were riding a 20-game home winning streak. Ranked No. 4 in the country, Oklahoma figured to extend their streak to 21 against Stanford. Stanford, however, shocked the college football world by taking a 31–0 lead before giving up two second-half touchdowns but still winning easily. Elway spelled the difference. He scrambled to avoid the rush, connected on short patterns that methodically moved the ball downfield, and threw three touchdowns while running for a fourth one. "John Elway put on the greatest exhibition of quarterback play and passing I have ever seen on this field," Barry Switzer, the Sooners coach, said after the game.

Stanford had three wins and only one loss after that game. The following week, Stanford defeated the San Jose State Spartans, coached by Jack Elway. By midseason, they were ranked No. 15 in the country. But Stanford won only two of its final six games.

Against USC, in the 10th game of that season, Elway performed a Houdini-like bit of magic that fans would talk about for years. With Stanford at the USC 46-yard line, Elway dropped straight back 10 yards. A Trojans defensive lineman took an outside rush and hemmed in Elway from his right. He stepped up to avoid the sack but then saw another Trojans defender closing in from the left. Elway sprinted right, toward the sideline. He reached the right hash mark still in trouble. Two USC lineman were rushing straight at him with bad intent.

Elway's answer? He turned around and began running with his back to the line of scrimmage, retreating past the Stanford 40 and then the 35-yard line. Unable to see his pursuers, Elway faked right, cut left and at the Stanford 30-yard line, wheeled around and reversed his course by running back upfield. The two Trojan defenders chasing him couldn't keep up. Elway raced past a third USC lineman at the 35. Reaching the 40-yard line, still behind the line of scrimmage, Elway spotted flanker Ken Margerum in the end zone, 60 yards away.

When the typical quarterback is scrambling under pressure, receivers run back toward him to become a more accessible target. Given his bazooka of an arm, Elway's receivers were taught the opposite—keep running downfield. Elway would find them. Margerum had run into the middle of the end zone. He was wide open only because USC safety Ronnie Lott, at the Trojans 10-yard line, calculated he had gone far enough to stop any Elway pass. Lott would go on to star for the San Francisco 49ers and be voted a first-ballot Hall of Fame selection. But on this play, Lott's instincts betrayed him. Elway launched a guided missile. The ball sailed over Lott's head into the arms of Margerum in the end zone, a 70-yard throw. The force of the ball nearly knocked down Margerum, but he caught it a second before Lott recovered to tackle him with teeth-rattling force. The sure-handed Margerum held on. Stanford touchdown! But emblematic of a season heading south, it was the team's only touchdown that day in a 34–9 blowout by USC.

The following week, Stanford lost its finale, the Big Game, 28–23 after Cal's Kevin Moen blitzed Elway and forced him to throw incomplete on the climactic play of the game. Stanford finished the 1980 season a lackluster 6–5.

CHAPTER 4

THE COACHES

Cal's narrow victory in the 1980 Big Game may have saved Roger Theder's job, but it was one of the few highlights of a disappointing season, which saw Cal finish with a 3–8 mark. Theder had made his name as an offensive-minded coach. But after the 1980 season, he decided his offense needed a makeover. And what he had in mind was a bold and risky move.

Like other coaches, Theder was always on the lookout for the latest trend. Along with Bill Walsh's "West Coast" offense, another formation was attracting attention. Called the "Run and Shoot," it was similar to the spread offense that Jack Neumeier had run at Granada Hills High School with John Elway. But it was most closely associated with the head coach at Portland State University. His name was Darrel Davis, but everybody knew him as "Mouse," a nickname an older brother had given him when he was in high school. Davis made all the plays on a ballfield, despite his small stature.

As a high school coach in Oregon, Davis employed the Run and Shoot and won 73 percent of his games while setting records for yards gained and points scored. In 1975, Davis moved up to become the head coach at Portland State, which played in a division one rung below the major conference schools. There, Davis installed the Run and Shoot. It was a pass-first offense that used four receivers, but no tight end, and a single running back. One of the receivers usually ran in motion parallel to the line of scrimmage just before the ball was snapped. This forced at least one defender to adjust his position and revealed to the quarterback whether the defense was employing a man-to-man or zone defense.

The offense was complex because it required receivers and the quarterback to make decisions on the fly, depending on how the defense was arrayed. It worked to near perfection under Davis. Portland State established yardage and scoring records behind quarterback June Jones and his successor, Neil Lomax. This success prompted other coaches to flock to Portland State to learn about this revolutionary offense. Davis believed it was unstoppable.

But with the success came frustration. No Division I school would hire him as head coach. Davis yearned to show what he and his offense could do on a bigger stage. Ultimately, he wanted to become an NFL head coach. To get there, he decided to step down as head coach at Portland State to become Theder's offensive coordinator at Cal for the 1981 season. Theder promised Davis a free hand in running the new offense.

The Bears' Run and Shoot era began auspiciously. Cal's defense couldn't stop it during preseason practice. The starting quarterback, sophomore Gale Gilbert, had a strong arm and the football smarts to make the necessary adjustments on the run. In the season opener against Texas A&M, Cal scored on its initial drive, which included a fake punt where the second-string quarterback, J Torchio, who served as the upback in the formation, threw a pass for a first down. Cal was driving for a second touchdown behind Gilbert when disaster struck—the quarterback tore his knee on a broken play. He left the game and didn't return.

The next man up was Torchio. He had led Cal to victory in the previous year's Big Game. Torchio led Cal to three more touchdowns and a 28–16 halftime lead against Texas A&M. But the offense couldn't score in the second half as the Aggies adjusted to the new scheme. Cal lost 29–28.

Gilbert's knee required surgery. His season was over after only 19 plays. With Torchio now the quarterback, the Bears lost four of their next five games. The sophomore's abilities were ill-suited for the new offense. Under the Run and Shoot, the quarterback was supposed to sprint several yards to the left or right to get a clearer view downfield. Torchio was more comfortable as a dropback passer. And he couldn't match Gilbert's accuracy and arm strength.

The Run and Shoot relied on small, speedy wide receivers who were too quick for linebackers to cover. When it was effective, it succeeded by stretching the defense. But it often stalled close to the opponent's end zone when the defense had less ground to cover, and the running game became more important.

Throughout the first part of the season, Davis refused to heed suggestions from Theder to modify the offense. It would work, Davis insisted, if the players executed it properly. Hearing Davis repeat this over and over—it was essentially the players' fault, he was saying—sapped Torchio's confidence in his own abilities.

Cal played UCLA in the seventh game of the 1981 season. The result was their worst defeat yet—34–6. On the Tuesday after the game, Theder told Davis he had decided to move to a hybrid model that included both the Run and Shoot and the traditional pro-set offense. Davis refused to go along, reminding Theder that he had promised him total control of the offense. Yes, agreed Theder, but the Run and Shoot wasn't working. "Here's the deal," Davis said after much back and forth. "Why don't I just go down the road?"

Davis resigned and drove back to Oregon.

Torchio played like a star in the hybrid offense in Cal's next game, as the Bears crushed Oregon State 45–3. Had Cal found the right path by junking the Run and Shoot?

Not quite, as it turned out. The next week, USC shut down Cal 21–3. It didn't get any better the week after that. Washington State shut the Bears out 19–0. Torchio threw for a meager 79 yards in that game.

That set up the 1981 season finale between the 2–8 Bears and the 3–7 Stanford squad. Despite the two rivals' mediocre records, it still counted as the Big Game, with 84,563 fans in attendance at Stanford Stadium. A divided team, Cal players held a meeting at their hotel the night before the game. Most of them backed Theder, who was an honest and decent man. Other players said it was time for him to go.

Stanford settled the question the following day behind Elway. He threw three touchdown passes, and Stanford won 42–21 to reclaim the Axe. "In the Cal locker room, players and coaches talked quietly in darkened hallways, and a pack of reporters hovered over coach Roger Theder like vultures on a telephone line waiting for carrion," the *San Francisco Examiner* reported the next day.

Dave Maggard, Cal's athletic director, fired Theder less than 24 hours after the game. Two weeks later, Maggard announced his new coach: Joe Kapp. He was a Cal legend, having quarterbacked the Bears the last time they qualified to play in the Rose Bowl in 1959. Kapp then starred in the Canadian Football League before leading the Minnesota Vikings to the 1970 Super Bowl. Kapp won renown by refusing to accept the Vikings' Most Valuable Award at a team banquet that year. What mattered, he said, was a team-first approach where all 40 players performed as one unit for the entire 60 minutes of a game. "There is no most valuable Viking," Kapp told the stunned crowd. "Forty for 60...I just can't accept this," he added and handed back the trophy.

Swashbuckling, macho, a man's man, a winner—those were the words that others used to describe Kapp. "His spirit and focus were magic," Alan Page, a Pro Hall of Fame defensive tackle for the Vikings, said years later. "He may not have thrown the prettiest passes, he may not have been the fastest runner, he may not have been a lot of things—but when things got tough, he was there for everybody."

One word, however, had never been used to describe Kapp—coach. Maggard handed him the reins, even though Kapp had never coached before.

"Don't worry," wrote Glenn Dickey, a sports columnist for the *San Francisco Chronicle*, and Kapp's biggest booster. "The real reason for Maggard's decision was that he knew that it was important for the Cal football program to go in a different direction, and to bring in a man who really wanted the job, who could be depended on to be optimistic about the program from beginning to end," Dickey wrote. "He also knew it was important to bring in a man who could sell a prospect on Cal because he himself is entirely sold on the university. When Joe Kapp tells a player that Berkeley is the best place to come for an education, his message will come from the heart."

No one doubted that. Joe Kapp was all heart. But what was in his head? That question would come up repeatedly.

Born in 1938, Kapp was the product of an unusual union. His mother Florence was a Mexican American who picked lettuce in the fields and worked as a waitress. His father Robert, a son of German immigrants, held a series of jobs that he constantly lost due to a drinking problem. Money was tight. It fell to Florence to raise Joe and his siblings mostly on her own. As a boy, Joe saw the abuse she took from people who tried to take advantage of her. The mistreatment lit a fire in her son. He would always stand up for what he thought was right to protect others, and he would never back down an inch, no matter the cost to himself.

Kapp was living with an aunt's family in Newhall, north of Los Angeles, when he graduated from high school. Years earlier, he had set his sights on attending Cal after his seventh-grade homeroom teacher took his class to visit the Berkeley campus. He fell hard for it. With his hardscrabble background, he had never seen anything like it before. "Its setting on the Bay was impressive," he wrote in a first-person piece for *Sports Illustrated*. "It was immense; the eucalyptus trees, the buildings, the Campanile, Memorial Stadium, the students, the color—the whole scene captured my imagination. I wanted someday to belong to all this."

Cal recruited him to play both basketball and football. On the basketball court, he became a valued reserve who dove for every loose ball and took no guff from the opposing team. In one game, a USC player was playing rough against one of Kapp's teammates, Earl Robinson, and spat a racial epithet at him. At halftime, all the Cal players trooped to the Bears' locker room—except Kapp. He found the Trojans locker room, got everyone's attention, and shouted, "This is a warning to all you fucking rubbers! You mess with my teammate verbally or physically, and I will beat the shit out of you before you get to the bus." The Trojans let up in the second half, and Cal stormed back to win the game.

Kapp didn't get off to a good start as a member of the frosh football team. In those days, players went both ways. So Kapp played both quarterback and defensive back. Against UCLA, a sprinter on the Bruins track team named Craig Chudy repeatedly raced past Kapp, catching three long passes for touchdowns. Kapp was despondent after the game, believing he wasn't good enough and ought to quit. The coach talked him into staying.

Kapp became Cal's starting quarterback late during his sophomore season in 1956. The team went only 3–7 that year but won the Big Game 20–18 to give a triumphant send-off to its venerated coach, Pappy Waldorf, who had resigned. The Bears' 1957 team won only a single game, however.

In Kapp's senior year, the 1958 squad lost its first two games but then surprised naysayers by turning its season around. Kapp led Cal to the Pacific Coast Conference title, earning the team a spot in the 1959 Rose Bowl. Their Cinderella season came to an end there when the University of Iowa clobbered the outmanned Bears 38–12.

Kapp won awards as the top collegiate player on the West Coast. But with a reputation as a plodding runner with a below-average arm, he wasn't selected by a pro team until the 18th round of the NFL draft. He received a better offer to play in the Canadian Football League. His time there didn't begin well, however. While he was a rookie in the CFL, a drunk teammate smashed a bottle of beer against his jaw one night and raked it against his throat. Kapp was so bloody that when two other teammates carried him to the trainer's room, the trainer took one look and fainted. A hospital patched him up with 108 stitches. Kapp played in the following week's game and went on to star in the league. He never missed a game despite separating a shoulder, dislocating a finger, and twisting his knee. In 1964, he led the British Columbia Lions to their first victory in the Grey Cup, Canada's Super Bowl.

In 1967, wanting to play in the NFL, he signed with the Vikings. In the team's second game that season, the Los Angeles Rams were slaughtering the Vikings. Coach Bud Grant inserted Kapp late in the game. He took his position behind the center, began calling signals, and then, wanting to shake things up, yelled across the line of scrimmage, "Fuck you, Rams! You're not much! Here I come!" The Rams' defensive line, known as the Fearsome Foursome, smothered him. That didn't faze Kapp; he reveled in the combat.

In a game later that season, the Vikings were tied with the Green Bay Packers, who would go on to win the Super Bowl. With only minutes left in the game, Kapp fumbled, and Green Bay went on to kick the winning field goal. "I felt so bad I was almost sick," Kapp wrote later. "So did the other guys. But I had this lifelong rule about never missing a post-game party, and I didn't intend to miss this one."

After the game, the players gathered at a fan's house. Kapp grabbed a bottle of tequila and headed to the basement. A teammate had already settled there. He was Lonnie Warwick, who had worked in the coal mines in West Virginia and as a railroad worker in Arizona before signing with the Vikings and becoming their starting middle linebacker. Kapp and Warwick drank tequila, commiserated and told each other that despite the loss, the Vikings were on the way to becoming a great team. Then each player blamed himself for the loss. "It's too bad I had to blow that game for us today," Kapp said.

"You didn't blow the game," Warwick said. "The defense lost the game."

"No, no, Lonnie," Kapp replied. "Don't try to make me feel better. I blew it!"

Warwick climbed to his feet, glared at Kapp, and said, "Listen, you crazy Mexican, I told you we lost the game, not you! Stop feeling sorry for yourself!"

Kapp stood up. Now the two were nose to nose. Warwick suggested they go outside to settle their dispute like men. Kapp, of course, agreed. They whaled at each other for about five minutes before teammates pulled them apart.

As Kapp wrote later, "When it was over, with him on top, Jim Marshall and Roy Winston made us get up and shake hands. 'Good night, Lonnie,' I said, and Lonnie said, 'Good night, Joe,' just as if we were both normal in the head."

The next morning Warwick called and said, "Jeez, Joe, I don't know what got into us."

"I know what got into us," Kapp replied. "Tequila."

"Yeah," he said. "I don't know about you, but I got to go to the dentist."

"Well, I'm on my way to the eye doctor," Kapp said. "One of my eyes won't open."

"I got a bad eye, too," Warwick said. "Let's go to the eye doctor together."

It was a bizarre incident. But it was quintessential Kapp, a scrapper who wouldn't back down from a fight. At 6'3", 218 pounds, he had the size to handle himself. And that long scar tracing his jawbone thanks to the CFL teammate with the broken beer bottle? He wore it like the badge of a badass.

Kapp's predecessor as the Vikings quarterback was Fran Tarkenton, who was known for his ability to scramble and avoid tacklers. Kapp was the rare quarterback who seemed to enjoy hitting as much as the middle linebacker. "Other quarterbacks run out of bounds," said Coach Grant. "Kapp turns upfield and looks for a tackle to run into."

With his never-stand-down spirit, Kapp won his teammates' respect, and they rallied behind him as the Vikings' leader. Kapp had learned a key lesson from Pete Newell, his basketball coach at Cal, who repeatedly praised Kapp for playing tough defense against the starters in practice—and made Kapp feel like a vital member of the team. Kapp went out of his way to make all of the Vikings, even the reserves, feel like their role mattered.

Kapp didn't impress anyone with his style, but he got the job done, one way or another. In 1969, he tied a league record by throwing seven touchdown passes against the Baltimore Colts, the NFL champion the year before. "At least five of them were spirals," Kapp joked later.

After plowing through most of the competition in 1969, Minnesota found itself matched against the Cleveland Browns for the right to advance to the Super Bowl. One play in that game epitomized Kapp's career. He was supposed to throw a short pass but didn't find an open receiver. Looking to make something happen, he scrambled to his right and then headed upfield. He quickly encountered an obstacle in the hulking shape of Jim Houston, Cleveland's toughest linebacker, a 250-pound tackling machine. Minnesota was safely ahead in the game. Just about any other quarterback would have raced to the sidelines and safety. Not Kapp. He put his head down, crashed into Houston. The quarterback flipped over and landed on his back.

One player lay prone after the fearsome collision. It was the Cleveland linebacker, out cold. He had to be carried away, done for the game.

But in that year's Super Bowl, the Chiefs whipped the Vikings. They even knocked Kapp out of the game, the first time that had happened during his 11 years in the CFL and the NFL. "We didn't party enough, didn't have enough fun," Kapp said in *Sports Illustrated*, in explaining the loss in his typical go-against-the-grain approach.

Kapp could take small satisfaction in becoming the answer to an arcane trivia question. Who was the only quarterback to play in the Rose Bowl, the Grey Cup, and the Super Bowl?

In advance of the 1970 season, Kapp demanded more money than the penurious Vikings would pay him. They chose not to re-sign him, and he went to the Boston Patriots, who were awful. Playing behind a porous offensive line, Kapp's performance suffered. When the Patriots tried to reduce his salary before the next season, Kapp took the league to court. The case dragged on. In the end, he not only lost the legal battle, but he never played again. In the following years, Kapp invested in real estate and acted in several movies, including two football flicks, *The Longest Yard* and *Semi-Tough*. Burt Reynolds starred in both movies.

One day, Kapp asked Reynolds if he had the chops to become a serious actor. Reynolds mulled the question and asked, "Joe, did you ever see the Jim Thorpe story?" Reynolds was referring to a 1951 movie in which Burt Lancaster starred as Thorpe, a college football star at Carlisle Indian School who also won the decathlon at the 1912 Olympics.

Kapp got excited and grabbed Reynold's wrist. He said he had paid to see it five times when he was 12, even though his family didn't have much money. Reynolds said he loved the movie, too, and asked, "After you saw the movie five times, who did you want to be?"

"Jim Thorpe," Kapp replied.

"Burt, who did you want to be?" Kapp asked.

"Burt Lancaster," Reynolds responded.

Kapp got the message. Football remained his true pursuit. He set his sights on becoming the coach of Cal, with his love for the university undimmed. So after Theder was fired following the 1981 season, Kapp campaigned to replace him and was selected as the Bears' new head coach.

His hair was now salt and pepper, but the fire remained. The announcement of his hiring took place at the Cal Faculty Club. Afterward, Kapp sat with players, alums, and reporters for lunch when he spotted something that bothered him. A reporter was wearing a cap with the inscription "UCLA/ Pepsi Invitational track meet." Kapp snatched the hat and announced to the gathering: "Look at this! UCLA!"

"Kapp flung the hat disdainfully to the ground, stomped on it violently, and threw it out the door," the *San Francisco Chronicle* reported. "There," a satisfied Kapp said. "We'll have none of that UCLA stuff in here. They're the enemy."

At the first team meeting, Kapp called out to one of his coaches, "Get the picture! Get the picture!" The coach came back with a photograph of the Rose Bowl stadium in Los Angeles. "That's where we're going, men!" Kapp said. "We're taking the Bears back to the Rose Bowl!"

The players began screaming and hollering.

*   *   *

If anything defined the history of Stanford football, it was quarterbacks who mastered the passing attack. Frankie Albert was the first college football quarterback to run the T-formation, an innovation that led to a 9–0 record and a Rose Bowl title after the 1940 season. John Brodie was the top college quarterback at Stanford in 1956 and, like Albert, he went on to star for the San Francisco 49ers as a pro. In 1971, Jim Plunkett led Stanford to its first Rose Bowl victory in three decades and became the university's first Heisman Trophy winner. He went on to quarterback two Super Bowl titles. Mike Boryla starred for Stanford in 1973 and went on to a pro career. Each quarterback had a head coach who emphasized the forward pass.

Bill Walsh took the passing game to another level after he was hired as Stanford's coach in advance of the 1977 season. "We won't be conservative," he promised when he first met with reporters.

It wasn't just that Walsh wouldn't be conservative—he ushered in a whole new approach to running the offense, one he'd honed as an assistant coach for the Cincinnati Bengals. Walsh enjoyed great success there with one quarterback, Virgil Carter, who was mobile and accurate but didn't have a strong arm, by having him throw short and medium passes. Carter's successor was Ken Anderson. He had come out of tiny Augustana College in Illinois, playing at the lowest level of college football. When Anderson arrived in Cincinnati, Walsh had to teach him how to drop back. By his fourth year, Anderson was the league's leading passer. But Walsh parted ways with Cincinnati in 1976 after the owner passed over him when hiring the team's next head coach. Walsh moved on to the San Diego Chargers where he put quarterback Dan Fouts on the path to his Hall of Fame career. Stanford finally gave Walsh the chance to lead his own team. He was 45 years old.

Walsh's first star pupil was Guy Benjamin, the starting quarterback for the 1977 team. Benjamin had been the first stringer the year before, under Walsh's predecessor, running a pro-set offense with two running backs, a tight end, and two wide receivers. Benjamin's job then was to find the open receiver and get him the ball.

That changed under Walsh. He instituted a more sophisticated plan that in time became known as the "West Coast" offense. Up to that point, most coaches started off a game by trying to establish the run. If successful, this caused defenders to anticipate another handoff—which would set up passes downfield. Walsh turned that concept upside down. He sought to establish a passing attack that would give his team the lead. Then he'd finish off the other team with the running game.

Beyond that, Walsh was a technician. He drilled Benjamin on how to drop back and throw the ball through a series of precise movements. The quarterback had to bend his left, or lead, leg to generate more velocity when he threw a pass. He had to open his hips when throwing the ball to the left at a specific point in the throwing motion. When Benjamin dropped back, Walsh taught him to stop going backward on his next to last step. That way, the final step served to push him forward, which made it easier to throw a quick pass. Walsh, an exacting mentor, would correct Benjamin if his footwork was off by three or four inches. Walsh's West Coast offense also relied on timed routes. Benjamin would drop back three or five steps and immediately throw to a receiver who may not yet have even been look-ing for the ball.

All along, Walsh emphasized the importance of advancing the ball steadily through high-percentage, short and medium passes to make first downs. If executed properly, the receiver wouldn't just catch the pass, he would have room to run for more yardage. With this approach, the running back became an important additional receiver. In 1977, Stanford's Darrin Nelson became the first running back in college football history to run for more than 1,000 yards and catch at least 50 passes, and he became the second one to do it the following year.

When you controlled the ball, Walsh noted, either through passing or running, the other team could not score unless the offense committed a major mistake. Walsh's timed routes and short passes minimized that pos-sibility. At the same time, Walsh counted on the opposing defense to begin making mistakes in frustration at the offense's steady success. Those lapses set up long completions.

After a decent season as a junior in 1976, Benjamin won the Sammy Baugh Trophy in 1977 under Walsh as the NCAA's leading passer. Steve Dils followed Benjamin as Stanford's starting quarterback in 1978. During practice, Dils might complete a pass and then have Walsh tell him that he hadn't thrown it properly. Each pass was supposed to reach the receiver in a certain spot, Walsh instructed. So, despite the completion, the coach would require the offense to run the play over and over until Dils consistently threw it to the correct location. The insistence on precise execution paid off. Dils, a senior, also won the Sammy Baugh Trophy in his only year as a starter.

Walsh enjoyed such tremendous success at Stanford—his teams defeated LSU and Georgia in bowl games—that the woebegone 49ers hired him after Stanford's 1978 season. Walsh turned things around dramatically by winning three Super Bowls with the 49ers over 10 years.

Stanford replaced Walsh with his chief offensive assistant coach, Rod Dowhower. Everyone said it would be a seamless change. It wasn't. By the end of the 1979 season, Stanford's players were openly rebelling against the new coach. While Walsh limited full-speed hits in practice once the season began, Dowhower insisted on the old-school approach of players crashing into each other late into the year. Players felt like they were back in boot camp. Injuries in practice abounded, and the team wore down. Stanford tied No. 1 USC in a midseason game but lost three of their last four games to finish the season with five wins, five losses, and the tie.

Dowhower's final defeat came in the 1979 Big Game when Cal stopped Stanford on fourth and goal at the 1-yard line. Days later, center John Macaulay read a manifesto aloud to Dowhower signed by 30 players saying they would not follow his mandatory offseason drills. They knew how to take care of business themselves, the players said. That was the final straw for Dowhower, who wasn't a schmoozer and hadn't won any allies among the big donors or the press. He resigned about a week later.

The new coach for the 1980 season was Paul Wiggin. Stanford officials would have been hard-pressed to find anyone who better represented the university. He boasted a Stanford pedigree, carried an impeccable reputation, and even looked the part. "He looks like he might have been chiseled out of an old blocking dummy—craggy, semi-rough features…football features," wrote *San Mateo Times* columnist Dick Draper. "Strong, in command, an out-of-the-'50s flat-top haircut all bristly like an aging porcupine's quills and a still-athletic body and confident posture despite a little extra padding around the midsection."

Andy Geiger, the athletic director, told the *San Francisco Chronicle* after he hired Wiggin: "He is respected by everybody we talked to. Everybody."

Born in 1934, Wiggin grew up in Lathrop in California's San Joaquin Valley, only 75 miles east of San Francisco but a world away in terms of culture and sensibilities. A farm town, Lathrop offered only two commercial establishments to its 600 residents. One of them was Wiggin's Trading Post. This simple establishment consisted of a gas station, a bar, the Greyhound bus stop, a store that sold knickknacks—and the Wiggin family home, all on Highway 50. In what was normal for the time, Wiggin and his six siblings slept in two bedrooms, and the entire household shared just a single bathroom. Behind the structure were five acres of farmland. The children pumped gas, milked cows, baled hay, and fed pigs, chickens, and horses.

In their free time, the boys played football in a plowed field and basketball around a rim hung on the side of a barn.

Early on, Wiggin showed athletic promise. But his father, who had played basketball in high school, thought he was soft. "Fat boy," he called Paul when he was in seventh and eighth grade. Before his junior year in high school, Paul's father arranged for him and his older brother Frank to work at the kind of summer manual labor job that it's hard to imagine kids taking on today—stacking 10,000 "wet" bricks a day apiece that had just been spit out of a machine onto a conveyor belt. Each boy had to pull two of the bricks from the conveyor belt, pivot, stack them on a pallet, then pivot back to grab two more bricks, and repeat the process 5,000 times per shift. Paul and Frank performed this task for eight hours a day in an open-sided shed without air conditioning in temperatures that reached 100 degrees. Their employer, the San Joaquin Brick Company, paid them $1.17 ½ per hour for a grand total of $9.40 per day.

There wasn't much to entertain teenagers in Lathrop. At night, friends might occasionally sneak onto a farmer's property and quietly move the family outhouse as a prank. Someone trying to use it later that night might fall into the cesspool. But Paul and Frank were too tired after their work each day to join in the fun. Back home, it was all they could do to crawl into bed and fall asleep. It's hardly surprising that Paul disliked the job. But, apart from the meager wages, the grueling labor paid off in another way. Over time, he noticed that the work strengthened his hands and his core muscles. After the first year, Paul saw the results on the football field at Manteca High School. He starred as a lineman on both sides of the ball and captained the squad.

The next year, Paul's father told him that the summer work had been beneficial and advised him to work there again. Paul never questioned his father, who was a respected city elder. He signed up for more of the brutal brick work and entered his senior year even stronger. If the team needed a first down, the play call was a run behind Paul's ferocious blocking. Paul also terrorized the opposing team's offense, tossing aside blockers to stuff the run and harassing the quarterback on pass plays.

One day, the town fire chief, a member of the Shriners organization, dropped by Wiggin's Trading Post. Finding Paul and his father in the backyard, he showed them a piece of paper that listed the top 100 high school football players in Northern California who would be eligible to play in the inaugural North–South Shrine football game scheduled for the upcoming summer. Paul was astounded to see his name on the list. He had no idea that anyone outside of his farming area knew anything about him or that he might be that good. Paul had never been recognized for anything. That year's North–South game would be played in the storied Los Angeles Memorial Coliseum, home to the USC Trojans, the UCLA Bruins, and the 1932 Olympics. A short time later, Paul learned that he had made the final cut of 28 players. "I've never felt more excited than anything in sports—even more than when I was part of the team that won an NFL championship," he recalled years later.

After his high school graduation, Paul requested permission to take a 10-day leave from his summer job at a shipyard to practice for the All-Star Game. The flight to Los Angeles marked his first trip on an airplane. Paul played well enough for the northern squad that USC, UCLA, and Cal all offered him scholarships. But Paul had already visited Stanford and had set his sights on going there.

However, Paul had let his high school grades slide. One day his father went out to talk to his son in the backyard, with a less-than-stellar report card in hand. "Do you know who that is out in the field?" his father asked, pointing off toward a lone figure at work.

"Yes, that's Ben Armstrong," Paul replied. "I've known him all my life."

"I went to high school with Ben. He was born on that farm. He's going to live on that farm all his life, and he's going to die on that farm. He's never going to know what this world is all about. And if you don't start doing better, you might find yourself ending up like Ben Armstrong."

Wiggin took the lesson to heart. After the Shrine Game, he wrote Stanford football coach Chuck Taylor and asked if Taylor would consider him if Wiggin attended Modesto Junior College and improved his grades and his football skills. Taylor agreed. After a standout year at Modesto, Wiggin enrolled as a sophomore at Stanford. He didn't take long to shine there, too. As a redshirt junior, Wiggin was one of 11 players chosen nationwide as an All-American. He repeated that feat in 1956, his senior year. His career at Stanford ended on a sour note, however. Stanford lost the Big Game that year to a Cal team led by sophomore quarterback Joe Kapp.

One day later on at Stanford, while he was still a junior, a fraternity brother woke up Wiggin. "Is there a team called the Cleveland Browns?" the friend asked.

"Yes," Wiggin replied, "but why would you wake me up to ask?"

"I think you've been drafted by them."

Wiggin knew little about professional football and hadn't imagined playing beyond college. He was planning to obtain a master's degree from Stanford and become a teacher. He didn't know anything about a football draft.

Two weeks later, Wiggin received a letter from Paul Brown, the NFL team's head coach. It explained how the Browns had drafted him in the sixth round to play for them after he had graduated. Professional sports were far less sophisticated then. Wiggin had never participated in a workout for the Browns—or indeed any team—to show how high he could jump or how fast he could run. He did have 17 unassisted tackles in a game against USC, however, which seemed like a pretty fair indicator of his potential as a pro.

Wiggin spent 11 years as the Browns left defensive end. Other players may have been faster or stronger. Wiggin made the most of his physical abilities by working harder and smarter than others. At a time when football had yet to become a refined sport, he was one of the few players who devoted hours to studying film on his opponents to learn their tendencies.

Wiggin learned to surge out of his defensive stance and put his hands under the right tackle's shoulder pads before the tackle could stop him. Then he relied on the strength fortified by the muscles he developed in putting those 10,000 bricks on a pallet each day during those two hot high school summers. At 6'3", 230 pounds, Wiggin wasn't big for a defensive lineman, even in his era. But his powerful hands and long arms prevented opposing linemen from easily brushing them away. They also provided the leverage he needed to steer even the largest offensive tackles out of his way. Another trick he developed was getting his hands underneath an opponent's shoulder pads, which allowed Wiggin to feel which way the lineman was going. This gave Wiggin the chance to get there first to disrupt the play.

Wiggin was a fixture on a team that, featuring running back Jim Brown, never had a losing record during his 11 years. In 1964, the Browns won the league championship, shutting out Johnny Unitas and the Baltimore Colts. Wiggin loved competing on the football field and the camaraderie of his teammates. He didn't get rich, though. His biggest paycheck was $27,000. He spent the offseason working as a teacher in the San Francisco Bay Area. After being named a Pro Bowler for the second time in 1967, Wiggin retired to become a defensive line coach with the 49ers. Later, he became their defensive coordinator.

In 1975, the Kansas City Chiefs hired Wiggin as their head coach during a rebuilding period. The general manager fired him midway through his third season, just after signing him to a two-year contract extension. The GM delivered the news on Halloween, as Wiggin would bitterly remember years later. Some trick.

As he packed his belongings, the team's players trooped into his office to express their sorrow, as *Sports Illustrated* reported six months later. The center cried. So did a linebacker. A 10-year veteran wanted to quit on the spot, as did a tackle named Jim Nicholson. "He came into my office," Wiggin said, "and he just stood there and started to cry. Picture a 6'6" guy with a beard crying. I went over to him and said, 'Nick, don't you feel bad. You paid the price. You did everything I ever asked you to do.' And with that, he threw his arms around me and gave me a kiss on the cheek. He continued to cry, and then he kind of let me go, mumbled something, and went out the door. It was the strangest period, maybe two minutes, where a guy expressed his emotions and never said a word. It was quite an experience."

The thing is, Paul Wiggin's players bonded with him because he loved them and treated them like men. They knew he would always have their backs. He would never sell them out. Outsiders might not have taken the full measure of the man—his looks could be deceiving, as Stanford officials learned during the 1980 and 1981 seasons. "He looked like he would be a tough, militaristic coach with his crew cut, but he was one of the most sensitive people I dealt with in sports," recalled Bob Rose, who was Stanford's sports information director. "He was a relative intellectual. He was a very curious person."

Here is another perspective on Wiggin, from Mike Nolan. Wiggin worked as an assistant coach for Mike's dad Dick with the 49ers and hired Mike to serve as his linebackers/defensive backs coach at Stanford in 1982. "Paul always expected people to be like him and be upstanding, respectful, competent without him having to get on them," Nolan said years later. "Paul was such a kind, honest, dedicated man. If Paul was your friend, he was your best friend. He'd give you his shirt off his back. We were more about preaching about how special our kids were instead of making sure the kids were in line. He was not a slave driver. He'd ask you to do things instead of saying, 'If you don't do this, you're out.' But that's how it is in athletics."

However, his admirable character didn't always translate into what school administrators and fans viewed as the key metric for a coach—a stellar win-loss record. Despite John Elway's heroics as a sophomore throughout 1980, Stanford finished the year 6–5, after just falling short in the Big Game with the Peach Bowl on the line. Elway starred again in 1981, but Stanford under Wiggin went 4–7, for their first losing season since 1963.

Here's another telling perspective on Wiggin: "If you could pick a coach for your son to play for, you'd choose Paul," offered Kevin Bates, a senior linebacker on the 1982 team. "But if you want to go to a Rose Bowl, I'm not sure he's your coach."

Stanford's head coach had to run a clean program that graduated the university's players. The other important measures of a Stanford football coach were his success in taking his team to a bowl—preferably the Rose Bowl—and winning the Big Game. With the Rose Bowl an unlikely goal for Stanford in the following season of 1982, the Big Game would loom large, not only for the Stanford players and fans, but also for Wiggin himself.

• CHAPTER 5 •

THE FATHER VS. THE SON

That's it, thought Claude Gilbert.

It was mid-September 1981, and San Jose State's next game was against Stanford. Gilbert, 49, served as the Spartans' defensive coordinator. It was his job each week to devise a plan to stop their next opponent's offense. And after hours and hours of watching video of John Elway, Gilbert had an aha moment. He'd figured out how to stop Stanford's star quarterback.

The two schools had been playing each other every year at Stanford Stadium since 1948. For Stanford, it usually amounted to an early-season warm-up before games against their tougher conference rivals. But most years it was the biggest game of the season for San Jose State, a public school where many of their students were commuters. The Spartans coaches never had difficulty in pumping up their players to perform their best against the elite private institution only 15 miles away up Highway 101.

But in 1981 Gilbert faced a major complication. The quarterback he wanted to stop was the son of his boss, head coach Jack Elway, the man who had hired him. Jack was in his third season at San Jose State and truly loved his players. But Jack had an uncommonly close relationship with his son, a bond developed over the years through their shared affinity for sports, and John considered his dad to be his best friend and his mentor. Jack wanted his team to beat John's team. There was no question about that. But as much as Jack the coach wanted to defeat Stanford, Jack the dad hoped he could do so in a way that stopped just short of jeopardizing his son, and without throwing shade on his incredible talent.

Gilbert's objective wasn't quite as complicated. He was simply a defensive coordinator who wanted to keep the other team from scoring, and that meant thwarting the quarterback. And, given the quarterback's last name, that put Gilbert in a quandary.

Gilbert was a first-year coach under Jack, so the two were still getting to know each other. But Jack had given Gilbert a license to run the defense while Jack focused on the offense. Besides, Gilbert had plenty of credibility and was not a man to automatically defer to others. He had spent three years as the defensive coordinator at San Diego State and performed so well that the school hired him as its head coach in 1973. Under Gilbert, the Aztecs won 70 percent of their games, but he was fired after his 1980 team suffered a downturn. That's when Jack hired him at San Jose State.

Now, after some thought, Gilbert told Jack at practice on a Monday in September 1981 that he wanted to discuss with him how the Spartans would defend Stanford in Saturday's upcoming game. Jack told Gilbert to meet him after practice at the S&H Keyes Club, an unpretentious watering hole near the San Jose State football stadium.

After they sat down, Jack ordered his usual, a vodka martini. Gilbert requested a beer. The two coaches exchanged pleasantries. Then Gilbert decided to get right to the point. He could tell that Jack was uncomfortable, but he plunged ahead. "Jack," Gilbert said, "I know this game is hard on you. But if we're going to have a chance to win, we're going to have to put pressure on John, and we're going to have to hit him. A lot."

Gilbert then outlined his plan. The film study had showed him that Stanford had no hot-read against a blitz. Most quarterbacks were taught to have an immediate target if the defense rushed extra players. Stanford offensive coordinator Jim Fassel had eschewed that approach—and for a simple reason. He had John Elway. John had shown phenomenal skill game after game in evading blitzers. And in doing so, buying a few extra seconds with his quick feet and his ability to shed would-be tacklers, he inevitably found an open receiver for a big gain.

Most quarterbacks, like John, were right-handed, and when they scrambled, they tended to run to their right since that permitted them to make an in-rhythm throw while on the move. John, though, had the ability to avoid rushers as he raced to the left, stop, reset his feet, and throw anywhere on the field, even back to his right. That's why John's unique move was so potent. Under pressure, John would fool the onrushing defenders by faking as if he was going to run to the right but then perform a clockwise reverse spin and run left. It worked time and time again. But Gilbert had figured it out and told Jack over drinks at the Keyes Club what he planned to do. Jack listened quietly. At the end, he said, "Yeah, Claude. I understand, but I don't want to hear it."

That's all Gilbert needed. He was free to implement his strategy, which he honed during practice over the next several days.

Gilbert had developed a two-pronged plan. In certain situations, a linebacker or a cornerback would blitz John from his right. This would likely prompt him to make his spin move to his left—putting him in the path of a linebacker named Bob Overly, who had waited a beat before running a delayed blitz from Elway's left side. With his strategy, Gilbert would be like a hunter who bagged his quarry by flushing it unwittingly into a trap. "Stay up the field and don't come inside," Gilbert told Overly. "He'll be coming your way."

Overly was a guy you didn't want in your face. He started his college football career as a walk-on at Snow College in Utah where he stood out during his second year there by disrupting offenses practically on his own. Now, as a 20-year-old senior at San Jose State, he was not particularly big—he was 6'0" and 220 pounds—but he was quick enough to evade offensive linemen trying to block him, and he was mean. Overly's teammates thought he was psycho on the football field. One day during practice, Overly, enraged because an offensive lineman had tried to block him below the waist, sacked a backup quarterback named Jack Overstreet. That was a no-no. Jack Elway yelled at Overly. "Fuck you!" he yelled back and sacked Overstreet on the next play for good measure.

Jack didn't like the disobedience, but he loved Overly's over-the-top aggression. Now Coach Gilbert planned to employ it against Jack's son.

In the meantime, the local press had been playing up the Elway versus Elway angle. Both John and Jack said all the right things, but it was a predicament for each of them. It was even worse for Jack's wife Jan and their two daughters. They could only watch the contest without choosing sides. Their solution was to wear T-shirts or hats emblazoned with both teams' logos.

Another factor added to the drama: John had sprained his right ankle in the 1981 season opener the previous week against Purdue. He had played brilliantly, setting a career mark by throwing for 418 yards while completing 33-of-44 passes. But Stanford lost the game by eight points, and John's ankle hurt so badly afterward that he couldn't practice before the San Jose State game. Jack suggested to John that he sit out the game so he could be at full strength the following week for Stanford's big match-up against Ohio State. After all, Stanford was a 20-point favorite over San Jose State. But John, who had spent years competing against his dad in intra-family battles, was determined to play against the Spartans. He had led Stanford to victory over San Jose State the year before, and he badly wanted to do so again. Fassel told John that the decision whether he could play would be up to Stanford's team doctor. The doc gave a thumbs up.

Years later, John would wish that he hadn't. As planned, Gilbert blitzed John from his right. He headed left—and Overly, with a delayed blitz, sacked him for a 10-yard loss, stopping one drive late in the first quarter. Overly dropped him again on the first play of the second quarter and a third time a few minutes later. Overly's blitz confused the Stanford players. Rob Moore, the fullback, had been drilled that if no defender on his side of the field was blitzing, he was to leave the backfield and become a receiver. Moore repeatedly made his read a moment too soon, only to have Overly rush into the backfield that he'd vacated, making a beeline toward his quarterback.

John couldn't hide his frustration. On one play, he was calling signals when he stopped, turned around, and yelled to Moore, "Rob, block that guy!" He pointed at the linebacker. "He's right over there."

At halftime, San Jose State led 14–6. John had only completed 3-of-10 passes for 36 yards.

It would only get worse for the Stanford quarterback. He threw an interception on Stanford's second possession of the second half, and the Spartans scored another touchdown. On Stanford's next possession, Overly intercepted John, and San Jose State notched seven more points three plays later.

John was hobbling, but he wouldn't give up. He should have. He threw two more interceptions. In an extraordinary act, Jack, unable to contain his fatherly instincts, walked several yards onto to the field and yelled at Stanford head coach Paul Wiggin to remove his son. "Get him out!" he shouted. "Get him out!" At another point, Jack waved a white towel at Wiggin, trying to get his attention.

On one play in the third quarter, Overly hit John just after he threw a pass. As Overly was disentangling himself from John on the ground, the linebacker yanked John's little white towel from the front of his uniform pants. "I told you it was going to be a long game," Overly spat at John and threw the towel into his face. The quarterback didn't respond.

But Jack did. "Get him out of the game!" he shouted at Gilbert.

Overly ran off the field, frothing with anger. He had not been benched before that season. "You pull me from the game?" he screamed at Jack. "Now I'm going to fucking kill John."

Overly inserted himself back into the game on the next play.

Several plays later, Overly sacked John a fourth time, for a loss of 19 yards. On the next play, John threw yet another interception. Mercifully, he didn't return for Stanford's final two drives.

The Spartans won 28–6, in what was perhaps the biggest victory ever for San Jose State's football program. It was John's worst game at Stanford. He completed only 6-of-24 passes for a measly 72 yards. He was intercepted five times and sacked seven times. Stanford's only touchdown came on a run. This snapped Stanford's record-setting 37-game streak of scoring a touchdown on a pass.

Jack put his arm around John on the field after the game, and they walked off together. Jack wanted to console his son. He also knew he needed to show some compassion after the beating John had taken, knowing that his wife Jan would be angry at what his defense had done.

The Stanford dressing room was about 400 yards from the stadium. Players had to walk through departing fans to get there. A little boy asked John for an autograph.

"Are you sure you want mine?" he asked.

John was despondent when he met with reporters in the locker room. "I was two steps slow all day," he told the *San Francisco Examiner*. "They were ready to play, and they wanted to win 10 times more than we did. They were the aggressor. This was the most frustrating day of my life. I couldn't pivot, and I couldn't plant my back foot [to throw]."

Jack, of course, was happy with the victory. But he couldn't hide his anger at Wiggin when he spoke to reporters. "John wasn't even operating at half-speed out there," Jack said. "He didn't work out all week. I'm not sure he should have been playing at all—what do you have to do, have him in a wheelchair to get the second quarterback in there?"

Afterward, father and son met in a secluded area outside the locker room. "Why don't you just come to the house tonight?" Jack asked, trying to make amends.

"No, I don't want to do it tonight," John replied.

Jack asked again.

Again, John said no. He wanted to return to the Delta Tau Delta house where he lived and hang out with his fraternity brothers. He said he would come home the following day.

Jack asked a third time. He was getting desperate. When John said no once again, Jack played the parent card. "You're coming down tonight," he said firmly.

"Dad, why do I have to come down tonight?" John asked.

"If you don't come home tonight," Jack replied, "your mom is not going to let me into the house!"

John came home that night. He actually had an important reason to be there the next day. In June, the New York Yankees had selected John in the first round of the Major League Baseball draft after he had hit .361 with nine home runs and 50 runs batted in during 48 games as a sophomore outfielder for Stanford. Now they would be coming to the Elway home to sign him to a professional contract with a $150,000 bonus. Elway would play for a Yankees' minor league team during the following summer, while keeping his eligibility to play football during his senior year at Stanford in 1982. "We project him as a superstar," Bill Bergesch, the Yankees executive who signed him, told *Sports Illustrated*. "He's got everything a scout looks for—he's big and strong, he can run, he can hit and hit with power, and he's got that strong arm. We see him as our right fielder down the road. Unfortunately, we are also aware he has some talent in football."

Yes, despite his terrible performance against San Jose State, John Elway still had some talent in football.

• CHAPTER 6 •

THE BANDS

The strike was on. Not the kind of strike where disgruntled union workers carried placards as they marched in a circle, chanting slogans. No, this was a strike by the Stanford band, who wanted to signal their absolute displeasure with the administration by *not* marching, or playing for that matter. And so they simply didn't show up for the football season opener, without giving advance notice to the university administration.

It was the fall of 1963, and leaders of the Stanford band were incensed that the music department had sacked the band's part-time director, a genial fellow named Jules Shuchat. For the students, ousting the popular Shuchat marked the final straw after years of neglect. The university-supplied instruments were ancient. The band had been relegated to practicing in a building that had been condemned years earlier. Their sheet music came from Palo Alto High School, where Shuchat served as the band director. Band members were forced to purloin paper from the music department late at night to print pregame and halftime formations for rehearsals before upcoming games.

Like virtually all university bands, the Stanford band had for decades marched in regimented lines, with dignity and reverence for traditional school songs and patriotic marches by John Phillips Sousa. But change was afoot. The band had junked its military-style uniforms the year before in favor of red blazers, gray slacks, and Tyrolean-style felt hats with a single jaunty feather. They looked like Austrian hotel managers on a musical outing.

Now, not only had the music department dismissed Shuchat, but university officials were moving to limit the band's autonomy. To make matters

63

worse, Shuchat's replacement had made no effort to reach out to the band and organize activities in advance of the 1963 football season.

Band leaders responded by spreading the word to skip practice and sit out the first game of the 1963 season, against San Jose State. The band's absence from a game—for the first time in 47 years—caused an uproar. University officials met with the band's student officers and cajoled them to return. Band leaders also heard soothing words from Shuchat's replacement, a 33-year-old Midwesterner named Arthur Barnes. The band was placated enough to regroup and play in the stands for the third home game and on the field for the fourth game, against Notre Dame in late October.

To their surprise, as the football season progressed, band members learned that having Barnes as their director was actually better than expected. With the sophisticates at Stanford's music department wanting nothing to do with the pep-musical organization, Barnes became their only adult supervisor. But he made no effort to impose his will over the band. Instead, the savvy Barnes realized he could exercise tacit authority by giving control to the students. Band management organized the rehearsals, halftime shows, and outside events. Barnes, who was also working on his doctorate, simply showed up to direct the music and make sure the band sounded good and loud.

Essentially, Barnes allowed the inmates to run the asylum—and it sparked a revolution with far-reaching implications for the student-run Stanford band, up to and including the famous ending of the 1982 Big Game.

In 1963, the band was set to perform for the season finale at the Big Game on November 23. The day before, however, saw one of the country's darkest days with the assassination of president John F. Kennedy. The Big Game was postponed a week. The nation remained in mourning for the popular president when Cal and Stanford finally met at Stanford Stadium. During pregame ceremonies, Cal's marching band "formed an anchor and played the fanfare from 'Victory at Sea' as a tribute to the late president's background as a World War II Navy officer," the *San Francisco Examiner* reported.

The Stanford band took the field and honored the fallen leader by forming the outline of the United States while performing "America the Beautiful." Next up was "The Star-Spangled Banner," in a special arrangement by Barnes. All 82,000 spectators stood up. The stadium grew quiet.

A 20-year-old trumpet player named Gary Wilson took his spot on the 50-yard line, close to the sideline facing the press box, with the Stanford band in formation behind him. Wilson had been chosen for a special role because he played well, and he played thunderous. Upon Barnes' signal, a loud drum roll began and quickly died out. Wilson lifted his horn and began sounding the anthem's familiar opening lines, solo. The trumpet's mournful sound filled the hushed stadium as Wilson played the first and second stanzas. Midway through the anthem, the woodwinds joined in, quietly, and finally the brass and drums added their muscle, leading to a rousing finish.

Loud cheers normally greet the end of the national anthem. But Barnes' version with the lone trumpeter eight days after JFK's death left the crowd stunned and silent for what seemed to be an eternity. Many spectators could not hold back tears.

The Stanford band would continue to chart a unique path in the following years. Rock 'n' roll was becoming popular and so were jazzy tunes. Students went to Barnes and asked if he could arrange songs playing on hip radio stations. In fact, he could. Blessed with perfect pitch, Barnes could take a hit song and, within two or three days, arrange a version of it for the band. Out went Sousa. In came The Beach Boys, The Beatles, and The Rolling Stones.

The band kept pushing boundaries in matters of taste and decorum. Within a couple of years, band members would dutifully march row by row out of the end zone during their pregame show—but during halftime shows, they would scream loudly while scattering like a forcibly broken rack of pool balls and coalesce into formations. Band members now wore red blazers, white shirts, black pants, white shoes, and white bucket hats with short brims, the kind an elderly duffer might wear on the links. In time, band members added the ugliest tie they could find to the ensemble.

Ivy League bands also had begun scattering and moving away from their traditional approaches. But no other university band sounded like Stanford's or dressed like them. Then again, no other school band had as much freedom to do as they pleased. And no other university band seemed to have as much fun.

The times they were a-changin' and so was the band. Fewer and fewer members wanted to be governed by convention when anti-war protests were gripping college campuses, kids were growing long hair, drugs were getting introduced, and the sexual revolution was underway.

Across the bay, Cal kept with the traditional military-style, precision-marching band, even as the Berkeley campus was becoming the country's counter-culture epicenter.

By the late 1960s, the Stanford band's halftime shows no longer saluted patriotic subjects or society's heroes. Instead, the shows satirized political or social topics of the day. When the band offered a tribute to someone or something, it was often with a double entendre about sex or drugs. When the band formed a penis, the band announcer insisted they were honoring Hoover Tower, a campus landmark, or some other phallic-shaped building.

In a show about Planned Parenthood, the band purported to form a Roman Catholic bishop's crosier with a coiled top. But as the band announcer slyly indicated, they were actually forming a Gynecoil IUD birth control device. The students got it. Most adults didn't. It was sophomoric humor that would further clash with the politically correct culture that became fashionable years later.

After Monday night rehearsals, band members drew up the pregame and halftime shows in what were known as SMUT meetings, which band members said—wink, wink—stood for Stanford Marching Unit Thinkers. Alcohol fueled the creativity process, and pot added to the mix in later years.

Stanford students loved the band. So did some alums—emphasis on *some*. More traditionally-minded alums wanted a band that would march in crisp formation and play fight songs (i.e., be more like Cal's band). Hate mail poured in to the Stanford band. The more hateful the missive, the funnier it was to band members. They reveled in disrespecting authority and rules.

The Stanford band dismissed the Cal band as a bunch of weenies. But they saved their worst insults for the marching band of archrival USC, with its martial-sounding fight songs and Trojan-style helmets and uniforms. "Each halftime, the [Trojan Marching Band] presents a new and exciting field show that is a powerful blend of popular music, precision drills, and crowd-pleasing dance routines," proclaimed the USC band's website.

The Stanford band's disdainful retort: "After all, if God had wanted us to act like the USC band, the Germans would have won the war."

In the fall of 1970, Stanford was scheduled to open its football season against the University of Arkansas in Little Rock. At that time, only one or two college football games were televised nationwide each week. ABC chose to broadcast the Stanford–Arkansas game. The then-Stanford Indians were led by quarterback Jim Plunkett, a Heisman Trophy candidate, while Arkansas had fielded a top team the year before, despite their loss in the Sugar Bowl.

An intrepid group of 69 Stanford band members traveled to Little Rock and designed a halftime show with a California surfing theme featuring songs from The Beach Boys. The drum major, a pre-med senior named Geordie Lawry, lined up all the band members on the sideline while he wore a wet suit and flippers and used his snorkel as a baton. "Drop trou!" he commanded, and down came the pants of each member in the all-male ensemble. Then all of the band members stepped out of their pants and performed the halftime show showing off their surfing trunks and bare legs. ABC's television cameras immediately cut away, and conservative Arkansas fans were scandalized.

Behind Plunkett, Stanford won a spot in the Rose Bowl during the 1970 season for the first time in two decades. During the Rose Bowl parade on January 1, 1971, band members flaunted convention by sauntering along the route, handing out roses to comely women in exchange for kisses, and drinking beer while they strolled. Their halftime show began with Lawry riding a tricycle onto the field wearing a yellow slicker and a rain hat. When he reached midfield, he tipped over, a riff on a popular skit from *Rowan & Martin's Laugh-In* show. Lawry doffed the rain slicker. He led the show wearing only an oversized diaper with a 1971 sash—he was the new year's baby.

That year, Lawry introduced an unlikely fight song for the band—"All Right Now" by the rock band Free. The Stanford band began playing Barnes' arrangement of the song to celebrate touchdowns and victories. "The world's largest rock 'n' roll band," they labelled themselves. And, in an ironic and self-mocking nod to what they saw as their growing legend, band announcer Hal Mickelson introduced the group as "the one, the only, the truly incomparable Leland Stanford Junior"—and here he would pause—"University Marching Band."

A year or two later, the band was banned from Disneyland after a swarm of members gathered for the Storybook Land Canal Boats, and the tour guide unwittingly handed over the microphone. "I was then forced by peer pressure to take the instrument into my humble and trembling hands and thereupon describe the scenery from a slightly different perspective," Mickelson related later. "After all, when you consider Snow White alone in the forest with seven dwarves, the possibilities are really staggering."

The band, which added women in 1972, operated out of a stucco building on campus that was considered so disposable by administration officials that it formerly housed the ROTC shooting range. Upon entering the Band Shak, as it was lovingly known, bandsmen and visitors could pass through a turnstile stolen from the Houston Astrodome. A vending machine in one corner dispensed beer for 25 cents a can. The walls were lined with countless signs pilfered from road trips, many of them with the unintended double entendres that the band members loved. "Beaver Crossing 3 Miles," read one road sign. "Moaning Cavern Park," read another.

One sign had nothing to do with drugs or sex. It curiously read: "Stop: If you have sick pigs at home or brought sick or dead pigs for disease diagnosis, please do not enter this swine barn."

The band's hijinks in the mid-1970s included satirizing a major Bay Area front page story: the kidnapping of Patty Hearst, a newspaper heiress. The band formed a "Hearstburger"—which, the announcer helpfully informed spectators, consisted of two buns and no patty.

The death of Mao Zedong in 1976 prompted a "Salute to Chairman Mao" halftime show. The band began by sprinting onto the field and forming an obscene Chinese symbol. Then, mocking a recent famine in China, band members formed a fish bone and played "Down to the Bone." They also formed the Chinese symbol for Mao and played "China Grove" by the Doobie Brothers. After the game, the university administration was hammered by conservatives and liberals alike, who simultaneously believed the band had glorified Mao and disrespected the great leader.

In 1978, the Stanford band offered a whimsical salute to office supplies for one halftime show. During one song, the band changed their formation from DIC FON to DIC FOR. In the press box, one puzzled sportswriter turned to another and asked, "What's a DIC FOR"? A moment later, they both burst out laughing.

Sitting in the stands of the 1979 Big Game, a Cal freshman named Mark Stevenson watched the Cal band carry out its meticulous performance and felt his chest swell with pride. The band made him feel good to be a Cal student, especially compared to the chaotic Stanford band. Stevenson decided at that moment he wanted to join the Cal outfit. He faced only one problem—he didn't play an instrument. So Stevenson took drum lessons during the spring semester and over the summer while home in South Pasadena. That fall, he passed muster to join the band.

Like other newbies, Stevenson had to undergo the week-long Fall Training Program. This consisted of learning how to march during the day and playing the music during evening rehearsals. From the get-go, the upperclassmen emphasized tradition, reverence, and pride in the Cal band and the university. "Remember who you are and what you represent," they were told time and time again. People typically accept the culture of a group they join, and that's what happened with the new Cal band members. For most of them, this simply meant taking the precision and discipline they had learned in their high school bands and elevating it to the high pageantry and performance standards of the Cal band.

On the final day of the Fall Training Program, each band member had to march across the football field, beginning four beats, or two-and-a-half yards, after the preceding person. By now, Cal band members had been told repeat-edly that each step should measure 22 ½ inches, or eight steps per five yards. All of the members had to follow that exact regimen while marching the full length of the field, carrying their instrument as if they were playing. Band leaders judged each person's composure, posture, and pacing. Each year, around 10 would-be band members didn't make the cut.

By contrast, regimentation wasn't exactly the Stanford band's thing. A promotional flyer for its band camp showed a photo of a seemingly crazed trombone player smashing his horn against the ground, a la Pete Townshend of The Who, with other band members laughing in the background during one post-game show. "Does this picture appeal to you for some TWISTED UNKNOWN REASON?" the flyer asked. "WHAT COULD DRIVE A MAN TO THIS?"

The Stanford band had nothing like Cal's Fall Training Program. At night after their first rehearsal, Stanford band leaders began showing mov-ies of past halftime performances in the Band Shak. "Training films," they were called. But after a while, a hard-core pornographic movie was spliced in. Doing that held a certain warped logic—freshmen had to be able to handle the band's anything-goes ethos.

Initiation into the Cal band followed a more traditional script, thanks to a custom led by upperclassmen, who were, no matter their gender, known as "old men." On a morning near the end of the Fall Training Program, the old men would point up to Big C, a gold-colored concrete block built into the side of Charter Hill above the campus, and proclaim to their charges with feigned shock and dismay that it had been painted red. And they knew who the culprits were—"Those dastardly Stanford students!"

Actually, the old men had done the dirty deed the night before in preparation for a ceremony that night involving the band's first-year mem-bers, who were led up the hill in the dark where they found buckets of gold paint. The old men told them they had to erase the handiwork of the Stanford students—the thing is, they weren't given any brushes. With no other options to apply the paint, the new bandsmen began thrusting their hands into the buckets to turn Big C from red to gold. At some point, after the consumption of more than a few six-packs, new male band members would typically dip their butts into a bucket and slide painfully down the concrete block to add more gold gloss. All the while, the old men would sing bawdy songs and yell encouragement to the freshmen. When they were finished and had straggled back down the hill, tradition called for everyone to stop at an old dorm and perform a yell. "Fuck you, Bowles Hall!" it began, followed by a string of profanities and nonsense words.

It was a night of good, clean college fun that could have taken place in the 1950s, or the 1930s for that matter. That's how the Cal band rolled.

Rehearsals took place Tuesday through Friday and on Saturdays before the game. Cal band members played the same pregame show each game—the crowd loved this convention—but had to learn a new halftime show each week with music they memorized. On game day, band members proudly donned their classic uniforms: black shoes; navy blue pants and coats; a white vest, spats, gloves, and citation cord over the shoulder; a gold cape with a block C in the middle; and a cap with a white plume and Cal emblem.

The Cal band modeled itself after the tradition-minded bands of Ohio State and Michigan. Alcohol was permitted—but only after hours and out of sight.

The Stanford band had a different model, more along the lines of Hunter S. Thompson, the gonzo journalist and author who wrote chronicles of his coverage about politics while fortified by alcohol and drugs. On game days beginning in the 1970s, Stanford band members started their Saturday mornings with beer and doughnuts. Next, they might have a few stiff drinks while mingling with tailgating alums before the contest. They would keep the party going during the game, whipping up their favorite concoctions, courtesy of bottles of liquor and blenders they would bring into the stadium.

But by the early 1980s, the band was having trouble being consistently clever every week. All too often they were simply obscene. More and more they relied on Mickelson to entertain the crowd during shows with his booming, over-the-top voice and glib one-liners. But even Mickelson, now an attorney for Hewlett-Packard in Palo Alto, was becoming worried about the band's direction. "What do rebels do when the establishment they want to topple has toppled?" Mickelson said in *The Stanford Daily* before the 1982 football season. "What do satirists do when what they satirize gives up and goes away? Because of the Stanford band, many other college bands around the country had changed their style and format: In that sense, the Stanford band was a success. What could the band do now that is genuinely new?

"The band became a victim of its own success," Mickelson added. "Some of its members became less interested in entertaining their audience and more interested in having a good time of their own. Some of the staff didn't want to cut back on people's spontaneity. The result was a kind of self-indulgence."

Unlike their Cal counterparts, Stanford band members were likely performing in an altered state. Not surprisingly then, when a few band members went astray, quite a few more often followed.

The leaders of the student-run outfit for the 1982 football season were well aware of the problems. The drum major was Ray Gruenewald, a 21-year-old trombonist who was known for playing loud and hitting notes in a high register. Everybody knew him as Disco, a nickname he earned after wearing a shiny shirt and bell bottoms to practice one day as a freshman. The band manager was John Howard, another trombone player. While the flamboyant Disco led the band during rehearsals and on the field, the more reserved Howard handled all of the logistics and management issues.

Taking the complaints of Mickelson and others to heart, they decided they would focus on cleaning up the band's image that year. And they would succeed—until the final four seconds of the season.

• CHAPTER 7 •

THE SEASON

One afternoon in the summer of 1982, Pat Gilbert answered a knock on the door at her home in Red Bluff, California. Outside were two men. One introduced himself as Joe Kapp, the coach of the California Bears football team. The other was Lary Kuharich, the team's quarterback coach. Kapp offered Pat a bouquet of red roses and said he was looking for her son, Gale. She said she would try to find him. Gale had gone to work out with friends.

Kapp had been on the job for six months, and the upcoming season was in danger of derailing. Gilbert, his best quarterback, had quit the team and was looking to transfer to Brigham Young University—because of his unhappiness with Kapp. A sophomore, Gilbert was 6'3", 215 pounds, with a strong and accurate arm. He'd shown considerable promise but hadn't had the opportunity to demonstrate it. Gilbert had begun the preceding year as Cal's starter but had torn knee ligaments 19 plays into the first game and missed the rest of the 1981 season.

The replacement for Gilbert had been J Torchio, a former walk-on who led Cal to victory in the 1980 Big Game but had quarterbacked the Bears to only two victories in the 1981 season amidst an avalanche of criticism from Cal rooters. Torchio would be the starter for the 1982 season if Gilbert didn't return.

That was not the only troublesome sign for Cal football. Four assistant coaches had gone elsewhere after Kapp took over in December 1981.

One of them was Al Saunders, the holdover offensive coordinator. Shortly before leaving, he met with Torchio and wide receiver Andy Bark one morning to diagram possible plays. Kapp poked his head into the office

73

as Saunders drew a play on the grease board that showed a receiver going in motion before the ball was snapped. "What are you doing?" Kapp asked.

"We're talking Xs and Os," Saunders replied.

"You're messing with me!" Kapp exclaimed. "You can't move before you hike the ball! We're going forward, not sideways."

Saunders said it was allowed.

"We're going to line up and hit them in the mouth!" Kapp said. He departed, leaving the others shaking their heads. Saunders resigned his position at Cal to become the offensive coordinator and quarterbacks coach at the University of Tennessee in 1982. He said he couldn't pass up the opportunity to coach at such a great program.

After replacing Roger Theder as Cal's coach, Kapp had met with his new players one by one. Each one heard the same enthusiastic spiel. Kapp would point to a photo of the Rose Bowl stadium and tell them that playing there was the goal. To emphasize the importance of his conviction, Kapp would point to a bottle of tequila on his credenza. It was his favorite drink, he noted, but he would abstain until they qualified for the Rose Bowl by winning the Pac-10 conference title. It was not lost on the players that Cal had not returned to the storied game since 1959 when Kapp quarterbacked the team. Now, 23 years later, Kapp was a terrific salesman—fun, personable, and full of promise that better days lay ahead. Most players left the meeting fired up.

One exception was Harvey Salem, Cal's best offensive lineman and a potential first-round pick in the next NFL draft. Salem had started every game for three years at Cal and had captained the team during his junior year. But Kapp seemed to question his dedication, telling Salem he had to quit the track team to avoid missing spring football practice, even though Cal officials had said he could play both sports. This left Salem disappointed and torn between his love for football and his love for throwing the shot put. After the meeting, Salem recalled that Kapp had played both football and basketball at Cal. Why couldn't he do the same? Salem went out for spring ball but disregarded Kapp's wishes and left after a couple of practices to rejoin the track squad. He felt validated when he finished seventh in the shot at the Pac-10 championship track meet.

The Cal team saw Kapp in action for the first time when spring practice began. He gathered the players around him and emphasized that they needed to perform as a single unit and that they would have to compete for their jobs every day. Then he sent them off to their position coaches for individual drills. Five players stayed put. Kapp had yet not hired a special teams coach, so they had nowhere to go. They were the punters and kickers.

"Is that all you do?" Kapp asked.

"Yes," they replied. "We're specialists."

"Are you guys on scholarship?" Kapp asked.

"Yeah," they replied.

"That's no way to run a team," Kapp said, shaking his head. He turned to the previous year's starting punter, Mike Ahr, and told Ahr that when he had played quarterback for Cal, he had also punted. Ahr felt like an afterthought.

So did Joe Cooper, the place kicker. During spring practice, Kapp insisted on replacing the center and holder on field goals, even though they worked cohesively with Cooper. The new center was a guard who couldn't get a good grip on the ball to make a consistently accurate long snap because he taped his hands for blocking. When he did get the snap right, the new holder had trouble putting the ball on the kicking tee. If he managed to place it correctly, he often didn't spin the laces toward the goal posts as Cooper preferred. And when the new holder spun the ball, it sometimes fell off the kicking tee.

All of this pointed to Kapp's major shortcoming—he had never coached a football team at any level before. And it left players feeling like Kapp's thinking about football remained stuck in the 1960s—when pro teams had only 40 players and simple playbooks.

The alums, however, couldn't say enough good things about Kapp, given his mythical status. Defensive coordinator Ron Lynn saw this when he accompanied the new coach to a restaurant in San Francisco shortly after the hire was announced. When Kapp entered, patrons stood up and applauded.

Kapp also excited David Lewis, Cal's tight end who had been marginalized during the preceding year's failed experiment with the Run and Shoot offense. Lewis had sat out that 1981 season despite having more receptions than any other Pac-10 tight end the year before. In 1982, Kapp emphasized in team meetings: Lewis would be a primary target for the quarterback.

Lewis became so excited at the prospect of catching passes from Gilbert that he and a wide receiver made the three-hour drive north from Berkeley to Red Bluff during the summer of 1982 to try to convince Gilbert to return. "We need you," Lewis told the quarterback. "Get your ass back to Berkeley."

Gilbert remained noncommittal. He had been in tune with Theder but felt lost with Kapp.

Perhaps only an hour after Lewis left Red Bluff, Kapp and Kuharich arrived. They spent three hours with Gilbert, pumping him up, touting his chance to become one of Cal's great quarterbacks. Gilbert remained uncertain. The decision weighed on him. All he had known was family, friends, and sports in Red Bluff. His dad worked for the California Highway Patrol. Gilbert had starred in three sports, but he showed the most promise in baseball, playing catcher on the Red Bluff team that advanced to the finals of the Little League World Series when he was 12. The town honored the boys with a parade.

In high school, Gilbert decided to concentrate on football. Nothing could match the thrill of throwing a touchdown pass before an excited crowd. Now, with Kapp and Kuharich sitting in his living room, pitching him on why he should return to Cal, Gilbert felt like a small-town boy being asked to make a big-time decision.

That night, Gilbert lay in bed and contemplated how Cal's first game of the 1982 season was only 39 days away. He had barely played the previous year before suffering his season-ending knee injury, and now he might miss another one. He couldn't bear that thought. The next morning, he called Kapp to tell him he would re-enroll in school.

During fall practice, Kapp told reporters that Gilbert and Torchio would compete for the starting job. Just before the season began, Gilbert won the nod over Torchio.

With Gilbert calling signals, Cal's fortunes in 1982 looked bright, a year after the disappointing 2–9 season under Theder. Most of the starters were returning with an extra year of seasoning. Plus, the Bears were scheduled to play seven of their 11 games at home. Lynn, the highly-regarded defensive coordinator, would serve as ballast to the unpredictable Kapp.

Among the returning starters was the leading tackler in 1981, outside linebacker Ron Rivera. He would be a junior in 1982.

Rivera had an unusual background. His father was a commissioned officer in the United States Army who was originally from Puerto Rico. His mother was of Mexican descent. His father's postings meant the family moved frequently before settling just outside of Monterey during Rivera's high school years. When his father got orders to transfer again overseas, Rivera's high school coach advised his parents that their son would probably lose any chance of winning a college football scholarship if the whole family moved. Rivera stayed with his mother—she filmed his games and sent the videos to her husband overseas—and his exploits on the field earned him 28 scholarship offers.

Rivera turned down Notre Dame, Ohio State, and Michigan on the same day. After the constant moves while growing up, Rivera wanted to attend college in California so his parents could see him play. His parents had always stressed academics, so Stanford and Cal topped his list. Rivera attended the 1979 Big Game as a Stanford guest. Cal won 21–14 in dramatic fashion when the Bears defense stopped Stanford quarterback Turk Schonert on fourth and goal from the 1-yard line. Rivera was ushered into the Stanford locker room after the tough defeat. As Rivera looked around, he noticed numerous Stanford players cracking jokes and openly making plans to party that night. That didn't seem right to him.

Outside, he bumped into Cal coaches by chance. They escorted him into the jubilant Bears' locker room. Theder spent a few minutes with him touting the benefits of Cal. His timing was perfect. The emotion of the Bears' last-minute victory washed over Rivera. He would play for the Bears.

But just after he arrived at Cal, Rivera's grandfather suffered a stroke. The linebacker wanted to quit school and return home immediately. He was his grandfather's favorite grandson. His grandfather hadn't missed any of Ron's high school games and afterward would give him $1.50 to buy hamburgers at McDonald's, while he handed out only 75 cents to the other grandchildren.

Rivera checked the Greyhound bus schedule to go home and went to inform Theder of his plans. The coach urged Rivera to re-think his decision. Rivera returned to his dorm room. A senior defensive back stopped by and said he, too, had wanted to leave school at one point but had made the right decision by staying. Rivera went to practice. Two other teammates urged him to remain.

Then Rivera's parents showed up. Theder had called them. They soothed Ron by telling him that his grandfather was recovering and wanted Ron to remain in school. Rivera heeded their advice. Later, when he was contemplating going home one weekend, Theder offered his car to Rivera. He ended up not needing it, but the gesture warmed the linebacker. Theder had his back.

But in December 1981, Cal had a new coach. Given his close connection to Theder, Rivera didn't take to Kapp immediately. Kapp, sensing this, stressed their shared Mexican heritage. Kapp endeared himself to Rivera after that by always asking about his studies. At one point, Kapp arranged for Rivera to meet with a law school professor to discuss school and life.

Rivera spent the summer before the 1982 season living at the home of his girlfriend north of San Diego. He worked construction from 6:00 AM to mid-afternoon for $5 per hour and afterward worked out with weights and ran wind sprints. The day's activities left him so exhausted that he fell asleep by 8:30 PM.

In August, Rivera went to Berkeley to work out with teammates for a couple of weeks before fall football camp began there. He learned that some of them were making $16 per hour at jobs arranged by the school. Rivera confronted Kapp. "What the hell?" he demanded. "You talk about this bond and connection that both of us have. What about taking care of me?"

"Was it hard work?" Kapp asked.

"I liked it, but it was hard work, too," Rivera conceded.

"Get your education and graduate," Kapp said.

In the following days, Rivera realized Kapp had given him a life lesson. He would do well in his studies. And at 6'3", 225 pounds, he was ready to lay waste to blockers and ball carriers during the 1982 season.

*   *   *

Few people gave either Stanford or Cal much chance of winning the Pac-10 title and playing in the Rose Bowl the following January 1 against the Big Ten conference champ. The *Contra Costa Times* pegged Stanford to finish sixth in the Pac-10, one spot ahead of Cal.

The University of Washington was heavily favored to win the conference and return to the Rose Bowl for the second year in a row. Loaded with veterans, the Huskies were ranked No. 2 in the country behind the University of Pittsburgh, led by senior quarterback Dan Marino. Other contenders for the top national ranking were Alabama, Nebraska, North Carolina, and Georgia, which featured running back Herschel Walker. He and John Elway were the favorites to win the Heisman Trophy.

Elway, of course, guaranteed that Stanford would be entertaining game after game. His astounding success—and Stanford's abysmal failures with him—highlighted coverage of the team leading up to the season opener. Commentators breathlessly called him the greatest quarterback in college football history. But they also noted Stanford had gone only 6–5 behind him in 1980 and 4–7 in 1981, including the humiliating loss that year to San Jose State, coached by Jack Elway. John Elway had not even led Stanford to a bowl game yet. Maybe he would in this, his senior year. But Stanford's fate wouldn't depend only on Elway, of course. Everyone knew Stanford could score. But could they play defense? The same qualities that make a great defensive lineman were not necessarily the qualities that made someone want to go to the library.

Elway, however, was so confident in his talent that he didn't even devote the entire summer of 1982 to preparing for the upcoming football season. Instead, he spent six weeks playing for a New York Yankees farm club. He batted .318 and showed such promise that Yankees owner George Steinbrenner envisioned him as the team's future right fielder for years to come. First, of course, Elway had 11 football games to play for Stanford.

If John Elway was the hook for sportswriters covering Stanford, Joe Kapp could be counted on for great copy for the writers covering Cal in the Bears' 100th season of football. Cal opened the 1982 season in Boulder against Colorado, which had won only three games the year before. In his first pregame speech in the locker room, Kapp borrowed exhortations from some of the tough-guy coaches he admired as he tried to pump up his team. Then he went wild and maybe a little crazy. "Let's kick the Buffaloes' ass!" he ranted. "I'm here to tell you it's just ass! No one is going to save us! There's no Rudolph the Red Nose Reindeer and a sleigh coming to save us!" Bears players muffled a laugh. *What the hell was Kapp talking about?*

Cal took a 21–0 lead during the first quarter following three turnovers by the Buffaloes. Kapp then inexplicably substituted his second-team defense. Colorado came roaring back. But the Buffaloes committed more turnovers, and Cal won 31–17. "I made a lot of rookie coach mistakes," Kapp told the *Contra Costa Times*. "Thank God my players were able to overcome the bad coaching."

A week later, they benefitted from more gifts as San Diego State fumbled five times, threw one interception, and had one punt blocked—all in the first quarter. For the second week in a row, Gale Gilbert and the offense didn't impress anyone but capitalized on the other team's errors as the Bears won 28–0. Reflecting on the dismal history of Cal football, reporters noted Kapp was the first Bears coach in 35 years to win his first two games.

The Bears' third game of the season, against Arizona State, posed their first real test. And they failed. The Sun Devils blitzed and blitzed and blitzed. Kapp never had an answer. In all, Arizona State sacked Gilbert and Torchio a total of 12 times, and Gilbert threw three interceptions. The final result: Arizona 15, Cal 0. "I don't think you can say we outcoached Cal," Arizona State's defensive coordinator told the *Oakland Tribune* afterward. But he was just being charitable. It was Kapp's responsibility to make sure Cal had plays to counter the blitz.

The following day, during what was normally a light, day-after practice at Memorial Stadium, Kapp told the offense to join him at Section OO. "Stadium stairs," he called out. The players began running up and down, up and down, up and down. After 11 punishing sets of stadium stairs, Kapp called a halt. Players hunched over on the field, hands on their knees, some on the verge of vomiting. "I guess you wonder why I brought you to Section OO," Kapp told them. "It's because yesterday you were an awful offense!" The Cal players rolled their eyes in disbelief. *Did Coach think awful was spelled with an O?*

San Jose State, the Bears' next opponent, had traditionally been a patsy. But they were a different team under Jack Elway and had already defeated three Pac-10 schools. Oddsmakers made the Spartans a 12-point favorite.

That didn't sit well with Fred Williams, a four-year starting corner-back for Cal. Williams had grown up hauling manure, driving a tractor, and irrigating the hay and corn fields on the family dairy farm outside of Chowchilla in California's Central Valley. Everyone was expected to do their share. Williams loved playing all sports, but he had an added incentive—if he didn't have practice in the afternoons, he would have to perform additional farm work. Williams' father, who hadn't finished high school, saw the bigger picture. "We work this hard," he told his son, "because that's what we had to do to make it, given our opportunities. So if I were in your shoes, I'd take advantage of education and school."

Williams made it to Cal but was overwhelmed by its size. He was also overwhelmed when two starting cornerbacks flunked out as his freshman season began. Williams didn't know how to backpedal as a defensive back or how to read offenses. But he reflected on his roots and how his upbring-ing had shaped him. He was "Chowchilla Tough." He resolved to resist the urge to go home, where a shovel in a field was waiting for him. He vowed to make it at Cal. Learning his position quickly on the practice field, he became a starter for the Bears' first game of his freshman year.

Now, in the fourth game of his senior year, Williams covered a wide receiver in motion on San Jose State's second play. Watching the quarterback's eyes, Williams pounced on the throw, intercepting the pass, and running it back 28 yards for a pick-six. On the offensive side of the ball, Gilbert enjoyed his best day at Cal by throwing two touchdowns without an interception as the Bears thwarted the Spartans' blitzes, and Cal defeated San Jose State 26–7.

Cal was now 3–1, already with one more victory than they had notched the entire preceding year. The media hailed Kapp as a coaching genius. To be sure, Kapp fueled the team, with his innate charisma and passion for competing. The Bears were starting to believe in him—and themselves.

But if Kapp's coaching chops had improved, he hadn't lost any of his weirdness in the process. He handed out cloves of garlic to his defensive linemen on game days, telling them to eat it and then breathe on the other team's offensive linemen. At one practice, after several receivers dropped passes, Kapp brought out a bucket of water with an unidentified white substance mixed in. He told the receivers the milky water would soften their hands and make it easier to catch the quarterback's passes. When an alum would visit practice wearing a red tie, Stanford's color, Kapp would grab a pair of scissors and snip the tie in half. The players learned to look for these moments and cheered them.

*   *   *

Stanford opened the 1982 season on the road against Purdue, who had beaten the Cardinal a year earlier. This time, Elway threw touchdown passes to four different receivers as Stanford won, 35–14. At the time, Midwestern teams were built to stop the run, with beefy defensive linemen and line-backers. Purdue's defenders simply ran out of gas trying to get to Elway, a nimble and elusive scrambler.

The next week featured the fourth and final installment of Elway versus Elway as John played San Jose State, his father's team. In 1981, the Spartans' defensive coordinator had detected a flaw in Elway's game that he could exploit, and the quarterback played with a sprained ankle. The result: San Jose State sacked Elway seven times and picked off five of his passes. He completed only 6-of-24 passes for 72 yards. It was his worst performance at Stanford. Now, leading up to the 1982 game, both John and Jack expressed relief that they wouldn't have to play against each other again. "I know it's been tough on Mom," John told the *San Francisco Examiner*. "She's been asked the question of who she's voting for for the last six months, and about 50 percent of the time she breaks into tears."

It was a seesaw battle. San Jose State scored the first 14 points. Stanford roared back for 21 behind Elway. Finally, a Stanford fumble late in the game led to a Spartans touchdown and a four-point San Jose State lead. Elway had a final chance to pull it out for his team. He brought Stanford to the San Jose State 26-yard line with three minutes left in the game. But on first down, his primary receiver ran the wrong route, and he was sacked for 14 yards. On second down, he was sacked again. On third down, he was sacked a third time. On fourth and 35, Elway rolled right. Two tacklers were about to grab him, but he escaped by carrying out his reverse spin to the left. He looked downfield but didn't see anyone open. He ducked under another would-be tackler and scrambled to the right again—and was sacked for the fourth play in a row. Time had run out on Elway. San Jose State won 35–31. But he had played spectacularly, completing 24-of-36 passes for 382 yards, two touchdowns, and no interceptions.

The loss meant that for the second season in a row, the father and his scrappy state school had dealt a humbling blow to the Stanford princelings. "Don't worry about it," a Stanford alum told one player afterward. "One day all of them will be working for you." That type of arrogance pointed to what many thought was the team's Achilles heel—they weren't as hungry as the lesser opponents who all too often defeated them.

There was no underestimating 13th-ranked Ohio State a week later in Columbus in a game televised nationally that would give Elway broad exposure. With 2:35 left, Ohio State was leading 20–16 and had the ball on the Stanford 25-yard line. All the Buckeyes had to do was run out the clock. They had already pounded out 176 yards on the ground. Stanford was down to its last timeout.

But on second and 14, Ohio State head coach Earle Bruce inexplicably sent in a pass play. Quarterback Mike Tomczak rolled left, saw an open receiver streaking to the end zone, and threw a floater that one Stanford defender tipped and a second intercepted.

Elway had one last chance.

With 34 seconds left, he had advanced Stanford to the Ohio State 18-yard line. Taking the snap, he rolled left. Stanford's offensive linemen held fast against the rushing Buckeyes as Elway drifted further left, buying time, surveying the field. Finally, having lured the Ohio State secondary into focusing on the left side of the field, Elway set his feet and threw a 50-yard strike across the field to a wide-open receiver in the right corner of the end zone. Touchdown, Stanford! An elated Elway felt like he had just hit the game-winning home run with two outs in the bottom of the ninth inning. Afterward, Bruce faced a torrent of criticism for the last-minute interception. Bruce said, "I knew it was a bad play right away when I met my wife, and she said, 'That's a bad play.' I knew then it was a bad play because in 27 years of coaching, she's never said that."

To be fair, in his 27 years of coaching, Bruce had probably never come up against a quarterback as skilled as John Elway.

Stanford's 23–20 upset of Ohio State left them with a 2–1 record. A week later, they played winless Oregon State, who tried to confuse Elway by playing nine down linemen and only two defensive backs just before the snap. It didn't work. Elway threw five touchdown passes while playing only two-and-a-half quarters as Stanford romped 45–5. "I'll be damned if anybody is better than Elway," Oregon State's head coach told *The Stanford Daily* after the game.

* * *

The Bears, rejuvenated under Kapp, traveled north to take on Washington in their fifth game of the season. The Huskies were 4–0, ranked No. 1 in the country, and seemingly on the path to their second straight Rose Bowl. But the Bears were feeling good after three victories in four outings. They also remembered they had nearly defeated Washington the year before, losing only after a last-second field goal. "We're going to try to wear them out," outside linebacker Ron Rivera said before the 1982 contest. "Hopefully, we'll get an early jump on them and keep the pressure on."

Instead, it was Washington that got the jump on Cal—and before the game even began. As the Cal players exited their locker room, they entered a dark and narrow tunnel, waiting for the signal to run onto the field. Suddenly, the Bears heard a guttural chant rising from behind them. The Washington players had entered the tunnel and were engaged in their favorite pregame intimidation technique.

"Say who?" they chanted.

"Say what?

"Say who say Dawgs ain't bad motherfuckers!"

The Huskies chanted it over and over again, the deafening sound ricocheting off the concrete walls. It unnerved the Cal players. For added measure, the Huskies pushed the Bears to the side while exiting the tunnel first. When the Bears followed a minute later, the cascade of boos almost seemed to push the team back into the tunnel.

The Huskies scored early, and the Huskies scored often, with an inadvertent assist from Cal's backup punter, who, rattled by the ferocious crowd, shanked five punts. Part of the blame could be pinned on Kapp. Unhappy with the starting punter, he brought his backup to Seattle instead. Cal finally scored late in the fourth quarter—way too little, and way too late. The final score was 50–7.

Afterward, the Bears could find only one pathetically small consolation—the game was supposed to be televised across the country, which would have been a disaster for Cal's reputation. But a rain delay in a baseball playoff game kept the contest off the air until only six-and-a-half minutes remained. Afterward, Kapp was asked if the Huskies were better than Arizona State. "All I can say is that last truck to hit us hurt the most," Kapp told the *San Francisco Examiner*.

Next up was Oregon, and the Ducks were winless. It was a painful game to watch. Neither team scored in the first three quarters. In the final quarter, Cal kicked a field goal. Oregon finally punched across a touchdown with two minutes left, and then, with just under a minute remaining, Gale Gilbert hooked up with tight end David Lewis for the winning score. Cal won 10–7.

The defense had kept the Bears in the game once again. At the heart of its solid play was a defender who had taken perhaps the unlikeliest path to Berkeley. He was Gary Plummer, the nose guard. His size—6'2" and 230 pounds—made him stand out in most places but not at his position. Typically, nose tackles were built like commercial refrigerators, and used their bulk to clog the running lanes. Every center he played against far outweighed him, as did the other offensive linemen. To top it off, Plummer had come to Cal not as a recruit but as a walk-on without a scholarship.

At Mission High School in Fremont, Plummer played both ways, winning All-Northern California honors by demolishing defensive linemen as a guard on offense and wrecking offenses as a linebacker. He received hundreds of recruiting letters. But when coaches showed up to meet him, they discovered he was only 5'10" and 180 pounds, not the 6'2" and 220 pounds as listed then. The coaches fled as soon as they saw him. Plummer was deemed too small to make it in the brutal trenches of college football.

He was devastated. With money tight in his family, his only chance to attend a four-year university was through a football scholarship. Besides, Plummer wanted desperately to keep playing the sport he loved at the next level.

Plummer knew how to work hard. He had been earning spending money for years, and he was always the best-conditioned player on his team. But working harder wouldn't make him taller. This was a problem he could not solve, for now anyway.

Plummer signed up to play at Ohlone, a junior college in Fremont, under coach Mike Cowan. Quick as a cat, Plummer dominated on offense and defense there in his sophomore season. By now he was 6'0", 200 pounds.

George Seifert, Stanford's defensive coordinator, called Plummer and told him he was the best junior college linebacker in California and was good enough to start at Stanford next season. Seifert made plans to visit Plummer at Ohlone. Plummer couldn't contain his excitement. When the appointed day arrived, Seifert walked up to his potential recruit, and his face registered surprise. "You're Gary Plummer?" he asked. "You're not big enough to play in the Pac-10."

It was the lowest moment of Plummer's life. "I'm done," he told Cowan after Seifert left. "I'll never play another down of football as long as I live."

"Fuck 'em!" Cowan said. "You're the best football player I've ever coached in my life. You're not quitting."

At Cowan's urging, Plummer took a weightlifting class for the first time. He also secured a side job working at a grocery store. One of the side benefits of working there was access to groceries—and Plummer put away enough that within nine months he had gained two inches and 28 pounds.

Cal defensive coordinator Ron Lynn encouraged Plummer to enroll at Cal to play linebacker—as a walk-on. "Am I going to get a scholarship?" Plummer asked.

"Of course, if you do well, if you become a starter," Lynn replied.

"That's all I need," said Plummer.

After the first day of spring practice in 1981, the coaches told Plummer they would have to move him to a new position. They had too many line-backers and needed another nose guard. Plummer felt crushed. Coaches had always said he was too small to play college football and now they wanted to move him to a position where you were supposed to be a behemoth?

Plummer returned to his sixth-floor dorm room and stood on the ledge. Two thoughts ran through his mind. One was: "I've been lied to by coaches again." The other: "Nobody would give a shit if I fell off now." But a third thought pushed its way through the gloom. He heard Coach Cowan's voice. "Fuck 'em, Gary! Fuck 'em!"

Plummer went to practice the next day, his blood boiling. He would teach the coaches not to underestimate him again, and he was determined to take out his rage on the first player in the first drill. The unlucky candidate was a junior backup center named Steve Pas. It was during a one-on-one drill, where Pas had to block Plummer. As soon as Pas hiked the ball, Plummer exploded from his four-point stance so quickly that the top of his helmet hit Pas' chin even before the center could lift his head. Pas tumbled over backward, and as he did, Plummer ran over him into the coach who was acting as the quarterback. "Ooooooh!" the other linemen murmured. The new kid was good; he'd just made the play of the practice.

As Plummer walked away, he told himself, "I will never play another down of football without that intensity." He had learned how to harness his fury. It would be one of the most empowering moments of Plummer's life. Two days later, the coaches named him Cal's starting nose guard.

Plummer's quickness and determination to succeed made the difference against larger opponents. He learned to outfox them by honing his knowledge of what defensive coaches call "pre-snap awareness." Plummer taught himself to watch the centers and other offensive linemen before the ball was hiked. If the center's knuckles turned red, that invariably meant he was leaning on his hand to block for a run. A lineman sitting too far back usually indicated a pass. With the analytical approach of a physicist, Plummer studied angles and leverage and figured out how to find space to get by the bigger line-men, time and time again. Equally important, he was also willing to take the punishment meted out game after game by his larger opponents. He may have been smaller, but he was smarter. And he was tougher.

*   *   *

Stanford's victory against Oregon State gave the team a 3–1 record. Next up was 11th-ranked Arizona State. The game would pit the nation's best passing offense against the best passing defense. Obviously, something had to give. For three quarters, Arizona State limited Stanford to 10 points and was poised to take an 11-point lead as the Sun Devils advanced toward the Cardinal goal line. But, with three minutes left, an Arizona State running back fumbled the ball away in Stanford's end zone. John Elway drove Stanford downfield and threw a 15-yard touchdown pass—the first given up by Arizona State that year. Stanford now led 17–14. Only 49 seconds remained in the game. It looked like Elway had pulled out a last-minute victory against a ranked opponent for the second time that season.

But the Cardinal went into a prevent defense that didn't prevent any-thing. It took the Sun Devils only 38 seconds to drive the length of the field for a touchdown. The final result: Arizona State 21, Stanford 17. "It was a heartbreaker of a game to lose," Stanford coach Paul Wiggin told the *San Francisco Examiner*.

Now 3–2, Stanford was manhandled on their home field by their next opponent, USC. The Trojans sacked Elway six times and intercepted three of his passes as they smacked the Cardinal 41–21. "When I had time," Elway told the *Contra Costa Times* afterward, "my receivers weren't open. When I had guys open, I didn't have any time to throw."

*   *   *

After defeating Oregon, the Bears' record was 4–2. They next hosted 11th-ranked UCLA, which had lost only four times to Cal since 1950. This meant, as the *San Francisco Chronicle* pointed out, the "Berkeley campus has produced more Nobel Prize winners since 1950 than football victories over UCLA." And so it went again in 1982. Cal's offense had its best game of the year, but the defense couldn't stop Bruins quarterback Tom Ramsey. UCLA won 47–31.

A week later, the Bears defeated hapless Oregon State 28–14. That left Cal with a 5–3 record.

USC, ranked 16th, was next. Because of injuries, the Trojans had to use their second-string quarterback and their fourth-string tailback. No matter. USC's defense—featuring four players who would go on to the NFL—made Cal look like a JV team. Cal quarterbacks Gale Gilbert and J Torchio threw a combined eight—*eight*—interceptions. The Trojans buried the Bears 42–0.

Of course, Joe Kapp threw more wackiness into the mix. When Gilbert came to the sideline at one point, the coach told him, "Green 8! Run Green 8! It's a message from God! I just heard it. We need to run this play!" It called for the two outside receivers to run deep routes while the tight end ran a shorter pattern over the middle. Kapp had introduced the play only that morning at the hotel. The offense had practiced it in the hotel ballroom, hardly the ideal setting. Gilbert dutifully called Green 8 in the huddle and then threw a pass over the middle that was intercepted. "God must have been a Trojan," a teammate told him as he came off the field.

For all of Kapp's weirdness, he was just the coach to settle down Gilbert after the USC debacle, however, in the days leading up to Cal's next game, against Washington State. As a player and a coach, Kapp wasn't shy about highlighting his own shortcomings. "I remember a game against Detroit when I was quarterbacking the Vikings when I threw three interceptions to Lem Barney in the first half," he said after the USC game. "The key is how a quarterback reacts to interceptions."

To help Gilbert put things in perspective, Kapp lightly recalled his dismal 1970 season with the Boston Patriots when they won only one of the 10 games that Kapp started. He threw 17 interceptions to only three touchdown passes. "I remember a game in Boston when I came all the way across an icy field to make the tackle," he said. "That was the highlight of my season."

Gilbert rebounded against Washington State. Poised, sharp, and opportunistic, he threw three touchdown passes and no interceptions as the Bears rolled over the Cougars 34–14. "I had been too tentative in my passing," he told the *Oakland Tribune*. "I was trying to put too much touch on the ball. Today, I just threw that football. Hard. That was the difference. That and the fact we weren't facing USC."

The victory in the 10th game of the season left Cal with a 6–4 record, with one game remaining.

*   *   *

Stanford, 3–3, played Washington State in its seventh game, in Pullman, where the conditions were wet and dreary. The Cougars had lost six of their top eight linebackers to injury. This forced Washington State's coaches to deploy six defensive backs, daring Stanford to run the ball.

This meant Stanford would be best served by highlighting the running game. The onus would be on Mike Dotterer, a senior running back who was probably even better on the baseball diamond than on the gridiron. Dotterer, who had turned down offers to sign with the New York Yankees and the Oakland A's, played left field on the Stanford team that had advanced to the College World Series in the spring of 1982. His father Dutch had been a major league catcher.

Dotterer was also known as the chattiest member of the Stanford football team. He had an opinion on every subject. "He talks almost as quickly as he runs, which by his own admission is deceptively fast," the *San Francisco Examiner* reported, noting that Dotterer served in the student senate at Stanford. On the football field, Dotterer, 6'0", 190 pounds, was a slasher who liked to run over defenders downfield rather than around them.

With the Cougars playing for the pass, John Elway handed off repeatedly to Dotterer. With three minutes left in the game, Washington State scored to take a 26–24 lead. Dotterer then carried the ball seven times on Stanford's final drive, scoring the winning touchdown with 22 seconds left. The victory left Stanford with a 4–3 record.

Up next was No. 2-ranked Washington at home. The night before, the Stanford squad watched Sylvester Stallone's first Rambo movie, *First Blood*. The stirring images left them fired up. But midway through the second quarter the next day, the Rambo effect had faded, and Washington was leading 17–7, seemingly on track to notch yet another victory. Dotterer broke off a long touchdown run, however, and Stanford went on to stun the Huskies by scoring 23 more points in a row.

But the game wasn't over, and no one was counting Washington out. With 5:30 left and Stanford leading 37–24, the Cardinal set up to receive a punt. Stanford coach Paul Wiggin sent running back Vincent White onto the field, taking the place of their No. 1 returner, who had fumbled a punt earlier.

White had grown up in Denver, the son of a teenage mother and a father who was frequently absent. He was raised by her and her parents, who stressed academics. They raised hell with Vincent when he came home one day with a B on his report card.

White was small but quick and shifty, in the mold of Stanford's All-American running back Darrin Nelson. When White was a high school senior, several schools offered him money under the table, and one university flew him in for a school visit on a private plane, which was probably an NCAA violation. The schools he visited treated him like a star, showing off their gleaming athletic facilities and putting him up at the best local hotels. Stanford took a decidedly different approach. White, like other recruits, toured the library, attended classes, and talked with professors. He also slept on whatever space was available in his host player's dorm. On his visit, it was a couch. The low-key approach worked. The mix of high academics and competitive sports at Stanford swayed White.

He was having a strong senior season at Stanford in 1982. Following in Nelson's footsteps, White gained big yardage on runs around the end and took advantage of defenders guarding against Elway's ability to throw deep by finding openings underneath the defensive coverage for short passes that his speed could turn into long gains. He would lead the NCAA in catches that year.

When Wiggin sent White in to receive the punt against Washington, he gave his player a strict instruction. "Just fair catch it," Wiggin said. But when the punter outkicked his coverage, White decided to disobey his coach's orders and run with the ball. He thought he had room to roam. He juked one Washington defender, then another, found a wall of blockers along the right sideline, put a move on the punter, cut left just ahead of two pursuing Huskies, and raced to complete a 76-yard touchdown. His punt return sealed the outcome. Stanford defeated Washington 43–31.

Several thousand jubilant fans stuck around for the Stanford band's post-game concert. The scene became even more festive when the Cardinal players, led by Elway, ran out from the locker room to salute the crowd and dance with the band. Backup tight end Jim Clymer borrowed an upright bass from one band member and plucked along with the music. Seeing the players party with them inspired several band members to resolve to celebrate with the football team on the field if given another chance that year. And how sweet would it be if they did it at the end of the Big Game in several weeks?

In the meantime, the victory against Washington landed Elway on the cover of *Sports Illustrated* after what the magazine called "this season's biggest upset." The victory left the Cardinal with a solid 5–3 mark. A bowl game for Elway and Stanford looked likely now.

But a week later, Arizona scored 28 unanswered points in the fourth quarter to defeat Stanford 41–27. In its 10th game, against UCLA, the Cardinal moved up and down the field, scoring at will. But so did the Bruins behind Tom Ramsey. Trailing late in the fourth quarter, Stanford's defense needed to force a punt to give Elway the ball one more time. The defense couldn't do it. UCLA ran out the clock and won 38–35.

And so in 1982, as in so many previous years, the final game of the regular season would become the most important game of the year for the two Bay Area rivals. Stanford was 5–5, while Cal was 6–4—no better than mid-conference also-rans. What now mattered most to both teams was the Big Game and the bragging rights it conferred.

CHAPTER 8

THE WEEK OF THE BIG GAME

Schools across the country had their own rituals and customs during their big game week. This might have seemed counterintuitive in 1982—that the traditions associated with college football rivalries could endure in a culture where so many young people prized iconoclasm and being different than their parents and where new technologies were speeding change more rapidly and consequentially than could be measured. But college students across the country then still embraced pep rallies, bonfires, and other decades-old rituals and customs related to the big games against their rivals—just as many fans do today.

Alabama and Auburn, separated by 150 miles in the state of Alabama, played in the Iron Bowl, frequently with the Southeastern Conference title on the line. The winner collected the Foy-ODK Trophy, named after a former dean of students at Auburn and Omicron Delta Kappa, an honor society on both campuses since the 1920s. The trophy was presented at halftime of the Alabama–Auburn basketball game later in the same academic year at the winner's home court. The student government president of the losing football team traditionally had to sing the winning team's fight song.

Michigan and Minnesota played for the Little Brown Jug in a rivalry dating to 1892. It was said to be the oldest trophy rivalry in college football. Michigan would be playing its other historic rival, Ohio State, on November 20, 1982, on the same date as the Big Game. So would Washington and Washington State, with Washington claiming the Pac-10's spot in the Rose Bowl for the second year in a row with a win. The victor of the Washington–Washington State game also would claim the Apple Cup, to be awarded by the state's governor.

The Oregon Ducks and Oregon State Beavers vied for the Platypus Trophy, which had been designed to include a duck-like bill and a beaver-like tail. But because the two schools regularly lost most of their games, no one cared much when Oregon students stole the trophy one year, and it hadn't reappeared by 1982.

In-state rivals Indiana and Purdue had been playing for the Old Oaken Bucket since 1925. Illinois and Northwestern, another in-state rivalry, had been playing for the Sweet Sioux Tomahawk since 1945.

One word described the Oklahoma–Oklahoma State football rivalry: bedlam. Oklahoma also played Texas in what was called the Red River Showdown. That game had taken place in October 1982 at a neutral site, the Cotton Bowl in Dallas.

Army and Navy would play their traditional game in 1982 at Veterans Stadium in Philadelphia, two weeks after the Big Game. In the preceding days, rumors were rife of attempts by Army students to steal the Navy's mascot, a goat named Billy, while Navy students were trying to nab Army's mascot, a mule. The cadets first stole Billy in 1953 in a plan that involved chloroform and a convertible. After his return, Billy appeared to be in good shape, and, according to Army, it was determined by testing that has never been adequately described that the mascot had suffered "no brainwashing at the hands of the cadets."

In 1982, the Midshipmen of the 13th Company were carrying the game ball from Bancroft Hall at Navy's campus in Annapolis to Philadelphia, a 128-mile trek that would become known as the Ball Run. The thinking behind it was that it would benefit the Midshipmen to get the "unlucky" 13th Company off the campus grounds so close to game time. Both schools would mark other traditions on game day. The Corps of Cadets and the Brigade of Midshipmen each would march onto the field hours before the game, creating a tableau of gray-suited Cadets or blue-coated Midshipmen. Once they completed what was known as the "march on," the students would take their seats for the game.

In 1982, Navy won the contest 24–7. Afterward, following tradition, the two schools showed their respect for each other. Navy's players stood alongside Army's, faced the West Point students, and sang the Cadets' alma mater. Then players from both sides faced Navy's students and sang the Naval Academy's alma mater.

The Harvard–Yale contest dated to 1875 and was called The Game. Its most famous matchup occurred in 1968. Both teams were 8–0 heading into the season finale, for the first time since 1909. Calvin Hill was a star running back for Yale, while Tommy Lee Jones, later a famous actor, played guard for Harvard. Yale seemed to have the game wrapped up when the Crimson improbably scored 16 points in the final 42 seconds to tie Yale. The headline in Harvard's student newspaper captured the post-game mood: "Harvard Beats Yale, 29–29." The two schools would meet for the 99th time on November 20, 1982.

One of the fiercest rivalries involved USC and UCLA, which are located only 12 miles apart in Los Angeles. From 1929 to 1981, both schools played their home games at the Los Angeles Coliseum. At UCLA, the days leading up to the game were known as "Beat 'SC Week." At USC, it was known as "Troy Week" or "Conquest." Both schools took steps to prevent vandalism of two major landmarks on campus. UCLA foiled potential USC saboteurs by covering its Bruin Bear statue with a tarp stating "THE BRUIN BEAR IS HIBERNATING. BEAT 'SC." USC countered by wrapping its Trojan Shrine (better known as "Tommy Trojan") in bubble wrap and duct tape and stationing students by it in a week-long vigil to prevent UCLA pranks. The two schools also would meet on November 20, 1982, with UCLA needing a victory and a loss by Washington to qualify for the Rose Bowl.

Big Game Week for Stanford and Cal in 1982 began with the two teams heading in opposite directions. For Stanford, the stinging defeat to UCLA in its last game meant the Cardinal had lost for the second week in a row because its defense failed to produce a fourth-quarter stop. "Those were both very, very tough losses," Stanford coach Paul Wiggin told the *Oakland Tribune*, "for the coaches, players, and their families."

The defeats were especially frustrating for Wiggin and the Stanford team because they came after the team's stunning 43–31 victory against No.2-ranked Washington. At that point, Stanford seemed to be rolling toward a big-name bowl game. Two weeks later, with a 5–5 record, they seemed to be fading out of the bowl picture entirely. Nonetheless, the Big Game always pumped up both schools. "For everyone involved, it is an important part of their lives," Wiggin told reporters. "I know it's important to mine."

Cal, meanwhile, had bounced back against Washington State in its preceding game, after a 42–0 thrashing the week before by USC. Quarterback Gale Gilbert had rebounded after throwing six interceptions against the Trojans to have his best day as a Bear against Washington State—completing 24-of-35 passes for 266 yards, three touchdowns, and no picks. The 33–14 victory against the Cougars put Cal at 6–4, guaranteeing its first winning record since 1979. This put the spotlight back on Bears coach Joe Kapp. "I believe he is doing an outstanding job," Cal athletic director Dave Maggard told the *San Francisco Examiner*. "To turn a 2–9 team around is a difficult chore. I think Joe has done that."

Kapp, known to be excitable, was especially hyped to play Stanford. "This is a bowl game," he told the *San Jose Mercury News*. "Everything that goes into a bowl game is in this one. This is something you take with you the rest of your life."

Coming into the 85th edition of the Big Game, the biggest story was legend-in-the-making John Elway, who would be playing his last game in a Stanford uniform, unless the Cardinal team righted itself and qualified for a bowl by defeating Cal. He had completed more passes than any quarterback in NCAA history and thrown for more yards and touchdowns than anyone in Pac-10 history. In the lead-up to the game, Cal senior defensive back Fred Williams conceded that the Bears could not hope to stop the phenomenal Stanford quarterback. But they had a plan to make his life difficult. "What we have to do is destroy his receivers," Williams explained. "Give him nobody to pass to. Ruin their routes. Intimidate them. Frustrate them. Make them hear footsteps every time they go to catch the ball. That's the only way to deal with Elway. Let him throw his 70-yard bullets. Just make sure no one is there to catch the football."

One of the traditions of the Stanford–Cal Big Game week was a Monday luncheon for the coaches attended by local writers, held in San Francisco. News accounts noted that it was the first time since 1914 that each team was coached by an alum who had played in the Big Game. In fact, Wiggin and Kapp played against each other in the 1956 Big Game. Stanford was heavily favored that year behind All-American quarterback John Brodie and Wiggin, an All-American senior lineman. But Cal won 20–18 behind Kapp, a sophomore quarterback, as the team rallied to give beloved coach Pappy Waldorf a victory in his final contest. At the luncheon 26 years later, Kapp, naturally, uttered the most memorable lines, embracing once again his bad-boy image. He recalled attending his first Big Game in 1955 as a freshman, when freshmen were not eligible to play varsity ball. Late in the contest, Kapp said he got in a fist fight with a Stanford fan in the stands.

On Monday night of Big Game Week, the Stanford band held its weekly nighttime practice at the Band Shak. As usual, they rehearsed songs, sometimes paying attention to instructions from drum major Disco Ray Gruenewald, sometimes engaging in general silliness. When the session ended at about 9:00 PM, about 40 members stayed to plan the band's pregame and halftime performances for the Big Game. To encourage the creative process, someone produced a pipe and a bag of weed, others grabbed beers from the vending machine in the corner. Within an hour or two, this is what they came up with: the pregame show would spoof their rivals by suggesting 101 things to do with a dead bear. The halftime show would be a satirical salute to childhood that was actually a sly attack on Cal. A bit later that night, however, several Cal students one-upped the band by sneaking into the Band Shak and stealing Disco Ray's trombone and parts of the outfit he had planned to wear during the Big Game. He gave chase but to no avail.

Stanford received good news the next day. Hall of Fame Bowl officials indicated to athletic director Andy Geiger that they would invite Stanford to play in their game on December 31—if the Cardinal won the Big Game. The likely opponent would be Vanderbilt University. Before the season began, the idea of going to the Hall of Fame Bowl in Birmingham, Alabama, would have seemed like a booby prize for Stanford. Now, after a so-so record despite Elway leading the offense, the possible bowl bid at the last minute seemed heaven-sent. It also elevated the stakes, even if it was a minor bowl game. In an era with a limited number of postseason matchups, getting to play in any bowl game mattered. For the Stanford players, it also meant they would get to go on a road trip and compete with their teammates one more time.

The prospect of spoiling Stanford's bowl hopes gave Cal players even more incentive to bury their foes on Saturday.

Elway met with reporters on Tuesday. He was typically bland, not wanting to say anything that would incite anyone. Talking to the press remained a chore for him. With football season ending, Elway said he was looking forward to more prosaic pursuits, like taking in *All My Children,* the soap opera that he and his buddies in the Delta Tau Delta fraternity house tried to watch every day at noon. The quarterback told reporters that he planned to graduate in June with a degree in economics and added, "I'm not going to worry about going out and getting a job." Elway wasn't trying to be funny, but his comment prompted reporters to erupt in laughter. Yes, Elway was definitely one prospective college graduate who didn't have to worry about getting a job. The New York Yankees and a yet-to-be-determined pro football team—Elway was expected to be the No. 1 pick in next year's NFL draft—would be competing to pay him millions of dollars to play for them.

In the meantime, Elway lived without flash on campus, despite his star status in the outside world. *Oakland Tribune* sportswriter Ron Bergman noted that he lived in a small room in the Delt house, with barely enough room for a king-sized waterbed, a bookshelf—he had textbooks on calculus and energy conservation—photos of his dad and his girlfriend Janet and a game ball from the 1981 Big Game. "A lot of people on campus think we're an *Animal House,*" Mike Aldrete, a baseball star and future big leaguer, told Bergman. "We do have a lot of football players [15], and they tend to be big and rowdy guys. But by the time they get home here, they're either too tired out from practice or they have to hit the books." Elway sought to fit in and be one of the guys. "I want to remain a kid as long as I can," he said. "I'm still in college, so I consider myself a kid."

The biggest news in sports on the Tuesday of Big Game Week came from the East Coast. The NFL announced that players and owners had settled a 57-day strike that had already forced the cancelation of seven regular-season games and the loss of $275 million in revenue and wages. Players had walked out following the second game of the season after owners balked at their demands—that they receive 55 percent of the NFL's gross revenues, that the NFL establish a minimum salary scale and provide better severance pay as well as improved medical insurance and pension benefits. With the settlement, the league announced plans to salvage a nine-game season.

On Wednesday morning, Cal nuclear chemistry professor Samuel Markowitz woke up at his home in Berkeley more excited than usual about teaching freshman chemistry 1A, the first course of a three-part series that introduced students of most technical majors to the fundamentals of physical chemistry. Markowitz donned a yellow dress shirt, his favorite blue blazer, and one of his many blue-and-gold "Go Bears" ties. For today was the day he had a special surprise, something he looked forward to all year, and a famous (to non-freshmen) highlight of the many Big Game week traditions at Cal.

Markowitz taught his class at the Physical Sciences Lecture Hall. For Markowitz, as for many chemistry and physics profs through the decades, the hall was their Roman forum, their Greek amphitheater. For the 1,000-plus Cal freshmen who took chem 1A each year, the lectures in the vast space were a rite of passage.

Wednesday mid-morning, 500 or so chem 1A freshmen filed in for what they thought was going to be a routine lecture. Indeed, for 30 minutes Markowitz talked about elements and atoms and covalent bonds—all that good chemistry stuff—and scribbled numbers and formulae on the blackboard. Then he paused and said that he wanted to remind new Cal students that Saturday marked the upcoming Big Game with Stanford. As he lifted a three-foot-tall cylindrical beaker from behind one of the center lecterns onto a low table, he announced that for the occasion, he would perform the "Big Game Color Change Titration." That was the cue for about 40 members of the Cal Marching Band's Straw Hat Band to burst into the lecture hall from a stage left basement hallway playing the school fight song, "Fight for California."

The freshmen, who were just getting into the swing of Big Game week, leaped to their feet and clapped to the music. "Go Bears!" they yelled. The line of high-stepping band members snaked between and around the blackboard wall and the demonstration tables, coming to a halt to fill in the space behind Markowitz, where they stopped playing.

The professor shushed the crowd and then turned to the tall beaker that held what looked like a parfait composed of red liquid on top and white below. He then explained the theory of "titration." The experiment he was about to demonstrate—assuredly, a closely guarded secret—would show how simply stirring the colors in the beaker while singing his special lyrics to another of Cal's many fight songs, "Big C," would produce oracular results. According to Markowitz, Big Game history proved that if the experiment was a success, Cal would win the game.

The students looked at each other, puzzled and more than a little skeptical. What did he mean? Markowitz then took a long stirring rod and slowly swirled the solution stack as he sang, a cappella, his special lyrics to "Big C." Gradually, the lower white layer in the beaker turned deep blue. The students began smiling. As Markowitz wrapped up with, "And when we stir this goo, the red will turn to blue, in an hour of Chem-is-try!"… the upper red layer turned gold. Blue and gold! Cal's colors! Take *that* Stanford! The students jumped to their feet again, and the band launched into an eardrum-rattling round of "Big C!"

At the same time, the Guardsmen, a social organization that raised money for at-risk kids, was hosting its annual Big Game luncheon in downtown San Francisco. Uniformed waiters were moving about the Grand Ballroom at the St. Francis Hotel, serving drinks to Cal and Stanford alums seated around about 40 round tables. Suddenly the chatter was interrupted as another set of members of Cal's Straw Hat Band marched in. Wearing straw boaters, blue jeans, white shirts, and vests, they high stepped into the room, playing

"Fight for California." Responding just as enthusiastically as the students on the campus, Cal rooters stood and clapped to the music.

Several minutes later, about a third of the Stanford band sauntered in, wearing their red coats, black pants, white shirts, and ugly ties, playing rock 'n' roll at maximum volume. Now the Stanford alums were on their feet. Things quieted down as the luncheon proceeded with cliché-filled speeches by Cal's Kapp and Stanford's Geiger. Afterward, the Straw Hat Band, yell leaders, and Rally Committee members went outside, commandeered a Hyde Street cable car, and played fight songs while riding toward Fisherman's Wharf. The pom-pom girls jumped off at stoplights to dance to the music and add to the merriment. "Go Bears!" called out passersby.

That night, Rally Committee members continued their watch outside The Campanile and other campus landmarks against any tomfoolery by their rivals from across the bay. They were joined by campus police, who, at 3:00 AM, stopped five Stanford students after finding a rash of red spray paintings on campus buildings. On a subsequent night, the police grabbed two Stanford students who had snuck into Memorial Stadium. But neither the Rally Committee nor the campus police could stop displays of school spirit farther afield. One set of Stanford students in London hung a BEAT CAL sign from the Tower Bridge over the Thames River while another did so by Checkpoint Charlie near the Berlin Wall in West Germany.

Still, one Cal Rally Committee member could take satisfaction in a prank that drew no publicity. Ken Raust and an accomplice duct taped the latch on the door of the Stanford locker room one afternoon to stop it from shutting entirely. After midnight, they snuck into the team's dressing room and found Elway's stall. They grabbed his sweatpants and sweatshirt and replaced them with Cal gear. As they left, Raust smiled as he imagined Elway's surprise the next day.

By now, members of Stanford's Axe Committee had taken the trophy from its normal home in a steel case behind an inch-thick of bulletproof glass at Tresidder Memorial Union on campus and stored it in a secure place. They knew that Cal students were likeliest to steal it during Big Game Week, or at minimum, damage the case in the process. So, several

nights earlier, after Tresidder had closed, Jon Erickson, the university official who oversaw the trophy, parked his red Bronco in front of the student union, in an area where cars normally were not permitted. It was a
three-man operation, reminiscent of a heist movie. One guy remained with
the Bronco and kept swiveling his head to make sure no suspicious types
lurked about. Erickson and Keith Light, who during daytime hours was an
admissions officer, went inside and barred the door so no one could enter.
It took them about 15 minutes to use an electric screwdriver to loosen the
six bolts, deactivate the two alarms, and then carefully lift the trophy out
of the case. Erickson and Light placed a black cloth over the Axe, received
the all-clear signal from the guard, carried it outside and into the back of
Erickson's vehicle, and then drove it to a secure location. The Axe would
remain there until game day.

On Thursday, only two days before the Big Game, Stanford received bad
news. Three key members of the football team had missed practice. Elway felt
lingering tightness because of a groin pull suffered against UCLA. Running
back Vincent White suffered stomach cramps from nerves and had to spend
the night at the campus medical clinic. Outside linebacker Garin Veris had
bruised his knee in practice the day before and was on crutches. Stanford's
chances of winning the Big Game without those three stars? Slim to none.

After practice that day, Stanford's offensive coordinator, Jim Fassel,
sought to fire up his players by introducing a special guest in the locker
room: Brad Williams, who as a tight end had caught the pass that set up
Stanford's game-winning field goal on the final play of the 1974 Big Game.
Williams was now a financial adviser in Palo Alto and looked the part in
a coat and tie. He smiled at the players, turned around momentarily, and
then whirled back to face the group. Suddenly, like the Incredible Hulk
transforming himself, Williams' eyes and veins were bulging, his face seemingly contorted in rage, and he looked even bigger than his 6'4", 235-pound
frame. Williams began hissing out a Big Game variant of the opening scene
of the 1970 movie *Patton*, about the famed World War II general. "I want
you to remember that no poor bastard has ever won a football game by
dying for his team," Williams spat out, looking from side to side. "He won

the football game by making the other poor dumb bastard die for *his* team. The California Bears are the enemy! Wade into that! Spill their blood! Kick them in the belly! You know, I actually feel sorry for those poor bastards. By God I do. We're not only going to murder those lousy Bear sons of bitches. We're going to tear out their living guts and use them to grease the treads on our cleats!"

By now, the players were cheering on Williams. He went on in the same maniacal vein before concluding, "Many years from now, when you're all sitting around your fireside with your grandson on your knee, and he asks you: 'Granddad, what did you do in the Big Game of 1982? You won't have to say, 'Well, I shoveled shit in Milpitas.' And you will thank God for it. Now you sons of bitches, now you know how I feel! Oh, and one more thing: I'd be damn proud to lead each and every one of you wonderful guys into this Big Game. Any time. And anywhere. May God bless you!" Williams swaggered out of the room as the players yelled their support.

Several hours later, with the traditional fireworks show on Lake Lagunita canceled because of rain, Elway appeared at a Beat Cal rally on the steps of the Stanford bookstore and promised he would indeed play on Saturday. Students cheered, and they cheered even louder when someone handed him the Axe, and he kissed the trophy. University president Donald Kennedy, wearing a bright red shirt, led the crowd to spell out S-T-A-N-F-O-R-D! Everyone left keyed up, swelling with school pride.

On Friday night, each school held a pregame event, but in very different ways and settings. Cal's took place at the university's Greek Theatre, near Memorial Stadium. It was a traditional rah-rah pep rally. As people streamed into the bowl-shaped theater, they could see dozens and dozens of wood pallets stacked in a rickety tower three stories high atop a sand pit in front of the stage. A "Beat Stanford" banner was attached to the frame. Newspapers soaked in kerosene were stuffed inside the pallets. Just after the ceremonies began at 8:00 PM, an electrical charge set them ablaze. The full house of about 5,000 students and alums whooped with delight. As the bonfire burned down, the Cal band marched onto the stage in full uniform, playing "Fight for California." Next the Cal Men's Octet sang several spirit songs.

Then a gray-haired woman wearing a 1930s Cal letter jacket strode onto the stage. The upperclassmen had seen her before and knew what was coming. "Granny," as they called her, was Cal's biggest and most enthusiastic football fan. Her real name was Natalie Cohen, and she had graduated from Cal in 1934. She was now 70 years old, wearing a Cal blue-and-gold sweater and as spunky as they come. Cohen announced she would lead the crowd in a yell. "Oski Wow-Wow!" she shouted, waving her arms. "Whiskey Wee-Wee! Olee! Muckie-eye! Olee! Berkeley-eye! California! WOW!"

Cheers shook the old structure as Cohen walked off the stage. The fire burned low. "Freshmen! More wood!" yelled out the upperclassmen. Freshmen scrambled to toss more pallets onto the fire.

Next onto the stage was a 1966 Cal grad wearing a blue blazer, a blue-and-gold tie, and a Rally Committee emblem on his jacket pocket. He was a mechanical engineering graduate named Tom Edwards Jr., and he was there to present a satirical history of the Axe. With a droll delivery, Edwards recounted Stanford's bad fortune just before the turn of the century, losing the 1898 Big Game and the first of three baseball games in 1899. The latter defeat, he told the Cal rooters, led Stanford students to create the Axe—only to have it "relieved" from them after Cal won the second match of the baseball series. The crowd cheered. Edwards went on to tell of the dastardly deed in 1930 when the Immortal 21 from Stanford stole the Axe back from Cal. The crowd booed.

The two schools, he explained, then agreed that the winner of the Big Game would claim the trophy for the following 12 months. For the 1982 game, Stanford held the Axe after squashing Cal the preceding year. "John Elway's Heisman hype has Stanford favored to easily defeat the Bears on Saturday," Edwards said, building to a close. "Only dedicated, deafening cheers from Cal fans could send the California team into a Bear Rage for victory." Deafening cheers rang out in the Greek Theatre.

Following Edwards was a 1966 grad who was introduced as one of the greatest yell leaders in the history of Cal. He was Jamie Sutton, and he had been elected to be the head yell leader for the 1964–65 academic year. Now Sutton walked deliberately onto the stage from the middle entry, carrying a metal chair. He stopped at the mic. Sutton was a San Francisco attorney and looked the part, wearing a bow tie, sport coat, and slacks. He bellowed his first words: "THIS IS THE GREATEST UNIVERSITY IN THE WORLD!" The crowd cheered its agreement. "Not only because it has more Nobel laureates than any university in the world and the greatest faculty of any university in the world and the most diverse and greatest student body of any university in the world, but it also has the greatest traditions of any university in the world, and the greatest of these is the Cal Haka." The crowd cheered again.

While playing rugby for Cal in the 1960s, Sutton had a teammate from New Zealand who told him about the "haka," the historic Maori challenge that the team performed before each game, meant to show their strength, unity, and pride. Sutton had come to the Greek Theatre to lead a similar ritual. "Before a battle," he began, "the two Maori tribes would line up on either side of the battlefield and in an effort to bolster their courage and intimidate their opponents, they would do a haka!"

Sutton grew serious and emphatic. "Cal's Haka goes, *Kamate. Kamate. Kaoro Kaoro!* which means, loosely translated, 'We are going to beat the hell out of your guys!'" As Sutton recited these words, he took off the bow tie and then the jacket, which he draped on the back of a chair next to him. He continued, "*Tiniti, Tangata, Fuhuru, Huru!* which means, 'And here are the muscles we are going to do it with!'" He unbuttoned the top buttons of his shirt.

Sutton stepped threateningly closer to the mic, rolling up his sleeves. "*Ahopane, Kopane, Ahopane, Kopane!* which means, 'And here is how we are going to do it!'"

Sutton rolled up his sleeves and said, "then there is the famous *Wakata, Wiki, Te Wraaaa!*" He stuck out his tongue, threw his arms straight up, and glared at the crowd. "Which means, 'We are the greatest damn Maoris in the world!'" The crowd cheered wildly.

Sutton loosened the mic stand and lowered it. "Everybody start clapping!" he commanded. Sutton bent over, stomped his right foot in an exaggerated fashion, and clapped slowly. He yelled for everybody to stand up and imitate him. Yelling at the top of his lungs, gesturing wildly, he performed the whole Haka. The crowd followed along, their roar rising to a crescendo. Sutton stuck out his tongue and repeated a line that brought more cheers.

Finally, he stood, raised the mic, and shouted, "The greatest university in the world!" He grabbed his tie and jacket, turned, and walked off through the center entry as the crowd roared once again.

Next, the Cal football team entered, stage left, led by Kapp. He positioned himself in front of the mic and talked about the importance of the Big Game's values—tradition and sportsmanship—and, above all, the need to beat Stanford! "The Bear will not quit!" he yelled. "The Bear will not die!" A fresh round of cheers rose into the night sky.

Kapp wanted to finish by spelling out the school's letters. "Give me a C!" he yelled.

"C!" responded the crowd.

"Give me an A!"

"AAA!"

"Give me an L!"

"LLL!"

"Give me an F!"

Oops. Kapp had misspelled California. Everyone laughed, including Kapp, and he walked away from the mic.

Ahmad Anderson, a senior defensive back, emerged from the crowd of players. He had created a new cheer, and he wanted to share it with fans. Anderson stood only 5'9", but his infectious energy captured the crowd's attention. He rapped, "You know it! You tell the story! You tell the whole damn world this is Bear territory!" The crowd hooted its approval. Anderson repeated it, again and again. Then the fans took over, yelling out the words without his lead. Cheers rang throughout the Greek Theatre as the team departed. They would spend the night at a quieter venue, the Berkeley Marriott Marina Hotel, four miles away.

Garff Wilson strode to the microphone as everyone at the Greek Theatre was instructed to light the candles they had received upon arrival. A retired professor of rhetoric and dramatic art, Wilson had come onto the stage to render tribute to Cal's greatest football coach, Andy Smith. Under him, Cal did not lose a game from 1920 through 1924. Smith died of pneumonia the following year at only 42. "He died while still at the height of his powers, and he was mourned as few sportsmen in our time have been mourned," Wilson told the crowd, with the Greek Theatre lit up with candles and the bonfire's embers. "His going has left a vacant chair around our hearthside which can never be filled."

While Wilson spoke, the Cal band hummed "All Hail Blue and Gold," the university's official alma mater song, and they began playing it after the professor's final words. Upon the last note, everyone looked at the back rim of the arena where the script *Cal* was spelled out in sparklers, one letter at a time. The Cal band rocked out on UFO's "Lights Out!" and the crowd filed out, fired up about the prospect of whipping Elway and Stanford the following afternoon.

Stanford had no organized activity that evening. Instead, it had a disorganized tradition that naturally revolved around the band. It was a parade in San Francisco, led by the band, followed by hundreds of students and anyone nearby who wanted to share their high spirits. It's safe to say that only a few in the parade were not drunk or high. The motley parade began at Union Square and then went along California Avenue to Larkin Street, where the throng turned right. They proceeded up the hilly street and then down, with the band performing, students dancing, and bars along the way doing a booming business. "Beat Cal!" the students yelled until they were hoarse. "Beat Cal!"

At 11:00 PM, the band had nearly reached its destination, Aquatic Park, by the bay next to Ghirardelli Square, when a mishap occurred. A 21-year-old man pulling out of a parking garage on Larkin Street panicked at the sight of the band and the revelers passing by. He gunned his 1973 Fiat and drove into the mob, injuring five students, but none seriously, fortunately. The driver also hit one bandsman, Stu Weiss, and ran over his saxophone, rendering it unplayable. Regrouping, the band made its way the final few blocks to Aquatic Park, where they performed before hundreds of students. But the accident left them rattled.

It would not be the last time that weekend that the band found itself in the wrong place at the wrong time.

In their final article before the game, *San Francisco Examiner* sportswriters John Crumpacker and King Thompson asked the coaches what fans should expect the next day. Kapp offered a macho response. "You make your statement on the field," he said.

True to character, Wiggin offered a more philosophical answer. "It's an emotional game, and sometimes in emotional games, bizarre things happen," he said.

• CHAPTER 9 •

THE PREGAME

It was finally game day, November 20, 1982. The 85th Big Game. A sell-out with 76,000 fans. Kickoff at Cal's Memorial Stadium was 1:00 PM. A general admission ticket to sit in the student section for either school cost $7.50. Reserved tickets seats cost $15.

The day started early for all the participants. Stanford football players began at Rickey's Hyatt House in Palo Alto, where the team traditionally stayed for home games. The players went through their normal pregame routine—breakfast, followed by meetings with coaches. By 9:00 AM, they were on the road for the 45-minute bus ride to Memorial Stadium.

Beginning at 7:00 AM, Cal's student team managers knocked on one door after another at the Berkeley Marriott Marina Hotel, waking up players. By 8:00 AM, all 90 players were downstairs eating breakfast. Then the team split up—offense in one room, defense in another, special teams in a third—before Joe Kapp brought everyone together for a few final inspirational words. By 9:15 AM, the players were boarding two buses—offense on one, defense on the other—for the four-mile drive through Berkeley to Memorial Stadium.

As the buses pulled out, a motorcycle escort led the way. Kicker Joe Cooper felt a stab of melancholy as he looked out at fans on Hearst Avenue, cheering on the team. As a senior, Cooper reflected on how he'd never get to do this again. The crowds thickened as the team turned right onto Piedmont Avenue and neared Memorial Stadium. When the buses stopped at the adjacent Maxwell Field, a throng of cheering fans—"Go Bears! Good luck!"—met the players as they disembarked, walking through North Gate into Memorial Stadium and up the concrete stairs on the right to the home locker room.

The seven referees also spent the night at the Marriott Marina. After breakfast and a final briefing, wearing coats and ties, they piled into two cars and drove to the stadium, arriving at about 10:00 AM. There, they encountered an unusual feature of Memorial Stadium. The officials had to walk past the Bears players getting ready because the officials' dressing room was in the recesses of the Cal locker room. At all other Pac-10 stadiums, officials had their own quarters away from teams. As they put on their uniforms, the officials expressed their excitement. Working a Big Game featuring John Elway was a plum assignment.

The seven men sat on folding chairs and benches in their cramped quarters while they reviewed their responsibilities. Led by Charles Moffett, the crew chief, they went over their assignments—including who to key on during pass plays, how to manage the clock, who would handle the ball after each play, and who would determine whether a runner crossed the goal line.

Moffett had been a Pac-10 referee since 1960. During plays from scrimmage, he would stand behind the offensive backfield. After penalties, he would signal the infraction to the crowd. The director of employment for Boeing Aircraft in Washington state, Moffett was considered by many to be the best official in the Pac-10. He wore a white cap signifying his role as crew chief while the others wore black caps.

The umpire was Walter Wolf, who played football and rugby at the University of Oregon in the early 1960s and then owned an insurance agency in Spokane. He would stand just behind the linebackers and watch for infractions by the offensive line—false starts, holding, illegal blocks, and ineligible man downfield—and he would note forward progress after each play.

Jack Langley, an electrical contractor in Belmont, just south of San Francisco, was the head linesman. He would stand where the ball was hiked, on the Cal sideline, and oversee the chain gang marking the line of scrimmage, as well as the down and distance to a first down. Langley would be responsible for calls near the line of scrimmage on his side of the field, such as whether a player was down or had gone out of bounds.

Gordon Riese, a high school mathematics teacher in Portland who had been a minor league pitcher for the Kansas City A's, was the line judge. He would stand on the Stanford sideline, opposite Langley, and perform the same duties on his side.

James Fogltance, an elementary school principal in Tucson, was the field judge. Like Langley, he stood on the Cal side but about 15 yards downfield and was responsible for ruling on long runs or passes.

Carver Shannon, who had played against Kapp in the Canadian Football League before a three-year stint as a defensive back for the Los Angeles Rams, was the back judge. Like Riese, he stood on the Stanford sideline and performed the same downfield duties as Fogltance. The alternate official was Ron Blum, who ran the Sonoma Golf Course north of San Francisco.

At 11:30 AM, Moffett and Wolf went to meet first with Paul Wiggin and then with Kapp to get the names and numbers of each team's captains and to be told of any possible trick plays so they could be prepared for them.

Kapp didn't mention one trick play that would take place during the game's final seconds. But then again, he had no reason to. It was unofficial, hadn't actually been practiced, and wouldn't be found in Cal's playbook.

The requirement that officials dress deep in the Cal locker room was only one of Memorial Stadium's quirks. Built in the side of a hill to resemble the Roman Coliseum, it had opened in 1923, honoring the Californians who died during World War I. The crowd scenes for a brilliant comedy called *The Freshman*, starring Harold Lloyd, were shot during the 1924 Big Game at Memorial Stadium.

In the following years, the stadium hosted the Big Game dozens of times. In 1962, it drew its biggest crowd, 88,000, to hear a speech by president John F. Kennedy marking the 94th anniversary of Cal's founding.

For this football game, 20 years after Kennedy's speech, most spectators still sat on benches with each seat's number carved into the wood. Those with higher-priced seats might sit on metal benches. The concourses were narrow, and there weren't enough bathrooms, but the seats were close to the field and offered good sightlines. The stadium's most unusual feature was one nobody could see—the Hayward Fault ran directly underneath the field, from goal post to goal post. When it was built, the stadium foundation was split in two to reduce the impact of an earthquake. Above the southeast corner were wooden houses perched on a hill thick with trees. Above the northeast corner was Tightwad Hill, which had been created with dirt excavated during the stadium's construction.

Tightwad Hill was the destination for another person who began the day early. His name was Mark Weigand. Although he would not set foot inside the stadium, he would play a pivotal role before the day ended. At 7:00 AM, Weigand drove to a secret location—actually, his mother's house in nearby San Ramon—where the Cal Rally Committee was hiding the Victory Cannon on a flatbed trailer in her garage. Weigand, a sophomore, was the cannoneer. He would fire the 900-pound Civil War replica every time Cal scored—and immediately after the game if the Bears won. But first Weigand had to transport the cannon, with its two blue wagon wheels and gold-painted barrel, up to Tightwad Hill, so named because hundreds of Cal fans would sit on the dirt slope where they could peer down and see all but the corner of the end zone closest to them—for free. Tightwads!

To their right on the hill was a wooden platform for the Victory Cannon. The big gun debuted in the early 1960s on the field at Memorial Stadium and subsequently moved to Tightwad Hill after the league banned cannons from stadiums in 1972, following a premature firing two years earlier at Stanford that hospitalized two of its students. To position the cannon in place, Weigand had to drive up a steep dirt road onto Tightwad Hill and then, with the help of 10 other Rally Committee members, carefully lower it 100 feet to its platform.

By 11:00 AM, they had completed their task, and Weigand made sure the cannon was ready to go. It looked fearsome but didn't actually launch a projectile. Instead, Weigand attached a firework to a metal rod that was fastened to the end of the three-foot-long cannon barrel. It was essentially a six-inch firecracker that would make a very loud bang and emit a puff of white smoke. To detonate the charge, Weigand would turn a key in a control box with his left hand while simultaneously pushing a button with his right. The resulting explosion boomed throughout the stadium. But it would be at least a couple of hours before he would get the chance to fire it. From his vantage point, Weigand had a clear view of most of the field directly below him.

The Cal band began its day at 7:30 AM after performing late into the evening before at alumni parties in San Francisco and around Berkeley. On game day, the 163 band members staged a final rehearsal of their pregame and halftime shows. Afterward, they gathered around the longtime band director, Robert Briggs. He was a traditionalist who loved leading the Cal band and wearing his uniform festooned with gold braid. But once a year, Briggs would briefly step outside his conservative persona to tell the same off-color joke to the band. After weeks of anticipation, that moment had arrived. It was known as the Broccoli Joke. It went like this: a woman walked into a grocery store and asked the clerk, "Do you have any broccoli?"

"No," he replied. "I don't have any broccoli."

She wouldn't take no for an answer and kept asking for broccoli. Increasingly exasperated, the clerk kept saying no, he didn't have any. Finally, he said, "Lady, spell 'ban' as in banana."

"B-a-n," she said.

"Spell 'straw' as in strawberry," he said.

"S-t-r-a-w."

Now, he said, "Spell 'fuck' as in broccoli."

Taken aback, she replied, "There is no 'fuck' in broccoli."

"That's what I was trying to tell you," the clerk said. "There is no fuckin' broccoli!"

The band members fell out laughing as Briggs smiled shyly.

At about 11:30 AM, with everyone in full uniform, drum major Bob Willis blew his whistle, and the band whooped as they ran onto the steps of Sproul Plaza in the heart of Cal's campus. It was the traditional "Noon Concert" before a home game. Willis blew his whistle again, and the band launched into their pregame show and then their halftime show before hundreds of students and fans, who stopped to see the performance before walking up the hill to Memorial Stadium. At noon, with the concert over, Willis stood in front of the band. "Give me a C," he yelled.

"CCCCC!"

"Give me an A!"

"AAAAA!"

"Give me an L!"

"Who are we?" Willis shouted.

"CAAALLLLL!"

"Who's going to win?"

"CAAALLLLL!"

Willis then blew his whistle one more time, and the band raced 100 yards to historic Sather Gate, where the Free Speech Movement paraded in 1964, in one of the first acts of civil disobedience on a U.S. college campus during the 1960s. But at this moment, Sather Gate belonged to the uniformed men and women wearing the Cal band's blue and gold. The trombone players lined up in the front row, with more than a dozen additional rows of musicians behind them. Willis stood in the front. "California Band!" he shouted. "Atten-shun! Atten-shun!"

"Hut One Two!" band members yelled in response while lifting first one knee, then the other. Willis blew a series of whistles, and the band went into a high-step march through Sather Gate and then switched to their normal marching step. Two minutes later, they turned right and began heading uphill on their way to Memorial Stadium. By 12:30 PM, the band members had reached the north tunnel at Memorial Stadium and were waiting for the Stanford band to finish so they could perform their pregame show.

Like their Cal counterparts, members of the Stanford band began their day early, after little sleep, following the unruly parade in San Francisco the night before. For the rest of game day, the Cal band would take one path, and the Stanford band another.

The Stanford band met at the Band Shak at 7:00 AM—for beer and doughnuts. "Breakfast of Champions," they called it. Doughnuts and Budweisers in hand, the band members walked across Campus Drive to Angell Field for a pregame rehearsal. It involved so much mischief and rule-breaking that it would have probably given Cal's traditionalist, Briggs, a heart attack.

Stanford student band manager John Howard took it in stride, however. He had seen it all before.

The band couldn't leave immediately afterward for Berkeley. First, band photographer Robby Beyers had to re-shoot the planned cover for the band's next album. So everyone, in uniform while carrying their instruments, trooped over to pose, more or less, in front of a wire sculpture next to a university library. Beyers shot the photos, but the usual difficulty in corralling the wayward band meant they left Stanford 30 minutes late. Not that the band members cared as they headed to Berkeley. They were too busy imbibing additional pregame libations and shouting bawdy limericks back and forth on the bus.

Aboard one vehicle, Gary Tyrrell, a trombone player, took swigs from a flask of Jameson Irish whiskey as he and a seatmate toasted Elway, the Big Game, Disco Ray Gruenewald, and anything else they could think of. Tyrrell was a superb trombone player from outside of Philadelphia. He had applied to Stanford not knowing much about the university other than it was part of a growing tech community and was on par academically with Ivy League universities. Visiting as a high school senior, he was captivated by students playing frisbee on a sun-kissed day, something he hadn't seen visiting Yale earlier in the year. On the night of his first visit to Stanford, Tyrrell followed the sound of drums and happened upon the Stanford band. Enthralled, he accompanied the group as it rocked students, moving from place to place on campus. *My God, this looks fun*, he thought.

By November 1982, he was a senior, not known as a hell-raiser. In fact, like a lot of other band members, he was a bit nerdy. Tyrrell was majoring in industrial engineering. But he liked having a good time, and the band definitely offered that.

The buses carrying Tyrrell and the other bandsmen parked near Memorial Stadium, just off Greek Row, at about 12:15 PM, only minutes before the group was to perform its pregame show. "Stanford sucks! Go home!" taunted Cal frat boys as band members disembarked and walked to the south tunnel to enter the stadium. For this game, the bandsmen were wearing white hard hats. They wouldn't need them outside. They would inside the stadium, however, when they began performing their pregame show, and the fruit began to fly from the Cal student section.

By the time the band arrived, two men from Birmingham, Alabama, were settling into their seats in the lower level of the press box, directly behind the sportswriters. They were Jim Simmons and Coy Collinsworth, representing the Hall of Fame Bowl. Simmons and Collinsworth hoped to phone Birmingham when the game ended to tell the officials there that Elway and his teammates would be coming to Alabama on December 31 to play Vanderbilt University. The Hall of Fame officials already had visions of a catchy title to promote the game. They were going to call it the "Brain Bowl."

Another person who was sitting in the press box was a tall slim man who left his Walnut Creek home with his son at 9:45 AM. It was Joe Starkey, Cal's play-by-play announcer. His son Jim would sit next to him during the game, identifying the players making tackles. On the way to Memorial Stadium, they picked up Starkey's statistician, Len Shapiro, and during the 45-minute drive, the three reviewed the key players, important stats, and the need for Shapiro to keep Starkey updated on Elway's statistics during the game. They arrived at Memorial Stadium around 10:30 AM and took the elevator up to the second level of the press box, which had booths for the broadcasters, assistant coaches, and university big shots on the west side of the stadium. The Cal radio booth was on the 40-yard line, nearest to the north end zone. Starkey, 41, would be calling the game on KGO-810 AM, which had broadcast Bears games since 1974.

Starkey was raised on Chicago's south side with the children of the city's outsized mayor, Richard J. Daley. For a time in high school, as the eldest in an Irish-Catholic family, he considered becoming a priest. But he discarded that idea and attended Loyola University in the mid-1960s, receiving an undergraduate and a master's degree in business. At times, he joined street demonstrations against the American involvement in the Vietnam War. But he also joined the national guard where he wore combat fatigues and carried an M-1 rifle when Chicago's streets, like those elsewhere in big cities, erupted in riots following the assassination of Martin Luther King Jr. in 1968. Starkey decided to relocate to California and ended up working as a campus recruiter for Los Angeles-based Union Bank. He was tear gassed during a student protest while on a recruiting trip to Cal in 1969.

All the while, Starkey harbored dreams of becoming a broadcaster. Beginning when he was about 10, he called Chicago Cubs games as he watched on the family's black-and-white television set, with the sound off. In high school, the nuns at his Catholic boys' school liked his voice and had him read announcements. In Los Angeles, he tried to break in as a sports announcer but failed.

In 1970, Starkey's bank transferred him to the San Francisco Bay Area. His dream to become a broadcaster remained unabated. Tape recorder in hand, he practiced calling the play-by-play while at games of the Golden State Warriors, the San Francisco Giants, and the California Golden Seals. At home afterward, he played back the tape to review his work. In 1972, Charles O. Finley, the inventive but bombastic owner of the Oakland Athletics and the Golden Seals, hired Starkey to be the hockey team's play-by-play announcer—but then fired him 15 minutes later when Starkey cheekily told Finley how he could reduce the high rate of employee turnover at his companies.

Weeks later, the station manager played Starkey's tape for Finley. The owner liked it but asked, "I think I've heard that voice. Is that that son of a bitch banker?" It was, but the station manager talked Finley into keeping Starkey. He quit his job at the bank, taking a pay cut. What mattered is that he had broken into the broadcasting ranks. In 1975, Starkey became the radio play-by-play announcer for Cal football games.

After entering the booth for the 1982 Big Game, Starkey followed his custom of taping notes, which contained players' statistics and items he wanted to mention, to the side window panel. Starkey also reviewed an oversized cardboard sheet with all the players' names and numbers that his son Jim would use to indicate to him who had made the tackle. At noon, Starkey went live on KGO with his pregame show.

He talked about the key matchups. When Cal had the ball, the most important question was whether first-year starter Gale Gilbert had turned the corner. The week before, the sophomore quarterback played well against

Washington State. But the week before that, he had thrown six interceptions against USC. Starkey then turned to Cal's receivers. Mariet Ford, the senior flanker, was only 5'9" and 165 pounds but quick enough to get open. Split end Wes Howell, playing his first year of football after three years of basketball, was tall, could jump, and was getting better every week. Tight end David Lewis, a senior, blocked well and was second in the Pac-10 in catches. Starkey expected the receivers to have a good day. They would be going up against a Stanford secondary that ranked ninth in the Pac-10.

When Stanford had the ball, Cal's fearsome right end, Reggie Camp, a senior, would take on left tackle Jeff Deaton, a junior and first-year starter. Camp was strong enough to fling offensive linemen aside as he pursued the ball. Gary Plummer, Cal's senior nose guard, was undersized for a defensive lineman at 6'2" and 230 pounds. His speed and strength, though, would present a challenge to Stanford's bigger center, senior Mike Teeuws. Besides Camp and Plummer, the other Cal standout was Ron Rivera, a junior outside linebacker who led the team in tackles.

Stanford tight end Chris Dressel, a senior who was completing a breakout season, would go up against Cal's Fred Williams, who was only 5'9" but was strong and tough. Williams had already promised that he and the other members of Cal's secondary would beat up on Stanford's two wide receivers, Emile Harry and Mike Tolliver. Neither of them weighed more than 175 pounds. Stanford featured a versatile running attack. Vincent White led the NCAA in catches, showing how the West Coast offense could employ a running back in the passing game. Mike Dotterer, White's equal as a runner, had gained 155 yards against Washington State, including the game-winning touchdown with 22 seconds left.

Elway, of course, was the main story. He provided the fuel that propelled the Stanford offense. That season's premier college quarterback—and in some estimations the best of all time—Elway would lead Stanford for the last time in a regular-season game, with a winning record, the Hall of Fame Bowl berth, the Heisman Trophy, and possession of the Axe all on the line.

The Bears defense was ranked only seventh in the Pac-10. With their offensive weaponry, Stanford players were confident they could move the ball.

Cal's defensive strategist, Ron Lynn, wasn't ready to concede a big day for Stanford's offense. He had developed a plan to deal with Elway. "We've got to be able to change it up," Lynn told reporters, without giving away the details. "We can't afford to give the quarterback the definitive pre-snap read—thereby not putting any decision in John's mind. If he can read what we're doing, bang, it's over."

Lynn wanted to confuse Elway by making him think he might face blitzes on any play from any direction. The Cal coach noted how Arizona State held Stanford to 17 points by constantly blitzing Elway, leaving him less time to find an open receiver. Lynn also knew that he could fool Elway only part of the time. Lynn, however, could also disrupt Stanford's quarterback by confusing his linemen and running backs. They were responsible for keeping blitzing linebackers, cornerbacks, and safeties from him. The danger for Cal, of course, was that Elway could throw a quick pass on a blitz and catch Cal without enough defenders near the receiver. White, who had scored two touchdowns in each of the last two Big Games, was especially dangerous when Cal blitzed. White could fake out defenders without slowing down.

Lynn instructed his outside defenders not to pinch inward when they rushed Elway on pass plays. This would help prevent the Stanford quarterback from scrambling outside of the containment zone, where he was especially dangerous, giving his receivers more time to get open or taking off on a run. At the same time, Lynn planned to put as much speed and athleticism on the field as possible to counter Elway. Lynn hoped to do this by frequently employing five or six defensive backs, not the typical four. Deploying five defensive backs was known as a nickel package while six was known as a dime. But in a dime package, Lynn would have to bench Ron Rivera, Cal's leading tackler.

The Axe, regained by Stanford after its victory the year before, arrived at Memorial Stadium at about noon, ferried to Berkeley in the trunk of a Stanford Police Department car, accompanied by three alums. Taking no chances, they quickly used a coiled bicycle lock to attach the vaunted trophy to two students, Kevin Wells and Max Scheder-Bieschin. The Axe, with its protectors, entered the stadium through the south tunnel, where Stanford fans were seated.

The Stanford band came dancing into the stadium a few minutes later through the same tunnel. Arriving late, they immediately charged onto the field to begin their pregame show. As expected, apples and oranges began flying at them from the Cal student section. But no band members were hit. For one thing, the band deliberately performed near the south end zone, to be farther away from the Cal students. And if anyone at Cal had a particularly strong arm, Stanford lacrosse players were positioned to intercept any of the high-flying fruit.

The band's show had the satirical theme of 101 things to do with a dead bear. One formation taunted Cal by spelling out "Axe," and another formed the shape of the Axe, while the band played the Journey song "Don't Stop Believing." Yes, the band was reminding Cal rooters that Stanford possessed the trophy, but, perhaps, if they just believed enough, the Bears might win it one day.

After finishing their show, Stanford band members ran to the south end zone to find their seats. On the other end of the field, Willis, the drum major, blew his whistle from within the north tunnel, and the Cal band came flowing out in a double-time march toward the back of the end zone. Each member had a specific path to follow while a drum cadence kept everyone in step. When the first band members hit the end zone back line, an explosion accompanied by a puff of smoke sounded at the 15-yard line. Everyone kept following their precise routes through the end zone and onto field. Within seconds, they had formed a giant wedge with saxophone player Ron Keimach at its point on the 24-yard line. On cue, everyone bowed. Willis then emerged on a run from within the wedge and leaped over Keimach. The drum major stopped, slowly bent backward, and touched the top of his shako—his tall, cylindrical, and furry cap—to the turf. Meanwhile, the band launched into the intro of the spirit song, "Big C." Just after Willis was upright again, the band marched forward, and the drum major tossed his baton high into the air and caught it. Cal rooters roared. They loved the tradition of their precision marching band. The pregame show ended with the band playing the national anthem.

At 12:45 PM, in Stanford's cramped visitors' locker room, Coach Wiggin finished a rousing address about the importance of winning the Big Game, exhorting his players, "Our people are here. And we're going to walk through them. Let's go, men!" Wearing their away game white jerseys with red numbers, Stanford players emerged from a back entrance of the locker room onto the concourse where they navigated alongside fans heading to their seats. The players turned right and then walked down the stadium steps through Section I, slapping hands with cheering Stanford fans as they made their way down to the field.

A minute later, Cal players, wearing blue jerseys with gold-colored numbers and pants, made a traditional entrance, racing from the north tunnel onto the field. The temperature was about 57 degrees, a crisp autumn afternoon with a dash of California sunshine—perfect football weather. Rain the day before made the turf slippery near the sidelines, thanks to the crowned field's drainage system.

Cal had a slightly better record, 6–4 versus 5–5 for Stanford. But the Bears had played a weaker schedule and feasted on have-nots, while the Cardinal had knocked off No. 2 Washington at home, No. 13 Ohio State on the road, and had barely lost to Arizona State and UCLA, which also were ranked in the top 20. Oddsmakers favored Stanford by seven points.

Nobody, of course, could be sure how this game would turn out. "Today's Big Game, if it's like the 84 others, should provide some bizarre and exciting moments," the *Oakland Tribune* reported that morning.

How little did they know.

• CHAPTER 10 •

THE FIRST HALF

Cal won the coin toss and elected to receive the opening kickoff. Stanford kicker Mark Harmon booted the ball to the goal line, and Mariet Ford returned it up the middle to the 19-yard line. The 85th Big Game was underway. Cal's offense began cautiously with a short run up the middle and a pass to the right flat that fell incomplete. On third down, quarterback Gale Gilbert sprinted four steps to his left, straightened his shoulders, and hit Ford by the left sideline for eight yards and a first down. From there, Gilbert mixed runs and passes as the Bears moved downfield. But the defense toughened and stopped Cal's drive at the Stanford 5-yard line. Kicker Joe Cooper ran onto the field to attempt a 27-yard field goal.

Cooper hailed from Fresno, California, and had starred as a safety in high school. His school's principal was one of the Immortal 21 from Stanford who had stolen the Axe from Cal in 1930. Both Notre Dame and the University of Washington recruited Cooper. But Cal wanted him as a kicker, and he liked the idea of being close enough to home for his family to attend games—Fresno was three hours away—but far enough away from them to do his own thing. Kapp's hiring, however, had not gone well for Cooper after the new coach insisted on replacing Cooper's holder and long snapper. Cooper was too intimidated by Kapp to object. He ultimately got them back, but the reshuffling had contributed to defenders blocking four of Cooper's missed attempts so far that season.

Now Cooper lined up for the field goal, soccer style. Second from the right on Stanford's defense was Barry Cromer, a junior safety studying to be a doctor. On the far right was another defensive back named Kevin

Baird. Also a junior, he was studying to be a lawyer. When the ball was snapped, Baird shot across the line of scrimmage trying to block the kick. Cal's outside blocker took a step left to stop Baird. That opened a more direct lane toward the kicker for Cromer. He knifed through and dove for a spot just in front of the ball.

Thud!

Cooper knew what had happened even before he looked up. It was another blocked kick. The ball fluttered to the left. No good.

Cal had moved the ball on its opening drive but came up empty. At the time, the loss of the three points seemed like a momentary hiccup for the Bears. But it would loom large later.

Stanford took over on its 20 and started strong when John Elway threw a dart down the middle to tight end Chris Dressel for a 17-yard gain. Two plays later, on second and 6, Elway dropped straight back. Cal right end Reggie Camp pushed left tackle Jeff Deaton backward, spun him around, and finally ran over Deaton as he crashed into Elway a split second after he released the ball. Elway and Deaton both picked themselves up. "Is it going to be a long day over there, Jeff"? Elway asked.

"Yep," replied Deaton. "It's going to be a really long day over here."

Deaton, a junior, was still learning the position as a first-year starter on the offensive line after playing defense the previous two years. Besides, he had broken two ribs against Washington three weeks earlier, but the coaches had not shared that with the media to keep other teams from knowing. Banged up, wearing hockey pads over his ribs, Deaton sought out the fullback as they huddled for the next play. "I'm going to need help on any pass protection with this guy," Deaton said. "Check in with me before you go out on your route."

"This guy"—Camp—was the single most feared Cal player. He scared even his own teammates. A senior, he had grown up in New Orleans with a mother who was deaf and mute from birth but liked to party and was often absent. Reggie learned American Sign Language before English. He could, for example, express his feelings toward his mother by placing his thumb flat against his chest and extending his little finger. Then he would make another fist and extend the thumb, the first finger and his little finger, signing, "I love you."

Kids can be cruel, though. Schoolmates taunted him by calling her "dumb." Reggie knew better—she had graduated from high school after all—and would show them with his fists. To add to his difficulties, Reggie's father walked out on the family when he was a baby. His grandfather filled the void. Reggie called him "Dad." The neighborhood in New Orleans was rough. Reggie and other boys played tackle football in the street, barefoot, and in shorts. At night, he could hear gunfire. Other kids tried to recruit him into a gang, but Reggie envisioned his grandfather's disapproval—he was a longshoreman and a deacon at a nearby church—and this dissuaded him.

On a trip to San Francisco when he was about 12, Reggie told his uncle he would like to meet his father, who lived across the bay. The uncle returned several days later and said, "Reg, I did everything I could. Your dad doesn't want to see you." Reggie was heartbroken. He changed his last name from Miles to Camp, his mother's maiden name. From then on, he referred to his biological father as "the donor."

After Camp's grandfather died in 1974, he and his mother moved to South San Francisco where they lived with her brother, Wallace. He, too, became a father figure for Camp. His Uncle Wallace accompanied Camp on his first day to Jefferson High School in Daly City for 10th grade. Before Camp went to class, Wallace asked the receptionist if she would fetch the football coach, Jack Burgett. The receptionist looked Camp up and down. He was a strapping 6'2", 190 pounds. "He's in class now," she said. "But give me a moment, and I'll have him come out here."

Camp had never played organized football before and told Burgett that he wanted to play running back or receiver. Burgett told Camp he could try that for three days, but the coach had another position in mind. After it became clear that Camp didn't know how to hit the hole or to run a passing route, Burgett told his new player that he could best help the team on the offensive and defensive lines.

Camp quickly learned to love the trenches. Smashing into other players offered the perfect outlet for the anger that welled up in him in reaction to kids' callous comments about his mother and the donor's rejection. Camp was aggressive—too aggressive, in fact. He fought with his teammates nearly every day. But Burgett would settle him down and helped him improve his reading and writing to grade level. Most Pac-10 schools recruited Camp, and he chose Cal because it was close to home.

Camp brought his unchecked aggression to Berkeley. Offensive linemen, who tried to control his rush by holding him or cutting his legs out from under him, incurred his wrath, even if they were teammates. One day in practice in 1980 during Camp's sophomore year, a freshman guard named Brian Hillesland caught Camp by surprise on a sweep and flattened him. Camp, thinking Hillesland had played dirty, grabbed his teammate by the helmet, twisted him around so they were face to face, and knocked him out with a punch. The coaches immediately ended practice.

On another occasion, Camp was engaged in a one-on-one drill on the sideline against a lineman who made a move that infuriated Camp. He retaliated by body blocking the lineman backward into the low wall that separated the field from the stands. A teammate saw the lineman in the locker room afterward, holding his shoulder and crying.

Camp became a starter during his junior year and a dominant player during his senior year as he channeled his anger into disrupting offenses. Majoring in social welfare, Camp was determined to obtain his Cal degree and play in the NFL.

Then, in the Big Game, Camp was taking out his aggression on Deaton, who was trying to ensure Camp didn't get to Elway. "That shows you the tremendous size and strength of Camp," marveled Stanford color broadcaster Gordy Ceresino, as Camp pulled himself off Elway on Stanford's third play. "That's what Cal's gameplan was: get Camp into the backfield."

The first quarter ended scoreless. Pressured by Camp and his teammates, Elway did not have time to find open receivers downfield.

When the second quarter began, Stanford started with the ball on its own 15-yard line. Two plays later, on third and 6, Cal defensive coordinator Ron Lynn sent in the play call: Jet Blitz 0. He had already called it several times with success. Lynn used Jet Blitz when he had six defensive backs in the dime package, and it called for two of them—Gregg Beagle and Clemont Williams—to blitz from each side. The "0" meant the other defensive backs would play man-to-man coverage. Elway took the snap and rolled right. Beagle raced in from that side. Fullback Greg Hooper went to block him, but Elway kept rolling to the right. Beagle followed Lynn's pregame instruction to stay outside to contain the quarterback. That worked to perfection as Elway tried to outrun Beagle toward the sideline. Elway was quick but not quick enough. Beagle dove, and down went Elway at the Stanford 2-yard line. Loss of 16 yards. For Beagle, a senior who had been a walk-on, it was the play of his career. But it would unexpectedly boomerang later because that sack would prompt a mistake by Beagle that would lead to Stanford's first touchdown later in the game.

Stanford punted after the 16-yard loss. Cal took over on the Stanford 44 and drove 30 yards before the defense stiffened. Cooper kicked a 31-yard field goal to put the first points on the scoreboard. Cal led 3–0 with 9:26 remaining in the first half.

When Stanford got the ball back, Elway threw for two first downs, but the Bears stopped Stanford's offense again. The Cardinal punted. After an unsuccessful series of downs, Cal had to punt, giving the ball back to Stanford. On third and 12, Elway dropped back. Once again, Camp beat Deaton on an outside rush and forced Elway to run up the middle. Two Cal players stopped him after a gain of only two yards. "John never even planted his back foot," Stanford broadcaster Ceresino told listeners. "Camp is tearing this football team apart. He is the single key factor in the game right now."

After Stanford punted again, Cal took over on its own 45-yard line. Gilbert dropped back to pass. Ford, lined up on the right, raced down the right sideline, past the underneath Stanford player in the zone defense. Before the safety could reach him, Ford leaped high to make a spectacular catch of Gilbert's throw. It was a 26-yard gain to the Stanford 29-yard line.

On the next play, Ford lined up split right again. Baird stood directly in front of him. Stanford was in a man-to-man defense because a linebacker and cornerback would be blitzing from the other side of the field. Gilbert dropped back, recognized the pressure coming from his left, and, a moment before getting leveled, threw a rainbow toward the right corner of the end zone. Baird ran stride for stride with Ford down the sideline. For a moment, Gilbert's pass looked overthrown. Both players dove headlong for the ball in the right corner of the end zone. Ford, with half a step on Baird, stretched out his arms, just above the artificial turf. He grabbed the ball, and, with Baird draped over him, the two players skidded out of the end zone. As they did, the ball tumbled away. Carver Shannon, the back judge, stood over the two players and raised his arms. Cal touchdown!

"A great catch!" cried out TV announcer Pete Liebengood. "They say he got it! Mariet Ford has come up with the catch of his career!"

Ford jumped up and raised his right arm in celebration. Baird, on one knee, raised both of his arms to the heavens, in disbelief. Baird had seen the ball pass through Ford's arms and bounce on the turf before the Cal receiver smothered it. Baird uttered an oath and cried out to the back judge, "Didn't you see the ball bounce?"

No, Shannon had not. He was following the play from the sideline, and the ball was thrown at an angle from the middle of the field. From his vantage point, it might have looked like a catch, but the backs of the two players had shielded Shannon from seeing whether Ford had actually caught the ball.

As Shannon turned away from Baird, inside linebacker Dave Wyman, who had run downfield when Gilbert launched the pass, raced up to the official. Wyman had a clear view of what had happened. "Are you fucking crazy?" he shouted at Shannon. "That fucking ball bounced off the fucking turf!"

"It's a touchdown!" Shannon replied.

"You've got to be shitting me!" Wyman said.

"If you don't get out of my face, I'm going to kick you out of the game!" Shannon told him. Wyman retreated to the sideline.

Kneeling a few yards behind the end zone, only a few yards away with a clear view of the play, was *San Jose Mercury News* photographer Michael Bryant. "He dropped the ball, but they got a touchdown," Bryant said aloud.

Sportswriters billed it as "Elway vs. Elway." After the September 1981 game, San Jose State head coach Jack Elway consoles his son, Stanford quarterback John Elway. (AP Images)

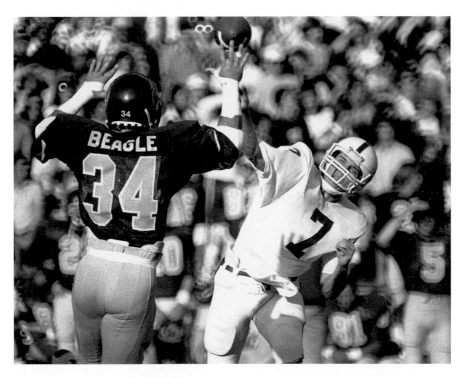

Stanford quarterback John Elway throws a pass over Cal defender Gregg Beagle in the 1982 Big Game. (ART STREIBER/The Stanford Daily Publishing Corporation)

After quarterbacking Cal the last time the Bears went to the Rose Bowl, in 1959, Joe Kapp returned as their head coach in 1982, with no coaching experience. (Cal Athletic Department)

Ron Rivera, an outside linebacker, was Cal's leading tackler during the 1982 season. (Cal Athletic Department)

Cal's traditional marching band, waiting to perform at the 1982 Big Game, was beloved by Bears fans and marked a sharp contrast with the Stanford band. (Robby Beyers)

Stanford's Mark Harmon kicks the apparent winning field goal with :04 remaining in the 1982 Big Game. (Robby Beyers)

Stanford students, in striped shirts, hold the Stanford Axe and celebrate Mark Harmon's field goal. All that's left was the kickoff. (Robert Stinnett)

With no time left on the clock, Cal's Kevin Moen, who is circled, receives the fifth and final lateral. Only the Stanford band stands between him and the goal line. (Andrea Geyling)

Cal's Kevin Moen has caught the final lateral. Unsuspecting Stanford band trombone player Gary Tyrrell is standing in the end zone. Meanwhile, a Stanford player, who is circled, ran onto the field, thinking the game was over and is now hurrying to get off. The referee has already thrown a penalty flag at his feet. (Chuck Machlin)

Cal's Kevin Moen, in the middle of the photo, closes in on the end zone as members of the Stanford band scatter out of the way. (Robert Stinnett)

Cal's Kevin Moen reaches the end zone. (Robert Stinnett)

Cal's Kevin Moen scores the game-winning touchdown and produces the most famous and lasting image from The Play. (Robert Stinnett)

Cal's Kevin Moen is about to barrell into Gary Tyrrell, a Stanford trombone player. (Robert Stinnett)

Cal's Kevin Moen keeps his feet after running into Stanford trombone player Gary Tyrrell in the wildest finish in college football history. (Robert Stinnett)

Only the sole of Gary Tyrrell's shoe is visible as Kevin Moen of Cal scores the winning touchdown a step away from photographer Robert Stinnett in the end zone. (Robert Stinnett)

While scoring the winning touchdown, Kevin Moen of Cal didn't know who or what he had bowled over. Gary Tyrrell didn't know what had happened either. (Robert Stinnett)

After "the most amazing, sensational, heart rending, exciting, thrilling finish in the history of college football," Cal fans celebrate with the Axe. (Robert Stinnett)

To mark the 25th anniversary of The Play, (from left to right) former Stanford quarterback John Elway, host Craig Hummer, former Cal safety Kevin Moen, and Gary Tyrrell, the former Stanford trombone player, relive it during a 2007 television special. (AP Images)

Stanford fans directly behind the end zone also had a clear view. For the rest of the game, every time a Cal receiver caught a pass, they would mock the officials by raising their hands in a touchdown salute.

What mattered most, though, was that Ford's catch stood. Cooper's extra point gave Cal a 10–0 lead with less than three minutes left in the second quarter. And after Stanford went three and out, that's how the first half ended. Elway completed two passes, but they were short throws to his backs, resulting in minimum yardage. That had been the pattern so far. In all, Elway had thrown for only 73 yards in the first half, and Stanford was 0-for-6 on third-down conversions. Before the game, the storyline was whether Cal could stop Elway. For the first 30 minutes, the answer was yes. Cal's defense had shut down Stanford's receivers. It was only the second time this season that Stanford had been shut out in the first half.

At halftime, offensive coordinator Jim Fassel gathered his players and said he would devise ways to better protect Elway against the blitzes that were confounding Stanford. Doing so could spring Vincent White out of the backfield. In spite of the score, Stanford players were certain they would overcome the Bears to win. "Hang in there. We'll get our shit together," one player on offense told cornerback Rod Gilmore.

Gilmore told Elway, "Just do your thing, and we'll do ours."

"Don't worry," Elway replied. "We got this."

In the Cal locker room, the Bears players felt good. They were in control. They were stopping Elway. But defensive coordinator Lynn cautioned them. "We have another 30 minutes to play," he said. Kapp, of course, was more ebullient. "We told you exactly what would happen," he told his team. "And now it has happened. Just keep doing it, and we will win the game."

Up in the press box, Jim Simmons and Coy Collinsworth were deeply concerned. They had come to Berkeley with the expectation that Stanford would win the game and secure their invitation to play in the Hall of Fame Bowl. Simmons called the chairman of the selection committee in Birmingham with the news: Stanford was trailing, and Elway had shown little to merit all the ballyhoo. Perhaps, the two men thought, Stanford's fortunes would change in the third quarter.

• CHAPTER 11 •

THE SECOND HALF

With 76,000 fans roaring in the background, Stanford received the kickoff to start the third quarter. On their first play, Cal defensive coordinator Ron Lynn blitzed two outside linebackers, a continuation of his first half strategy. But thanks to tweaks in strategy during the intermission, Stanford had begun to adjust. John Elway took a three-step drop and hit flanker Mike Tolliver on a slant over the middle for a 12-yard gain. This was the kind of call that could beat the blitz, both because it allowed Elway to throw quickly and because the two extra outside rushers created space over the middle.

Two plays later, Elway called 78X Hook in the huddle. It was a pass designed for Emile Harry, who lined up split left. If Cal was playing a zone defense, Harry would run out 18 yards, stop, and come back toward the quarterback in a pattern known as a hook. If Cal was playing man-to-man but with a deep safety, Harry would run 16 to 18 yards downfield and then cut across the field. If Cal was playing man-to-man with no deep safety, Harry would race downfield for 10 yards and then break at an angle toward the far goal post.

It turned out Cal was blitzing again, which forced man-to-man coverage with no deep safety. Safety Richard Rodgers and the middle linebacker blitzed up the middle. Rodgers broke through the line, but fullback Greg Hooper pushed him to the side. Left tackle Jeff Deaton slowed Reggie Camp long enough to give Elway time to step up and launch a pass 60 yards down field. Harry, running a post pattern to the far goal post, was open by two steps. But Elway uncharacteristically missed him by throwing too long.

Stanford had to punt the ball. But the series showed that the Cardinal was finally getting close to breaking one against the Bears.

Cal got the ball back and drove to the Stanford 16-yard line. On a fourth-down field-goal attempt, Joe Cooper committed the cardinal sin of looking up immediately after kicking the ball. He shanked it, sending the ball wide. After his second miss, the score remained 10–0.

On Stanford's first down, Elway hit Tolliver on the right sideline—literally. He had both feet out of bounds when he caught the ball. But it was ruled a catch for a gain of 22 yards. "These officials are having a bad day today," exclaimed color announcer Gordy Ceresino. "That's not the first bad call that we've seen."

Elway connected on two more passes. "For the first time this afternoon, Elway is somewhat into a rhythm," said play-by-play announcer Pete Liebengood. "He's like a pitcher. He's got his fastball working, and he's finding his spots."

On the next play, Elway hit Tolliver again, just inside the far sideline. The officials ruled him out of bounds—another blown call. "Things have a way of evening up in a football game," Ceresino said.

That left Stanford with second and 10 on the Cal 25-yard line. Lynn sent in the defensive play call—Jet Blitz Cover 1. Cal was in a dime defense with six defensive backs. One cornerback, Jimmy Stewart, would blitz from Elway's left, and another, Gregg Beagle, would come in from his right. In the Stanford huddle, the quarterback gave the call: 22 Halfback Option. Vincent White would be the primary receiver. Lining up to the right of Elway, he would race out of the backfield just outside of the right tackle and then choose one of two options, depending upon his defender, Rodgers, a safety. If Rodgers was playing White to go outside, White would cut inside over the middle. An inside position by Rodgers would prompt White to go outside.

As Elway called signals, Stewart, outside of the tight end on Elway's left, stood on the line of scrimmage, ready to blitz. Beagle, to Elway's right, was poised a couple of yards behind the line, trying to disguise his blitz. Elway took the snap. Stewart raced in from the left, unblocked, in hot pursuit of Elway, who rolled right to escape him. That would have put him in Beagle's onrushing path, but Beagle briefly collided at the line of scrimmage with Rodgers, his teammate trying to cover White. The collision delayed Beagle from getting across the line, giving Elway, racing away from Stewart, time to throw to White. The collision also knocked down Rodgers briefly, leaving White wide open 10 yards downfield. As Rodgers tried to recover, White put a move on him and sprinted toward the goal line. He juked another defender but was tackled from behind at the Cal 3-yard line.

Stanford had its first real chance to score.

"Seventy-eight Halfback Swing," Elway called out in the huddle. White, again the primary receiver, would swing left out of the backfield. Stanford went with a two-tight end set. Jim Clymer, the left tight end, would run straight ahead into the end zone as if he was on a pass pattern, but Clymer's real job was to block the middle linebacker from racing over to the left to cover White. The play worked to perfection. White was wide open when he caught Elway's swing pass and scooted into the end zone untouched. The score was now Cal 10, Stanford 7, with 5:29 left in the third quarter. "We got a ballgame," Liebengood said.

After an unsuccessful Cal series, Stanford got the ball back, and Elway completed two passes to put Stanford in Cal territory again. "John Elway has it heated up," Liebengood said.

"He is really snapping it off," chimed in Ceresino.

Stanford was now on the Cal 43-yard line, second and 8. Elway called the play: 22 Halfback Option—the same call that had sprung White several minutes earlier. On the other side of the line, the call from Lynn was again Jet Blitz Cover 1—six defensive backs—the same defensive scheme as on the Stanford touchdown. Cal would be throwing an all-out Red Dog at Elway, blitzing two cornerbacks from the edges and two men up the middle. The other two cornerbacks would play Stanford's receivers man-to-man. Beagle lined up again on the right of the quarterback. He would blitz again, unless White, at right halfback, went out for a pass. If he did, Beagle would break off the blitz and cover White. But after sacking Elway earlier on a second-quarter blitz, Beagle was determined to do it again and be the hero—an impulse more compelling than covering White.

Elway took the snap. Seeing a wave of blue jerseys sweeping toward him, he backpedaled to buy time. Beagle was one of the blue jerseys. But in his zeal, he overcommitted, taking one too many steps toward Elway. As he did, White raced out of the backfield. Beagle tried to grab him with his right hand, but it was too late. White sped past Beagle and snared a pass from Elway in the right flat. As White turned to run up the right sideline, Beagle tried to grab him from behind, but White shook him off. With a downfield block, he sprinted the rest of the way untouched into the end zone. Cardinal fans rose out of their seats and thundered their approval. The touchdown put Stanford ahead 14–10 with 1:42 remaining in the third quarter.

That was the score as the third quarter ended, leaving a final 15 minutes to settle the 85th Big Game.

After Stanford's second touchdown, Cal moved most of the way downfield behind a mixture of runs and passes by Gale Gilbert. On second and goal from the Stanford 4, outside linebacker Garin Veris sacked Gilbert on a blitz. On third and goal from the Stanford 12, Gilbert had an open receiver in the end zone. But he threw the ball slightly behind him, and Stanford cornerback Rod Gilmore reached out with his left hand to knock it down. It was a near miss for the Bears. Out came Cooper again. This time he kept his head down and kicked a 35-yard field goal. Stanford now led 14–13 with 13:28 left to play.

After the Cardinal failed to move the ball, Cal got the ball back and drove again into Stanford territory. On first and 20 from the Stanford 32, Gilbert turned to wide receiver Wes Howell in the huddle. "Be ready," Gilbert told him.

Howell, a senior, had originally come to Cal to play basketball after transferring from a local junior college. A rugged 6'3", 205 pounds, he didn't mind physical contact on the court, going man-to-man against 6'9" power forwards in Pac-10 basketball games for two years. It was good training, Howell thought, for his future as an NBA guard. But he went undrafted. Two teams invited him to training camp, but he turned down the opportunity, believing he had no chance to beat out the bigger name players. Then Joe Kapp called. The coach, who had been a hard-nosed backup guard at Cal

25 years earlier, had attended a basketball game where he had seen Howell display his leaping ability. Although Howell had used up his eligibility as a Cal basketball player, he could play one year of football, Kapp noted. "I know you love to play basketball," the coach told him, "but you have an opportunity to maybe get to the NFL."

Howell was doubtful at first. He had last played football as a freshman at Castro Valley High School seven years earlier and had caught only one touchdown pass that season. But he decided to put basketball's give-and-goes, 2-3 zone defenses, and backdoor plays behind him and learn how to run streaks, slants, posts, z-outs and to block. With his athleticism, Howell became adept enough to become a starter by the third game of the season.

Now Howell lined up split left. Opposite him, about 10 yards away, was Gilmore. A senior who had redshirted, Gilmore had deferred his admission to law school to play a fourth year of football. Gilmore was small—only 5'9", 175 pounds. But he was quick. He had been doubtful for the Big Game with a bruised thigh. But the adrenaline flowing from playing his final game at Stanford was a powerful pain reliever. Gilmore had hardly missed a play.

As Gilbert dropped back, Howell raced down the left sideline. Gilmore matched him stride for stride. Gilbert lofted a pass to the left corner of the end zone. By now, Howell had gained a step on Gilmore. But the defensive back had pinned him to the sideline. Howell reached out with his left hand as he dove for the slightly overthrown ball, pulled it into his chest as he hit the turf, and then skidded out of the end zone. The official raised both arms in the air. Touchdown! "And you thought the Mariet Ford catch was great!" shouted Joe Starkey. "This one was better!"

Gilmore couldn't believe it. *You got to be fucking kidding me*, he thought, questioning whether Howell had both caught the ball and caught it in bounds. What Gilmore thought didn't matter, of course. Howell raised his trophy aloft to celebrate the incredible catch. Cal fans screamed their approval.

Cal now led 19–14 with 11:24 remaining. Kapp made the fateful decision to try for a two-point conversion. If the Bears converted, Stanford would need a touchdown and its own two-point conversion to win the game. But if Cal failed, Stanford could conceivably kick two field goals to win the game.

Gilbert took the snap and was chased out of the pocket by Veris. As he rolled right, Gilbert threw to tight end David Lewis in the end zone. Safety Charles Hutchings knocked down the pass. Though no one could have known it then, the failed two-point conversion had just set up the game's incredible ending.

Stanford got the ball back, trailing by five. An Elway pass and a long run by White put the Cardinal at the Cal 30. On the next play, Elway started to drop back to pass but tripped and fell onto his back. But it wasn't clumsiness that sent him to the ground. For the second time in the half, one of his linemen had accidentally tripped him. Right guard Dennis Engel, the culprit this time, had stepped too far to his left as he set up to block. "Stay off my fucking feet!" Elway yelled at his friend as they walked back to the huddle.

Elway rebounded on the next play by tossing a pass to Tolliver that brought Stanford to the Cal 10. On third and goal, Cal blitzed up the middle once again. Elway took a three-step drop, and then saw an unblocked Cal lineman rushing toward him. He backpedaled six steps and, just before the blitz caught up with him, lofted a pass to the right corner of the end zone. Emile Harry leaped high and got both hands on the ball, but cornerback John Sullivan knocked it loose as they both came crashing down.

Should Stanford go for the touchdown on fourth down? Paul Wiggin decided not to, betting Elway could produce another score. Mark Harmon booted the 22-yard field goal. That narrowed Cal's lead to 19–17 with 5:32 left in the game. Now Kapp's decision to go for the failed two-point conversion began to loom large. Had Cal simply kicked the extra point, they would now be three points ahead, forcing Stanford to score a touchdown to win.

The Bears went three-and-out on their next series, as Stanford blitzed on third down, forcing Gilbert to overthrow an open receiver. Elway now had another chance to put Stanford ahead.

The Cardinal took over on its 37. A run gained a yard, and Elway, backpedaling once again to escape a blitz, threw a pass over the middle that nose guard Gary Plummer nearly intercepted. That left the Cardinal facing a third and 9, with about 3:30 remaining. It was no secret that this was a passing down. Tolliver lined up right. He raced out five yards and cut over the middle on a slant. The Cal defender slipped. Elway threw a bullet, Tolliver caught it and raced downfield before being tackled at the Cal 35-yard line. They were now within range for a long Harmon field goal that could win the game.

Up in the press box, veteran observers agreed this was becoming one of the best Big Games ever. Apart from winning the Axe, so much more was still at stake in the final minutes. Elway needed a victory to win the Heisman Trophy, and Stanford needed the victory to keep its season alive with a bowl game. The two Hall of Fame Bowl representatives, Jim Simmons and Coy Collinsworth, sitting directly behind reporters, felt renewed hope that Stanford could pull it out.

On press row, someone called out, "Three minutes left! Elevator down to the field!" Numerous reporters scurried to catch a ride down to field level to avoid the post-game crush leaving the press box and to quickly get to either team's locker room for interviews. Two *San Francisco Chronicle* reporters, Al Moss and Dave Bush, decided to stay in their seats upstairs to watch the final minutes, a decision they would later regret.

Stanford still had the ball. A run gained three yards. "Keep your eye on the clock," said Liebengood, as a TV camera showed the scoreboard. There was 2:50 and counting left in the game. Elway had plenty of time, especially since Stanford had all three of its timeouts to help manage the clock. Cal had only one.

On second and 7, from the Stanford 32, Lynn called yet another blitz. Elway took the snap, and linebacker Eddie Walsh knifed through to the left of center Mike Teeuws, who, having missed the block, turned around in dismay to see what would happen. Walsh crashed into Elway from behind and knocked the ball out of his hand. It rolled past the right hash mark toward the sideline. Nose guard Gary Plummer jumped onto it.

"Cal's ball!" shouted Liebengood. "Big play!"

"That's the same blitz they've gotten to him all day with!" exclaimed Ceresino, as Plummer held the ball aloft. Teammates mobbed him, and Cal fans jumped out of their seats with joy. "We want the Axe!" rose a chant from the Cal student section. "We want the Axe!"

They were on the verge of getting the prize back from Stanford. Cal needed only one first down to ice the game—against a defense that had been unable to make key stops throughout the season. At that moment, the Axe was located just behind the south end zone goal post. It was attached via the coiled bicycle cable lock to two Stanford students, Kevin Wells and Max Scheder-Bieschin. Standing with them was another Stanford student, Helene Leckman, who had also taken turns chained to the Axe. The three stood out not only because they were guarding the Axe but because they were wearing red-and-white striped polo shirts and white pants. Next to them was Jon Erickson, the "adult" who had overseen the Stanford Axe Committee for years. Erickson told them to be prepared to transfer the Axe if Cal won the game, which now appeared very likely. Erickson reminded them that he would unlock the chain that linked the Axe to the two students. Wells and Scheder-Bieschin were to place the trophy on the ground and then back away so Cal Rally Committee members could grab it. Erickson advised them that they should exit the stadium immediately afterward through the south tunnel, steps away, because their outfits would make them visible targets for any Cal students who wanted to engage in mischief.

Wells, Scheder-Bieschin, and Leckman were standing alongside members of the Stanford band, who had walked down half a dozen steps from the stands onto the playing field. Win or lose, they would perform the traditional "Hail, Stanford, Hail" and then rock out in a post-game concert for anyone who stayed to listen.

Even before Elway's fumble, the half dozen members of the Cal Rally Committee Axe Guard had left their seats on the 50-yard line in the Cal student section and walked behind the Bears' bench to the south end zone. They were wearing blue jeans, white button-down shirts, white sweaters with an embroidered patch, and driving caps with blue and gold stripes. They were now positioned about 20 yards from the Axe, which was still attached to Wells and Scheder-Bieschin, who were standing just behind the goal post.

"We want the Axe! We want the Axe!" thundered the Cal rooting section.

The Bears took over on their own 37 with 2:32 left in the game. Stanford had all three of its timeouts. The Bears needed one first down to win the 85th Big Game, deny Stanford a bowl game invitation, and send Elway back to Palo Alto with a loss in his final collegiate game. It was going to be just a matter of time before the Bears ran out the clock and celebrated a sweet victory.

Cal went with the same offensive set they had used the whole game. Stanford brought in two young linebackers who were strong against the run. On first down, the Bears ran a trap, one of the oldest plays in football, invented by the legendary coach Pop Warner decades earlier. After the snap, Cal's right guard would not make a real attempt to block the Stanford lineman across from him, John Bergren. The Bears hoped Bergren's aggression would take him into the Cal backfield, trapping him out of position after Gilbert handed the ball to running back Ron Story. The left guard would swing to his right to seal off Bergren while the center and right tackle would block Stanford defenders to create a hole for Story. That was the theory on paper. But Cal's offensive linemen missed their blocks, and Bergren and Veris, the linebacker, tackled Story after only a two-yard gain. The clock showed 2:22 left in the game and kept ticking.

On second and 8, Stanford put five men on the line, expecting another run, while Cal went with a pro, two-set back. Gilbert handed the ball again to Story who ran over toward the right side of the line, led by tackle Harvey Salem and running back John Tuggle. Story dodged one defender, then another before two more brought him down at the Cal 45-yard line, only two yards short of a first down. Stanford called its first timeout with 1:43 left in the game.

This set up a decisive play. Cal needed a first down to run out the clock. Stanford's defense desperately needed to stop them. On the Cal sideline, the coaches decided to give the ball to Tuggle, their senior running back, who was fourth on the school's all-time rusher list. At 6'1", 210 pounds,

Tuggle was probably the strongest player on the team, just the man to bull forward for the first down.

Playing the right corner for the Stanford defense was Gilmore, the undersized fifth-year senior. He called out to Kevin Baird, who was playing the left corner. "It doesn't matter what defensive coverage we're playing," Gilmore told Baird. "Cal is going to bounce it outside. Play run." Baird agreed. He and Gilmore would be going rogue by not covering their receivers, but they were sure of their instincts. They told the two safeties, Vaughn Williams and Charles Hutchings, of the plan. If they were wrong, Cal's receivers would be wide open, with only the safeties between them and the goal line. "Keep your ass deep," Gilmore told Williams as the Stanford players broke the defensive huddle.

Gilbert called the play: 25 Power G. The Bears broke their huddle and trotted up to the line. They were in the same pro-set, with split running backs and two receivers split wide. Stanford put five defenders on the line with two linebackers behind them. Lining up opposite Cal's flanker, Ford, Gilmore was standing just a few feet from Kapp on the Cal sideline. Gilmore glanced to his right and saw Kapp smiling at him. *That son of a bitch is going to run at me*, Gilmore thought.

He lined up in front of Ford as if he planned to blanket him. But when the ball was snapped, Gilmore sidestepped the receiver and raced into the Cal backfield. At the same time, Cal's tight end brushed past Veris, the outside linebacker, to block the middle linebacker. The assignment for obstructing the 6'6", 250-pound Veris belonged to Story, the 5'10", 195-pound halfback, a clear mismatch. Gilbert handed off to Tuggle to run over left tackle behind Story. Veris rushed in, bowled over Story, and then fell toward the ball carrier. His penetration forced Tuggle to take two steps sideways to the left before turning upfield.

Cal's chances of getting the first down still looked good. At that moment, only one Stanford player stood between Tuggle and the two yards he needed—Gilmore. Outweighed by 50 pounds, the smaller Stanford defensive back squared up and realized he had to hit Tuggle chest high, otherwise the running back might fall forward for enough yardage. Gilmore had one advantage—Tuggle had become off-balance to avoid Veris. Seeing Gilmore, the powerful Cal senior lowered his helmet and crashed into the defensive back's midsection. For a split second, it appeared that Tuggle, with his superior size and strength, would shake loose and make the first down. But Gilmore hung on, even as Tuggle spun around, trying desperately to find a way to wriggle free. He could not. Gilmore and Tuggle crashed to the turf. No gain!

Stanford had made perhaps its most important stop of the season. Gilmore had made the tackle unassisted. On his hands and knees, he raised his arms in triumph. "We were fucking right," Gilmore said to Baird as they ran off the field.

It was now fourth and 2 for Cal. Stanford used its second timeout. On the Stanford sideline, Wiggin held up one finger as he walked toward Elway. Stanford was down to its last timeout.

Kapp chose to punt. Stanford's White ran onto the field as the lone return man. The dangerous White had sealed Stanford's victory against the University of Washington three weeks earlier by juking several Huskies on his way to a 76-yard punt return for a touchdown. Now White positioned himself at the Stanford 20-yard line.

Cal's punter was Mike Ahr, a one-time walk-on who had followed a stellar 1981 season with an up-and-down year in 1982. Ahr fractured his right tibia in the season opener and had trouble fully extending his leg after that. After Ahr had a poor game against San Jose State, Kapp took the backup punter to Seattle for their game against Washington, leaving Ahr behind in Berkeley. But the backup was so rattled by the raucous Washington crowd that he averaged only 30 yards per punt. Ahr reclaimed his job the following week but had yet to fully regain Kapp's confidence. Now the Cal coach grabbed Ahr as he was about to run onto the field. "Whatever you do, don't let him catch the ball!" Kapp shouted. "Kick the fucking ball into the end zone!"

And that's what Ahr did. "He nailed one!" exclaimed Liebengood, as the ball sailed over White's head. The ball hit the turf five yards into the end zone. In his final kick for Cal, Ahr had hit the punt of his career. "Good time to do it!" Liebengood said.

"They say the Big Game brings out the best in everybody," added Ceresino.

With the touchback, Stanford would get the ball back on its own 20-yard line for a final drive. Elway would have one last chance to win the 85th Big Game, earn Stanford a bowl game invitation, and possibly snag the Heisman Trophy.

CHAPTER 12

THE DRIVE

John Elway trotted back onto the playing field with his teammates, as the sun began to sink below the rim of Memorial Stadium. It was about 3:45 PM in Berkeley. Elway was hyper-aware of the situation. He always was. Moments earlier, he had glanced at one of the scoreboards high above Memorial Stadium's end zones. It told him and everyone else that he had one minute and 27 seconds to pull out the victory. Cal still led 19–17. It didn't matter that Elway's exploits had established him as perhaps the greatest quarterback in the history of college football. That wasn't on his mind. Elway also wasn't thinking about how he had failed to complete a touchdown pass on the climactic play in his first Big Game two years earlier, giving Cal the victory, or how, if Stanford didn't pull off a victory in the final minute of play here, he would end his collegiate career without ever playing in a postseason bowl game. No, Elway was laser-focused solely on the first play of this final drive and how that would set up what followed. It was what he did every time he took the field with the game at stake.

In the huddle, the center, Mike Teeuws, was confident. Elway had already led them to last-minute touchdowns three times that season. And, after being shut out in the first half this day by Cal, Stanford's offense had struck for 17 points in the second half. When Elway entered the huddle and said, "Let's take it down and win this thing," Teeuws was sure it would happen. Every one of his teammates felt just as confident.

Elway called the first play. It would be a screen pass to Vincent White, the shifty running back who had scored both of Stanford's touchdowns on throws from Elway in the third quarter. It seemed like a good call—White was a threat to break loose every time he caught a pass.

Screen passes are a form of deception that count on an overeager defense. They had become an important weapon in Bill Walsh's West Coast offense because of the opportunity to fool a defense expecting a downfield pass. On this play, Teeuws, along with the right guard and the right tackle, would act as if they were trying to block Cal's defensive linemen, but then let the defenders slip past. While the defenders were focused on sacking Elway, Stanford's offensive linemen would charge to the right to set up a wall of blockers for White, the target of a pass behind the line of scrimmage. If executed as drawn up, White would have only one or two unblocked defenders in front of him, usually a cornerback and a safety, and he had already shown he could fake them out. Stanford's success on the screen pass would depend on Cal's defensive linemen stampeding toward Elway, putting them out of position to stop White but not getting close enough to the quarterback to disrupt his pass, or worse, throw him for a loss.

Cal did not have a conventional defense on the field. Looking down at the field from the press box, defensive coordinator Ron Lynn had sent in his "dime" package—six defensive backs instead of the usual four, along with one linebacker and four linemen. Lynn wanted his fastest defenders on the field. This meant benching strongside linebacker Ron Rivera, the Bears' leading tackler. This left Rivera cursing under his breath at Lynn and pacing up and down Cal's sideline.

The dime defense aimed to prevent Elway from throwing long passes to advance into field-goal range or score a touchdown. The Bears knew all too well what Elway could do—he had completed more passes than any other quarterback in the history of the NCAA, was about to rank second in total offense, and also held a number of Pac-10 passing records. Cal effectively had two cornerbacks on each side of the field in this defense. The Cal cornerback responsible for the deep zone on the right side was Ahmad Anderson, who at 5'9" and 170 pounds was undersized even for his position. Anderson had been a walk-on but had become a four-year starter by closely studying how to play the position. "Don't get beat deep," he told himself as Cal broke its defensive huddle. "Keep everything in front of you. Fly to the ball."

Elway approached the line of scrimmage, scanned the defense, and thought the screen pass could work. He saw seven defenders crowding the line of scrimmage. Yet another blitz call from Lynn would put Cal's defenders in the wrong place. White was bent over in a three-point stance behind and to the left of Elway, in a split formation with fullback Greg Hooper to his right. Elway crouched behind Teeuws. He barked the count, took the snap, and dropped back. With his back foot planted on the fifth step, Elway turned right and spotted White. But just as Elway started to throw, he saw Cal's left defensive end evade Hooper's block and stick his left arm up. Elway had to make a quick adjustment by throwing slightly behind White. The running back turned to his left to catch the ball but bobbled it. He gathered it in, but then slipped on the wet turf and fell face first untouched. A seven-yard loss. Up in the radio booth, Stanford's play-by-play announcer, Pete Liebengood, expressed the obvious: "Not the way you want to start off an 80-yard march!"

On the field, Elway winced but then quickly moved on to the next play. With the clock ticking, the Stanford players lined up without calling a huddle.

Lynn, the defensive coordinator, smiled briefly, thinking he might have confused Elway and his teammates with the dime package. Now Stanford faced second and 17 from its own 13-yard line. Lynn had no choice but to keep the six defensive backs on the field for the next play. But he had just enough time to send word via his headset to a coach on the sideline to have nose guard Gary Plummer play "spy"—meaning he would fake a rush and drop back a couple of yards, watching for Elway either to run or throw a short pass. At 6'2", 230 pounds, Plummer was an undersized nose guard, smaller than the centers he played against. But he was quick and could cover a back scooting out for a short pass or corral a quarterback attempting to run.

On the other side of the ball, Elway was thinking he wanted to complete a pass for a first down. But he knew he could settle for less since he would still have two more downs to gain the full 17 yards. As he lined up under center, Elway noted that Cal had four down linemen again, but the linebacker, a cornerback, and a safety stood just behind them. Elway quickly did a mental run-through of what to do in the event of a Cal blitz. He barked the signals, took the snap, and dropped back all the way to the 3-yard line. The blitz didn't come. This gave Elway a couple of extra seconds to find any opening in the Cal zone defense downfield, but he saw none. Looking to at least pick up a few yards, he threw a short pass to the 17-yard line. His target was again White, who had curled out of the backfield. From his spy position, Plummer saw the ball whipping his way. *I can grab this!* he thought to himself as he dove. But wearing cumbersome forearm pads, Plummer couldn't quite hold on, and the ball hit the turf. It was an incomplete pass. Plummer screamed in both frustration and elation. An interception would have ended the game. But Cal was still on the verge of stopping Stanford's quarterback and winning the Big Game. "We're down to two plays for the Stanford Cardinal!" exclaimed Liebengood.

The 76,000 fans in the stadium were standing now, rank upon rippling rank in the blue and gold of Cal or the red and white of Stanford. "We want the Axe!" chanted Cal fans. "We want the Axe!"

On the Cal sideline, Rivera tried to will his teammates to victory. "Come on, guys!" he yelled. "You can do it."

Elway had allowed himself a sigh of relief when he saw Plummer fail to hold onto his pass. He then immediately focused on the next play. It was now third and 17 for Stanford on its own 13-yard line A glance at the scoreboard told him that 58 seconds remained. Elway stood outside of the huddle waiting for a teammate to bring in the next play from offensive coordinator Jim Fassel. From his seat in the press box, Fassel had quickly scanned his options and then decided he needed another downfield receiver to counter all the Cal defensive backs. So Fassel took out White, the running back, and brought in Eric Mullins, Stanford's third receiver. Mullins had caught four passes that day.

On Stanford's next play, tight end Chris Dressel would line up on the right side of the line but would stay back and fortify the offensive line's blocking scheme in case Cal blitzed. Fassel was betting the additional blocker would buy Elway enough time to find one of his three wide receivers in a hole somewhere in Cal's zone defense. Fassel's play called for receivers Emile Harry and Mullins to line up on the left. Each would run about 15 yards, then curl right, and try to find a seam in the zone defense. Stanford's other receiver, split wide on the right, would race up the sideline, stop, and look for a pass if the other two receivers were covered.

Hooper, the fullback, would line up six yards behind Elway and to his left. He would be available to help left tackle Jeff Deaton stop Cal's fearsome right defensive end, Reggie Camp, who had menaced Elway and Stanford's offense all day.

The two teams broke their huddles and lined up. Cal showed blitz again, but just before the snap, linebacker Eddie Walsh started backpedaling, and safety Richard Rodgers ran to his right toward Stanford's two wide receivers. Elway took the ball and dropped back seven steps. Deaton and Hooper pushed the onrushing Camp past their quarterback. As they did, Elway spotted a small opening downfield to his left. He stepped forward in the pocket and fired a fastball toward Harry at the 29-yard line. But Rodgers, closing faster than Elway had expected, dove and knocked down the pass. As the ball bounded harmlessly downfield, a jubilant Plummer raced toward Rodgers, and the two slapped hands, high in the air. Cal cornerbacks Anderson and Fred Williams raised their arms in triumph and strutted away from Harry. The frustrated receiver jogged back to the huddle. *Damn, we can't lose this game!* he thought.

Stanford faced fourth and 17 on its own 13-yard line, trailing 19–17. Only 53 seconds remained. "Obviously, there will be no punt," exclaimed Cal radio play-by-play announcer Joe Starkey. "They wouldn't even think of it. Here's the game!"

In the few seconds he had to make the next call, Lynn thought about blitzing Elway for the first time during this crucial series of downs. But he decided that was too risky. He stuck with the Cover 3 defense, which called for two cornerbacks and a safety each to guard a zone deep enough to protect against a Stanford first down. It had worked for the last three plays, and he was betting it would work again.

In the huddle, barely able to hear himself over the crowd's roar, Elway was intense and focused. He wasn't going to concede. He called the play that Fassel sent in: Slot Corner X Post, Maximum Protection. The receiver on the right would run deep along the sideline, which should draw two defenders. The other two receivers on the left would run downfield about 15 yards and then cross their routes, hoping to confuse the defensive backs in the zone. Stanford's maximum protection package again kept the tight end in to block any blitzer, and the fullback again would help keep Camp from Elway. Seven men would block for the quarterback.

As they broke the huddle, Elway turned to his left and shouted, "Emile!" Harry paused to listen. "Get open!"

Damn! Harry thought. *He's going to throw it to me!*

It was do or die for Stanford. Elway took the snap, dropped back seven steps, planted his right foot on the 2-yard line, and took a step forward. He quickly scanned the progress of his three receivers against the Cal defense. Mullins appeared open to his left. Elway raised the ball above his shoulder with his right hand and quickly tapped it with his left as part of his throwing motion. Cal strong safety Clemont Williams, protecting the middle of the field, saw this and broke to his right to knock down a pass. But seeing Williams' move, Elway changed his mind, just as Reggie Camp spun away from his blockers. Elway quickly shifted his feet toward the middle of the field and saw Harry crossing from left to right, entering the space that Williams had just vacated. In the backfield, Camp, now five yards away and with no one in his path, closed in on Elway from behind. The quarterback stepped up to the 6-yard line—"he's got to get this one!" shouted Starkey— and threw a bullet, just before Camp crashed into him.

There were still six Cal defenders surrounding Harry. Linebacker Walsh, in front of Harry, saw the ball whizzing toward him and leaped, but it passed just above his outstretched left hand. Harry, in full stride, made a split-second calculation that he would get hit just after the ball arrived. That might jar it loose. The six-footer, who could dunk a basketball, jumped to catch the ball, which then arrived right on the red No. 10 on his white jersey. A split second later, Harry was drilled by Williams and immediately hit the turf. Harry began to get up, faltered, and rested on his knee for a moment. The hit stung. But what mattered is that he had held onto the ball. It was a 29-yard gain and a first down! No other quarterback in college football, or possibly even the pros, could have thrown the ball hard enough to complete that pass. Even Cal's radio announcer was impressed. "What a quarterback, John Elway!" shouted Starkey. "What a play!"

The clock stopped as the first down chains were moved. There were now 43 seconds left. Stanford was still alive, having advanced to its 42-yard line. Elway, however, didn't give himself the luxury of celebrating. He needed at least another 35 yards to get into comfortable field-goal range.

After the two passes to the left, he and Fassel figured that they could find an opening on the opposite side. The next play called for Dressel, the tight end, to line up on the right and run upfield. This would freeze Cal's deep coverage man on the right. Mike Tolliver, the wide receiver on the right, would race past the cornerback covering the short zone to give Elway the chance to hit him before the deep cornerback could rush over. The play would rely on the quarterback's exquisite talent once again because he would be throwing to the short side of the field, where he had less room to maneuver.

Elway dropped back five steps, then took three quick steps to his right. Tolliver found a seam in the zone. Elway had to put the ball perfectly between two defenders. And so he did. Tolliver caught the pass over his shoulder and fell out of bounds at the Cal 39-yard line. It was a gain of 19 yards. Stanford had advanced into Cal territory.

But wait. A referee had thrown a penalty flag. On the Cal bench, Rivera, his teammates, and his coaches pointed at the turf, screaming that Tolliver had gone out of bounds and then returned to the field before catching the pass. This was a rule violation. If the catch didn't count, Stanford would lose the 19-yard gain and even more yardage once the penalty was marked off. Stanford would be pushed back into its own territory with time running short. Charles Moffett, the head referee, instead of standing in the middle of the field to call the infraction, ran over to the sideline and huddled with the referee who had thrown the penalty flag. The crowd quieted as it awaited the verdict.

When it came, the ruling was good news for Cardinal fans. A third referee had seen a Cal defender push Tolliver out of bounds. That meant the receiver was eligible to return onto the field and catch the pass. Moffett waved his arms to signal no penalty. The play stood, and the clock had stopped. At the Cal 39-yard line, Stanford was now nearly in field-goal range with 31 seconds left and still had one timeout. "They still need to get a little further downfield," Starkey informed listeners.

On the Stanford sideline, field goal kicker Mark Harmon practiced booting a football into a portable net. He didn't look at the action on the field at all—he needed to focus on making sure he was ready to make the winning kick. But he could hear his teammates exhorting him. "Harmon, you're going to be going in!" yelled one. "You're going to do it!" said another. Harmon, however, just wanted to be left alone for now.

But, first, Stanford needed at least one more sizable gain. From his perch in the press box, Fassel had determined that Cal's defenders were overplaying against another Elway pass. He was certain a running play could work. Stanford could always take the final timeout if he was wrong. Even still, it was a risky gambit because if Cal stuffed the run, Stanford would have to burn the timeout it needed for a field goal.

Fassel decided to gamble. He called a pitchout to halfback Mike Dotterer that had worked repeatedly in the big win against Washington State four weeks earlier. "98 Pitch," Elway said in the huddle.

Under center, Elway could see that Cal had seven defenders on the line of scrimmage. *They're going to blitz*, he thought. And indeed, after two remarkable completions by Elway, Lynn was returning to his aggressive approach. He called for two cornerbacks to blitz, one from Elway's right and one from the left.

Elway took the hike and pitched the ball to Dotterer, who started toward the left, under control, waiting for the play to develop to dictate his next move. As Elway watched from the backfield, he saw several Cal defenders get sucked into the middle of the field. Simultaneously, the cornerback blitzing from Elway's left was blocked out of the play. The middle linebacker was cut down by Stanford's pulling right guard, Matt Moran. Suddenly, the left side of Cal's defense had collapsed. Dotterer, seeing the open space, threw it into high gear and cut outside. Untouched, he raced past the Cal 35-yard line, past the 30—"Dotterer may go all the way!" screamed Starkey—and at the 25 saw one Cal defender ahead to his right, desperately racing across the field. Dotterer cut inside. It was the wrong move. Two Cal defenders converged on him at Cal's 18-yard line. Elway couldn't believe his eyes. If Dotterer had cut outside, Elway and practically everyone else in the stadium thought he would have scored the game-winning touchdown.

Still, the surprise play call and its perfect execution by the offensive line and Dotterer had left Stanford easily within range for Harmon. Dotterer, thrilled, high-fived Elway as he hustled back to the huddle. Harmon, now standing next to head coach Paul Wiggin, tried to clear his mind, knowing he was about to enter the game.

Elway lined up his team for one last play. The clock, which had stopped for the first down, began ticking down the seconds again: 19, 18, 17…Elway took the snap and pitched it again to Dotterer, this time running to his right. Plummer broke through and stopped him for no gain. Elway had been watching the play unfold, and as soon as Dotterer went down, he whirled around and put his hands together in a T to signal a timeout to Moffett. Everyone looked up to one of the two scoreboards to see the time remaining: eight seconds.

Elway raised his arms in triumph as he walked toward the sideline. He had done it. He had put Stanford in position to win the Big Game with a field goal.

For Starkey, his love of college football overcame his hometown bias. "I'll tell you: this is something!" he told his listeners. "For John Elway to pull this out, after being fourth and 17 on his own 13-yard line with less than a minute to go, is one of the most remarkable finishes you'll ever see!"

But Harmon still had to make the kick. The distance was 35 yards, well within his range. Harmon had made 36-of-37 extra points that season while making 13-of-19 field-goal attempts.

Cal's field-goal block unit trotted onto the field, including safety Kevin Moen. Could he block the kick and be the last-minute hero, just as he had been at the Big Game two years earlier? Wouldn't that be something? But Richard Rodgers, also a safety, infuriated by Elway's incredible comeback, shooed away Moen. "I'm staying in," Rodgers told his teammate. Rodgers also desperately wanted to block the kick. Moen turned around, disappointed, and trotted toward the sideline. He wouldn't have a chance to deliver Cal a last-second victory, after all.

As Harmon ran onto the field, his stomach was fluttering. He had never been called on to kick a game-winner before at Stanford, let alone one in a hostile stadium, with a bowl game and perhaps Elway's Heisman Trophy on the line. He told himself he had made a kick from this distance hundreds of times before. All he had to do was follow the proper form.

Harmon placed his black, two-inch high kicking tee on the 25-yard line and looked toward the goal post to make sure he had put it in the right spot. His 10 teammates were in the huddle listening to Steve Cottrell, the holder and backup quarterback. "We have a chance to win it," Cottrell exhorted them. "Let's do it." He paused. "It's a field goal on my cadence." The 10 Stanford players clapped hands in unison and broke the huddle.

From the 25-yard mark, Cottrell placed his left hand on the tee, held his right palm above it, and turned toward Harmon, who paced off four yards at an angle from the ball and took a practice kick. "Ready Bigs?" Cottrell called out, in a routine the best friends had practiced too many times to count. Harmon nodded. He was locked in. He leaned slightly forward, his arms by his side, his left foot one step in front. Cottrell turned back toward Teeuws, the center. "Green! Green!" he shouted. "Set!" Teeuws hiked the ball, sending it tight up against Cottrell's chest. In one motion, he spun the ball to have the laces face the goal posts and placed it on the tee, tilted slightly toward him.

Elway was sitting on the bench. He felt spent and exhausted. He didn't look up—he would know from the crowd's reaction whether it was good.

"Here's the snap!" shouted Starkey. "Here's the kick…it is long enough… *it is good!* Stanford hits it with four seconds to go, to take the lead 20–19!"

When Elway heard the Stanford fans roar, while the Cal side of the stadium fell silent, he felt a surge of relief. They had pulled it off! Two dozen

Stanford players raced from the sideline onto the field in exultation, pounded on Harmon, and leaped into the air. When he had worked himself free from his teammates, Harmon turned toward the Cal bench. "Take that, you dirty Golden Bears!" he yelled.

The Cal defenders, who came off the field, were devastated, especially the seniors playing their last game. Camp, sitting on the bench, teared up. So did cornerback Anderson. They felt like they had let down their teammates. Rivera threw his helmet on the sideline, fuming that Stanford had scored and that he hadn't been on the field to stop them.

Steve Miller, a Cal fan at home listening to Starkey call the game, hurled his transistor radio against an apartment wall.

In the press box at Memorial Stadium, Gordy Cercsino, a star linebacker several years earlier under Bill Walsh and now the color man for Stanford's TV highlights program, couldn't contain his excitement. "Look out!" he shouted. "Stanford's going to take home the Axe! Book your plane tickets to Birmingham! The Hall of Fame Bowl is on the way!"

Stanford's president, Donald Kennedy, was watching the game from a booth on the same level of the press box. He stepped out and found Cal's athletic director, Dave Maggard. "Dave, it's too bad you had to lose this," Kennedy told him. "You played well."

Stanford right guard Dennis Engel, a fraternity brother of Elway's at the Delt fraternity house, rushed over to his buddy sitting on the bench. Engel had grown up in nearby Santa Clara, and every year on the Sunday morning after the Big Game, he had seen the *San Jose Mercury News* display a front-page photo of the seniors on the winning squad holding up the Axe. Now, finally, it was his turn. And he wanted Elway to be in the photo with him. But the quarterback, with tears welling in his eyes after their stunning achievement, waved him away. He needed a few moments to himself. Engel walked to a spot on the sideline closest to the Stanford students who had been brandishing the Axe throughout the game. Once the kickoff was over, he would race to the trophy, hoist it, and get a front-page photo suitable for framing and displaying for a lifetime.

The Axe was now locked via a looped cable to Kevin Wells and Max Scheder-Bieschin, the two Stanford students. They were jumping up and down next to the south end zone goal post, alongside dozens of red-jacketed members of the Stanford band who had climbed down unimpeded from the stands onto the turf several minutes before. With little room between the stands and the playing field, some of the band members had leaped into the end zone in a mad celebration when Harmon kicked the field goal at the other end of the field. They were as excited as any Stanford fan.

Trombone player Gary Tyrrell high-fived everybody in sight. *Bowl game!* he thought. *Awesome! I love the Big Game!*

Pressed up against the stands on the field, drum major Disco Ray Gruenewald blew one long whistle followed by four short whistles, and the band launched into an especially raucous version of "All Right Now," the school's unofficial fight song. Stanford had whipped the Cal weenies on their home turf to win the Big Game in a victory that Stanford fans would be talking about for years. In the meantime, the band would have a hellacious rolling celebration on the bus ride home to their side of the bay, followed by a riotous party at the Band Shak.

Rob Rawson watched all of this unfold across the field from his seat in the Cal student section. Rawson, who had graduated the year before, had played trombone in the Cal band. Now, like all other Cal fans, he was crushed by the defeat. To top it off, he had to watch the Stanford band's joyous antics. Like his mates in the Cal band, Rawson had no fondness for the Stanford band and its irreverent style. *They are so smug and arrogant*, Rawson thought. He turned to a friend. "Dammit," he said, "just once, I'd like to see their disrespect for the rules bite them in the ass."

Marsha Moen could see the Stanford band to her right from her perch on the opposite side of the field, where Cal alums and parents sat, below the press box. She had flown in from Iowa to watch her son, Kevin, play his last game. But now Cal had lost in dramatic fashion. Down on the Cal sideline below her, *Kevin had to be distraught*, she thought. Tears rolled down her cheeks.

The scoreboard now read: Cal 19, Stanford 20. Time left :04.

"Only a miracle can save the Bears!" shouted Starkey to his radio audience.

CHAPTER 13

THE PLAY

Members of the Stanford band could barely contain their excitement after watching the winning field goal soar through the uprights of the far end zone. They rocked out "All Right Now" while standing just behind and alongside one corner of the south end zone. Band members and Stanford fans were so pumped up that drum major Disco Ray Gruenewald waved his long baton in the air when they reached the end of the song. Keep it going, Disco Ray was signaling. Keep the party going! Trombone player Gary Tyrrell stood just behind the end zone, rocking with his mates. The five members of the Stanford Dollies—fetching in white tails, white boots, black cummerbunds, and red body suits—kicked up their legs and shook their hips as they danced to the band's energizing music.

Next to the band, beside the goal post, stood Doug Cohn. He was a Memorial Stadium maintenance worker. At halftime, he had cleaned the Hall of Fame donor reception area and emptied trash cans throughout the stadium. Each of the stadium workers had a specific responsibility at the end of the game. One had to retrieve the black yard markers that were placed every 10 yards on each sideline. Another had to grab the orange end zone pylons. Cohn's job was to untie the pad that covered the south end zone goal post and return it to the stadium's equipment shed. Cal had only two of the goal post pads—one at either end—and the cost of replacing one was not insignificant given the school's bare-bones athletic budget. But for the moment, he was focused on crowd control. "Get back! Get back!" Cohn yelled at the Stanford band members to his left who were crowding the back line of the end zone. Stanford still had to kick off, and four seconds remained on the clock.

Next to Cohn stood Max Scheder-Bieschin and Kevin Wells, the two Stanford students chained to the Axe. Only minutes before, they were disconsolate, preparing to surrender the Axe to members of Cal's Rally Committee. But now they were hoisting aloft the Axe, secure in the knowledge that Stanford would keep the trophy for another year.

Now it was the half dozen members of the Cal Rally Committee Axe Guard who were crushed. They were standing at the other corner of the south end zone, a few yards to the right of Wells and Scheder-Bieschin. Ken Raust, who had organized the spectacular bonfire rally the night before at the Greek Theatre, felt utter despair and utter disgust. Raust was a senior and he told himself he would never see Cal beat Stanford again as a student. A second Axe Guard member, Karen Lingel, felt awful, like a family heirloom had been stolen from her. But a third Axe Guard member, Gail Hoffmann, held out hope despite the slim odds. "Wait! Wait!" she called out to her mates. "The game's not over! We can still run it back!"

In the stands just above where the Stanford band had congregated, Mike Aldrete and Vince Sakowski, fueled by beer, were plotting how to jump onto the field, evade a security guard, and celebrate with their good friend John Elway. The three had played together on the baseball team before Elway signed with the New York Yankees and became ineligible to keep playing with them. Still, they all lived together in the Delta Tau Delta fraternity house and were best of friends. "I'm watching you! I'm watching you!" the security guard shouted at Aldrete as he stepped onto the concrete ledge that separated the field from the stands.

A few yards away, a father and son met briefly on the Stanford sideline. They were Robert Stinnett and his son Jim. The elder Stinnett was a staff photographer for the *Oakland Tribune*, and he had one assignment that day—to shoot the winning team holding aloft the Axe immediately after the game. A *Tribune* photographer the year before had failed to capture that iconic image. Stinnett didn't have to worry about taking photos of the game, which was fine with him. Truth be told, Stinnett had little interest in shooting sports. During several decades at the *Tribune*, Stinnett, 58, had specialized in crime photos and other breaking news. His Chevy

Nova was packed with scanners from police departments throughout the Bay Area—bristling with antennas, the car looked like a mechanical porcupine—to keep him abreast of the latest crime developments. Stinnett also liked shooting rock concerts and had taken Jim with him to see The Beatles' last live performance, at San Francisco's Candlestick Park in 1966. And he had invited Jim, then 30, to accompany him to the 1982 Big Game. The *Tribune* secured a press pass that allowed Jim to shoot his own photos down on the field. In the waning seconds of the game, father and son discussed their plans. "I'm going to run to the parking lot and get out of here before it gets too crowded," his son said.

"I need to stay here to shoot the Axe picture," Robert replied and added, "If I can, I think there might be a good Joe Kapp dejection shot. If I can get one of those, I'll follow him."

Wearing a blue windbreaker and a baseball cap, the elder Stinnett hurried back to the end zone to shadow the two Stanford students chained to the Axe. He was carrying a Nikon camera with a telephoto lens for close-up shots and a motor drive capable of snapping five photos per second.

In the stands, Stanford fans were clapping in time to "All Right Now" and jumping up and down in excitement. Many Cal fans were leaving their seats and trekking up the wooden steps to the exits. Jim Branson, a Cal rooter sitting on an aisle, decided to remain to the bitter end. But he couldn't help calling out to them, "It's not over! It's not over!" None of the departing fans paid any heed. They saw no reason to stay. Cal had just lost in heartbreaking fashion, 20–19.

Among the Cal fans crestfallen by the Stanford field goal were three buddies from the Phi Gamma Delta house. "Let's go drown our sorrows," Phil Neville told his friends, Steven Hinds and Chris Jones. A keg was waiting for them on the porch of the fraternity house just a few blocks away. The three joined the others heading to the exits.

Just outside the northeast corner of Memorial Stadium, with a direct view of the field from Tightwad Hill, Mark Weigand was despondent. Only a few minutes earlier, he was all set to fire the Victory Cannon to signal to Berkeley that Cal had won the 85th Big Game. And then...Weigand shook his head. Another Cal defeat. Still, he kept his eyes on the field 200 yards below. After all, the game wasn't over.

Fans of both teams had been listening to the game, either on KSFO-AM (Stanford) or KGO-AM (Cal). One of the listeners had a particular interest in the outcome. He was Jack Elway, John's father. He had been listening to the game while hiding out in the equipment room across the street from Spartan Stadium in advance of San Jose State's 7:00 PM game against Utah State. Jack was overseeing a program turnaround for the Spartans, who had a 7–3 record going into the Utah State game. But he was also intensely focused on the Big Game. A Stanford win would mean a bowl game for his son and possibly the Heisman Trophy. When Stanford got the ball back for its final drive, Jack walked to his car parked just outside of the equipment room. There, he could smoke and face no distractions. He cheered on John when he led Stanford on the incredible, final-minute drive to win the game with Mark Harmon's 35-yard field goal. Afterward, Jack lingered in the car for a few minutes, savoring what the victory would mean for his son.

In the lower level of the press box at Memorial Stadium, Jim Simmons and Coy Collinsworth also were as thrilled as could be. Stanford had won after all, and Elway had proved to be as spectacular as advertised. The Hall of Fame Bowl would have its dream match-up of Vanderbilt versus Stanford. The marketing folks would promote it as the "Brain Bowl," given the high academic standards of both universities. Immediately after Harmon's field goal, Simmons picked up a phone to call Birmingham. He gave the good news to Hall Thompson, the owner of Thompson Tractor Company and the chair of the bowl's selection committee. "All that's left is the kickoff," Simmons told Thompson.

One level up from Simmons and Collinsworth sat Mike Nolan, one of the six Stanford assistant coaches keeping track of the action down below and sending in offensive and defensive plays via headsets to Paul Wiggin and the other assistant coaches on the sideline. Amidst the congratulatory handshakes in the coaches' booth after Harmon's field goal, Nolan flashed back to a pro football game in 1972 when he was 13 years old. Nolan was sitting in the press box with his mother as they watched his father Dick coach the San Francisco 49ers in an NFC division playoff game against the Dallas Cowboys. With the 49ers leading by five points after a Dallas touchdown, a play away from going to the NFC Championship Game, the Cowboys attempted an onside kick. A San Francisco receiver named Preston Riley failed to corral the ball, Dallas recovered, and, behind quarterback Roger Staubach, went on to score the winning touchdown. "The game's not over," Nolan muttered in the press box. "The game's not over."

Down on the field, chaos reigned immediately after Harmon's field goal. Two dozen Stanford players rushed onto the playing surface to jump in the air and pound on Harmon in celebration. This was not permitted. It took officials several minutes to clear the field of the Stanford players and assess a 15-yard penalty against the bench for, well, exuberance. The infraction meant that Harmon would kick off from the Stanford 25-yard line, not the 40. Practically no one at the time understood the potential significance of this, but Cal would have a shorter distance to cover to the goal line.

On the Stanford sideline, Wiggin conferred with Fred von Appen, the special teams coach. They agreed Harmon would squib the kickoff, deliberately kicking the top part of the ball to boot a short line drive that would hit the turf at least once before a Cal player could collect it. They thought it was riskier to kick the ball deep and give Cal's speedy return man the chance to get up a head of steam. The squib kick had been popularized only the year before by Bill Walsh's 49ers kicker Ray Wersching. In theory, a squib kick would disorient the return team because the ball was likely to take an unpredictable bounce or two and cause the Cal player closest to the ball to have trouble gathering it in. It also could hinder the Bears from setting up a blocking scheme for a long return and give the Stanford players racing downfield an extra second or two to converge on the ball. But choosing to make a squib kick had one major drawback: the kickoff team had little familiarity with how to defend it. Stanford practiced it only occasionally. Instead, they repeatedly drilled the conventional kickoff, which they employed at least several times in the normal course of each game. In contrast, Stanford had used the squib kick perhaps only twice during that season.

"Kickoff team! Kickoff team!" went the call up and down the Cardinal bench. Stanford would use its standard kickoff team. As the players gathered around von Appen, he told them that Harmon would squib the kickoff to the right. Coach von Appen reminded the players to stay in their lanes as they ran downfield, to cover the entire field. He did not warn them that the Bears might lateral the ball. Had he done so, he would have told them to be extra careful to not over-pursue the ball carrier and avoid getting caught on one side of the field as the ball swung to the other side. Only the week before, unbeaten and untied SMU, the No. 2-ranked team in the country, had pulled off a miracle finish by lateraling a squibbed kickoff, fooling its opponent, and running the length of the field for a touchdown. But no matter. The Cardinal players were confident. With Stanford leading 20–19 with only four seconds left, Cal had enough time only to score a touchdown on this single play, but no team had run one back against Stanford all season. One tackle away from a glorious victory, the players jogged onto the field.

Harmon stood in the middle of the field and placed the football on a kicking tee. Five players were arrayed on a line to each side of him. Mark Andrew and Tom Briehl, to his immediate left and right, were backup linebackers who were quick enough to race past Cal's front line and big enough to break up the wedge of blockers that a return team typically formed in the center of the field. Andrew and Briehl were designated R-1 and L-1, respectively. Playing R-2 and L-2 were Mike Noble and Kevin Lamar, two more backup defenders who were both big and quick. Lamar, as he took his position, was certain he would make the game-ending tackle. At R-3 and L-3 were Dave Wyman and Jack Gilmete. They, too, were reserve linebackers with strength and some speed. At R-4 and L-4 were Barry Cromer and Steve Lemon, the gunners. They were backup defensive backs. Each would be the first player downfield on his side. If a kick returner was downed after a short advance, the tackler was typically either Cromer or Lemon. Playing R-5 and L-5, lined up against each sideline, were Darrell Grissum and Kevin Baird. They, too, were defensive backs, but they were responsible for outside containment, meaning they were supposed to avoid angling toward the middle of the field. Instead, their job was to position themselves to stop a ball carrier who tried to race up either sideline.

Meanwhile, chaos and despair reigned on the Cal sideline. Several of the defensive players were in tears. Gregg Beagle, a backup safety, was pissed off at being benched during the Cardinal's final drive, believing he could have stopped Elway's fourth-and-17 completion. And he was furious that Cal was going to lose his final game. Beagle dropkicked several chairs along the bench and took a seat, stewing in his thoughts.

With Stanford fans roaring and the Stanford band playing "All Right Now," Beagle did not hear the call on the Cal bench: "Hands team! Hands team!" Beagle was one of its members. Cal's coaches, expecting Stanford to squib the kickoff, had decided not to employ the usual return team, which included big men whose job was to open lanes for the speedy Mariet Ford, who typically stood near the goal line to receive the kickoff. Instead, the hands team consisted of players who were accustomed to handling the ball. Jimmy Stewart, who had played during Stanford's final drive in place of Beagle, also was on the hands team. With his helmet off and angry over the loss, Stewart also didn't hear the call.

One Cal player totally on top of the situation was Richard Rodgers, a safety who was the special teams captain. Rodgers, a junior, grew up in Daly City with his mother, a dispatcher for the San Francisco Police Department. His father expressed little interest in him. Rodgers had attended Jefferson High School one year behind Reggie Camp, the team's starting right end who burned with resentment and anger over his father's rejection. Rodgers wasn't angry at his dad, just disappointed in him. Besides, at Jefferson, he found father figures while playing football. Especially important to him was Jefferson's head coach, Jack Burgett, who provided guidance for Rodgers on and off the field. Burgett ran an option offense where the quarterback had to learn how and when to pitch the ball to a trailing back on plays when he didn't hand it off to a fullback or carry the ball himself.

Burgett, a former Marine, was a taskmaster. He blindfolded Rodgers during practice and made him run up the sideline at full speed while pitching the ball repeatedly to a back who was five yards behind him and to the side. Burgett not only taught Rodgers to make blind pitches, the coach also made him hold the ball just so—Rodgers had to have his right thumb underneath the ball to keep it from tumbling end over end when he tossed it to the right.

At Cal, however, Rodgers played defense only. He became known for his ferocious hits, even during practice drills known as "thud." In thud drills, the defensive player was supposed to make contact with the ball carrier but not tackle him. But Rodgers treated thud drills like live ones and slammed into his teammates. They nicknamed him "Rock," not only for his hits but for his sculpted shape.

Rodgers gathered the hands team players on the field at the Cal 35-yard line and barked out these instructions, "The game's not over! If you get the ball and are going to get tackled, pitch it! Don't go down with the ball! Don't fall on the ball! Keep the ball alive!"

Tight end David Lewis looked around the huddle and joined in: "If Rock says it, let's do it!"

Rodgers didn't mention it, but the Bears were well-schooled in the art of lateraling. Kapp had introduced a free-flowing activity on Sunday afternoons to loosen up after the previous day's game. It was a playground version of keep away, in T-shirts and gym shorts. There were few rules, but everybody who played had fun lateraling the ball as they tried to advance from one sideline across the field to the other. Kapp and the players called it "Grab Ass," but in public, to avoid raising any hackles, they called it "Grabazz," pronouncing it *Gra-bahz*, as if it were a French word.

Also in the huddle for the final kickoff were Tim Lucas, a backup linebacker; Garey Williams, a backup defensive back; Wes Howell, who had caught a touchdown pass earlier in the fourth quarter; and Ron Story, a fullback, who, upon hearing Rodgers words, thought: *I'm not going to pitch it. I'm going to run it all the way back!*

A seventh player in the huddle was Dwight Garner. He was a freshman running back in 1982 who had carried the ball only 30 times and hadn't scored a touchdown. Still, he did not lack for confidence. Like Story, Garner thought that if he got the ball, he would run it back for the winning score. He remembered Kapp's frequent admonition: give 100 percent for all 60 minutes and never give in until the last second had ticked off.

Ford did not join the huddle. He had already positioned himself as the deep returner, 20 yards away from his teammates. A senior, Ford had transferred to Cal the year before after two standout seasons at Diablo Valley Junior College in Pleasant Hill, near Berkeley. Ford was only 5'9", 165 pounds, but he was quick and could take a hit, and he'd overcome any doubts about his size. He had finished second in the Pac-10 in catches in 1981, his first at Cal. On this day, Ford had been awarded a touchdown in the first half on a pass that actually had hit the turf. But he had also made one spectacular sideline catch earlier in the game and had added more than 75 yards in punt and kickoff returns. A sociology major, Ford was planning a career as a child psychologist. "He is bright, affable and hard-working," *Sports Illustrated* would write later. "He made only one promise to his parents, he says, and that was to graduate from Cal." He was on track to achieve that goal. But as he stood waiting for the kickoff, Ford had a growing concern. He could feel his legs cramping up.

The ninth Cal player on the field was Kevin Moen, who had started the game at strong safety but then mostly sat on the bench while Rodgers played during dime and nickel packages. Moen was 21, a senior playing his last game for the Bears. He had attended games at Memorial Stadium as an elementary school student in Lafayette, outside of Berkeley, before his family moved to Rolling Hills, south of Los Angeles, when he was in eighth grade. The move was a godsend for Rolling Hills High School because Moen was a standout athlete. He was a four-year starter for the baseball team, and the Yankees scouted him. On the gridiron, Moen became a starter as a sophomore. In his senior year, he played quarterback on offense, cornerback on defense, and he also punted. He practically never rested while Rolling Hills went undefeated during the regular season. Afterward, Moen was chosen as the Most Valuable Player of the South Bay League.

At quarterback in high school, Moen didn't throw the ball much because his school ran an option offense. So, like Rodgers, he became adept at pitching the ball. Moen, however, loved tackling and hitting. As a boy playing in his front yard, he always imagined himself as Dick Butkus, the fearsome Chicago Bears linebacker. So he wasn't interested when several universities recruited him to play quarterback. He chose Cal because they wanted him to play defense. At the 1979 Shrine All-Star Game, where the best high school seniors in northern Los Angeles County played against the best from the south, Elway had thrown a touchdown pass that zipped over Moen. But Moen also had made several impressive tackles during that game. "It's going to be great to have you up there to play that kind of football for us," Roger Theder, the Bears' head coach, told Moen after the game.

As a sophomore in 1980, Moen made the climactic play at the end of that year's Big Game, with Cal leading by a touchdown. He blitzed Elway on fourth and goal and forced him to throw incomplete. That more than evened the score with the Stanford quarterback. During the next two years, Moen alternated with Rodgers. They were both a step slower than other defensive backs. But they could both hit. In 1979, Moen drilled an Oregon State receiver, leaving him with three broken ribs and a punctured lung. He laid out another guy five plays later. At practice a day or two later, one of the coaches told him, "Anyone else who comes to your area, they'll have to go to the morgue. We're going to start calling you 'the undertaker.'"

Teammates picked up on the nickname, and Moen liked it. His Christmas card one year showed him standing over a Washington State player he had just leveled. At 6'1", 205 pounds, Moen had the body of a defensive back but the mentality of a linebacker.

Moen's teammates liked him because he was steady and reliable and never sought to call attention to himself. They thought of him as a redneck surfer. Moen had spent summers on a farm while growing up and liked horses and chewing tobacco. But with his blond hair, blue eyes, and laid-back Southern California vibe, he could pass for a surfer, although he had only been out in the waves a few times.

Moen's parents were in the stands at Memorial Stadium. His mother, Marsha Moen, was despondent at how the game was ending with the Stanford victory. She was crying at her seat on the press box side of the stadium. Her former husband, Donne, was more stoic. Sitting a few sections over to her right, in row 61, Donne had always preached to Kevin the importance of bringing a level of humility to his athletic career. Much of what you accomplish, Donne had told Kevin repeatedly, starts with God-given gifts. After that it's patience, repetition, and a willingness to risk your neck by sticking it into potentially dangerous places. As Moen ran out on the field for the final kickoff, Donne, a senior credit officer of Union Bank, took solace from the fact that Kevin had played extensively during his four years at Cal and was set to graduate the following spring and enter the job market with a fine university degree.

Donne, a camera buff, had brought two cameras to the game, as usual. The long lens camera had run out of film before the final kickoff. The other, a Minolta, had a 300-millimeter lens extender, but wasn't as adept at shots from the stands. But that's all he had. Donne found Kevin on the field and trained his lens on him.

Moen didn't actually join his teammates in their huddle, so he didn't hear Rodgers' instruction to lateral the ball. He was mad and frustrated at being on the verge of losing his last game. Moen didn't have a lot of hope, and he certainly wasn't thinking that he might run back the kickoff. He hadn't scored at Cal and didn't have a me-first mentality. Moen had last scored a touchdown in his final game as a high school senior, on a quarterback keeper.

On the field at Memorial Stadium, Moen was focused on the task at hand. Moments before the final kickoff, he noticed two teammates were missing. The Bears had only nine players on the field! Beagle and Stewart had missed the call for the hands team. As the team broke the huddle, Moen ran to his spot in the third row of players, on the left side. But seeing a gap in the spacing, he moved five yards closer to the middle of the field. That, too, went unnoticed by anyone at the time but was about to become a crucial development.

On the Cal sideline, Kapp and his offensive coordinator were talking with starting quarterback Gale Gilbert and Gilbert's backup, J Torchio. Kapp wanted to know how far Gilbert could throw the ball. Kapp was thinking that the Cal player who received Stanford's kick, expected to be a squib, would down the ball to stop the clock. Cal would have one play for Gilbert to throw a Hail Mary—a last desperate heave, as much a prayer as a pass, toward the end zone where they might score a miracle touchdown on the game's final play. Three or four receivers would sprint to the end zone, hoping that somehow one of them would catch the ball for a touchdown. There would be no element of surprise. The defense would stack its coverage to make sure it didn't happen. The odds of completing such a long pass were so slim that a team was said to utter a prayer as the quarterback uncorked the throw. "Hell, we've got one more chance," Gilbert told Kapp and Torchio on the sideline. "I can throw it 70 yards."

The problem was that no Cal coaches had told Rodgers, Moen, or the others on the kickoff team to take the kick and then down the ball. They were going to try to run it back somehow.

As the players broke their huddle, Kapp and special teams coach Charlie West also noticed not everyone on the hands team had run onto the field. They grabbed backup halfback Scott Smith and pushed him onto the gridiron. Smith ran to an open space in the front row of Bears, directly facing Harmon, the kicker. He was the 10th Cal player onto the field.

The 11 Stanford players lined up for the kickoff, Harmon in the middle.

Briehl, in the L-1 position to the kicker's immediate left, called out, "Mark, you have to kick it deep. They have the hands team out there."

"No," Harmon replied, "the coach told me to squib it."

The rules required Cal to have five players in the restraining area, 10 yards from the ball at kickoff, between the Stanford 35 and 40. But in all the confusion, Cal had only four: Rodgers, Smith, Lucas, and Williams, from left to right, with Stewart's place, between Rodgers and Smith, unoccupied. Lewis, Moen, Story, and Howell were supposed to be five yards behind them at the Stanford 40-yard line. But Moen had dropped back and now stood 10 yards behind them, at the Cal 48-yard line, on the hash mark nearest the Cal sideline. Garner was farther back, with Ford even deeper.

Harmon, standing at the Stanford 21-yard line, held his arm aloft, signaling he was ready to boot the ball. Next to him was Walter Wolf, the umpire. Wolf lowered his arm a couple of seconds later to give the go-ahead.

At that moment, West pushed an 11th Cal player onto the field. He was Steve Dunn, a backup defensive back, and he didn't even have time to buckle his chin strap.

Harmon ran forward four steps and then kicked the top of the ball with his right foot. It did exactly what a squib kick was supposed to. It traveled a few yards, hit the turf, bounced over the front line of Cal players, then bounced a second time. The erratic football landed in Moen's arms at the Cal 45-yard line. He had to back up a couple of steps to catch it. Had Moen been playing in position, five yards upfield, the ball would have hopped over his head into an unoccupied area. Dunn, a skinny defensive back who was running onto the field when the ball was kicked, would have had to run upfield to corral it after another bounce, with Stanford players converging on him.

Moen caught Harmon's kick chest high and stutter-stepped five steps to his right toward the middle of the field, where he saw a horde of white jerseys heading toward him, led by Cromer and Wyman. Moen pivoted back to his left, and then the instincts of the high school option quarterback kicked in as he shifted the ball into his right hand. Hemmed in, Moen leaped to have a clear throwing lane and tossed the ball overhand and backward to his left to Rodgers, who had retreated from the front line to catch the ball near the sideline on the Cal 46-yard line.

Rodgers caught it and took one step forward as Dunn, who had raced up from behind, blocked Darrell Grissum. He had containment for Stanford on that sideline. But now Rodgers saw Stanford's Cromer and Wyman closing in on him. Moments earlier, Rodgers had told teammates in the huddle to lateral the ball if they were about to be tackled. Now it was his turn to put those words into practice. Rodgers turned backward and used both hands to shovel the ball to Garner, who was about four yards behind him.

With a freshman's bravado, Garner immediately thought he would run it back. He took two steps forward and faked out one Stanford player. But then four Cardinal players converged on him at the 50-yard line, near the left sideline. Wyman hit Garner first from the side, Mark Andrew grabbed him from behind, and Kevin Lamar slammed into him head-on. Garner didn't go down immediately: the force of Stanford players tackling him from all sides stood him up for a crucial second.

"Dwight, the ball!" cried out Rodgers, who had circled behind him. "Dwight, the ball!"

That crucial second would be pivotal to what happened next, in what soon enough would be called The Play.

As he toppled over, Garner flicked the ball to Rodgers.

An instant before, Lamar felt Garner's knee hit the turf. The Cal player was down! Lamar began to punch the air to celebrate the game-ending tackle. Harmon, several yards behind the pile, raised his arms in triumph. "The ballgame is going to be over with the tackle made at midfield!" exclaimed Ron Barr, broadcasting the game for KSFO-AM.

"And the ballgame is over!" shouted Jim Grundberg, calling the play-by-play action for KZSU, Stanford's student radio station. "It's all over! The Stanford team has won this ballgame!"

Stanford fans roared their approval.

A dozen Stanford players, led by their exuberant split end, Mike Tolliver, rushed from the Cardinal sideline onto the field to celebrate. Tolliver was particularly excited. He had grown up in Los Angeles and wanted to offer a postgame greeting to Kapp, a boyhood favorite of his when Kapp played quarterback against his beloved Los Angeles Rams.

Scheder-Bieschin and Wells, the two Stanford students chained to the Axe, saw the stop and the Stanford players dash out from the sideline. They, too, began sprinting onto the playing field, from a spot next to the south end zone goal post. Each student carried aloft his side of the trophy and wanted to bring the Axe out to the players. "We won! We won!" screamed Scheder-Bieschin. Jon Erickson, the adult supervisor of the Axe Committee, took off after them.

To their left, a half dozen other Stanford band members had lined up just behind the end zone back line at the kickoff, poised with one hand on the turf in a starter's position to sprint onto the field as soon as a Cal player was downed. They felt a special bond with the Stanford players, strengthened by their post-game celebration with the team and a wild throng of fans following the team's victory against Washington three weeks earlier. The thrill from that day remained fresh in their minds. Now the bandsmen saw the Stanford tacklers swarm Garner. It was as if a starter's gun had sounded. They, too, sprinted onto the field, toting their instruments.

So did Jim Kohn, who played tenor saxophone. In fact, Kohn was leading the charge. A gung-ho sophomore, Kohn wanted to be the first bandsman onto the field. He had even exchanged instruments with a trumpet player so he could run faster with the more compact horn. Band members sometimes augmented their uniforms with accessories. Kohn's stood out. He was wearing a giant cone underneath his white hard hat—in homage to a popular *Saturday Night Live* sketch on television about a family of extraterrestrials known as the Coneheads—that he had found discarded after a Halloween party and had repurposed for the Big Game. On the back of his red jacket, using masking tape, Kohn had spelled out "I heart France," a reference to the Coneheads' farcical explanation for their otherworldly behavior by saying they came from France. Seeing Garner's momentum stopped, Kohn lit out from the end zone.

Simultaneously, Elway's baseball buddy, Aldrete, jumped from the stands, eluded a security guard, and raced past the sideline onto the playing field, trailed by Sakowski, another baseball player.

Gina Moreno, Melinda Myers, and Diana Dobbs—three of the Stanford Dollies—also rushed onto the field from the sideline. Moreno—and numerous Stanford players—would swear later that they had seen a referee wave his arms above his head, or blow his whistle, to signal that Garner was down, and the game was over.

Two officials were positioned to make the call on Garner. One was Wolf, the umpire. His role on the kickoff was to stand just behind Harmon when he kicked off and then follow the kicker, who was typically the last defender. By the time Garner got the ball, Wolf was on the Stanford 44-yard line, with a direct view of the ball carrier just a few yards away.

The other official was Jack Langley, the head linesman. He, too, had been a Pac-10 official for a decade. Langley's job on the kickoff was to follow the ball carrier from the Cal sideline. Because Moen had lateraled the ball toward his side, Langley stood only three yards from Garner when the Stanford players swarmed the Cal player at midfield. Stanford's tacklers partially obscured his view. Langley tensed the muscles in his mouth to blow the whistle.

The game clock had ticked down to :00. Had the game ended? That would depend on the officials' call.

CHAPTER 14

"The Band Is Out on the Field"

Neither Walter Wolf nor Jack Langley blew his whistle. Neither official ruled that Dwight Garner was down. The play was alive. The game wasn't over. Now Richard Rodgers had the ball for a second time.

He crossed the left hash mark at the Cal 47-yard line, heading upfield to his right. Two teammates—Mariet Ford and Kevin Moen—instinctively moved behind Rodgers and to his right to be ready for a possible lateral. The gang of Stanford players, who had tackled Garner, jumped to their feet. One of them, Steve Lemon, grabbed at Rodgers but had a bad angle and came up empty.

Lemon and his teammates had made a critical mistake. In their excitement to claim victory, the Stanford players had over-pursued. In all, eight of the 11 players were between the hash mark and the Cal sideline just a few yards away. And now the action was swinging away from them, to a wide expanse of open field to the right, toward the Stanford sideline.

One Stanford player, Kevin Baird, had stayed home, maintaining his position after starting out as the closest player to the Stanford sideline. Baird now stood between Rodgers and the goal line. But Rodgers had been an option quarterback in high school, tutored to pitch the ball precisely while running blindfolded at full speed. Although he had been a defensive back at Cal, his muscle memory kicked in. Rodgers drew Baird toward him while holding the ball with both hands, rather than tucked under his arm.

At the Stanford 45-yard line, Rodgers pitched the ball in textbook fashion to his right. Ford caught the ball in stride at the Stanford 46. He raced past Baird and cut to the right. The 10 other Stanford players angled across the field in desperate pursuit. Ford sprinted past Mike Tolliver at the Stanford 35-yard line. The Cardinal receiver, realizing the kickoff return had unexpectedly remained alive, had dropped to the turf, hoping no one would notice his trespass from the bench. But Gordon Riese, the line judge, had seen him and other Stanford players dash illegally onto the field. Slowing momentarily, Riese grabbed his yellow penalty flag from his pocket and tossed it in the air. Then he resumed running full speed down the right sideline in pursuit of the action.

Ford kept going past the Stanford 30-yard line, trailed by Moen a step or two behind him and to his right. But Ford couldn't keep going. His cramping legs could give out at any moment. More importantly, three Stanford players—Lemon, Tom Briehl, and Mark Harmon—were converging on him from his left. Ford dove into them, and as he did, he made a blind pitch over his right shoulder, sensing Moen was there. *We got this guy! Finally!* Lemon thought as he, Ford, and his two Stanford teammates crashed together to the ground. Lemon did not see what happened next. Moen had to slow down, but he grabbed the lateral from Ford. The kickoff return remained alive.

Still, one final issue loomed, one that nobody could have predicted. "Oh, the band is out on the field!" screamed Joe Starkey.

About 100 bandsmen had scampered onto the field from the behind end zone and the sideline. Leading the way, Jim Kohn and his conehead had reached the 17-yard line. So had Kevin Wells and Max Scheder-Bieschin while toting the Stanford Axe.

By now, only one thing stood between Moen and the goal line: the red-jacketed Stanford band. Shocked at seeing the players thundering toward them, they stopped playing "All Right Now." Drum major Disco Ray Gruenewald, standing just off the playing field next to the stadium interior wall, turned around to see why the music had suddenly died.

As Moen raced past the Stanford 20-yard line, one player had a shot at him, Darrell Grissum, a sophomore defensive back who had raced across the field from the far sideline. Moen had a blocker, Wes Howell, but Howell didn't have a good angle on Grissum. So Howell reached out with his right hand and pushed Grissum toward the right sideline, potentially an illegal block. No referee threw a flag, however.

As Moen crossed the 15, he cut left to avoid Grissum. This gave a final Stanford player the chance to tackle him: Mike Noble, a freshman linebacker, who also had been racing across the field diagonally from the left sideline. But Noble was disoriented from seeing band members around him and hesitated for a split second. That was long enough for Moen to gain two steps on the Stanford player. Moen crossed the 10-yard line and then the 5 as Noble chased him from behind. Stanford band members and three Dollies scattered out of the way. This created a narrow corridor for Moen through the sea of red to the promised land.

One bandsman didn't get out of the way as Moen crossed the goal line. He was Scott DeBarger, a sophomore saxophonist. He spied Moen coming toward him only at the last moment and thought he was a sore loser acting as if he were scoring a touchdown. Except this one was going to count. DeBarger tried to get out of the way, but Moen clipped him, knocking DeBarger's tenor saxophone to the turf. Now in the end zone, Moen took three more steps and leaped forward, holding the ball aloft in celebration—click!

Robert Stinnett, the *Oakland Tribune* photographer standing in the end zone, snapped a picture, only a step away from the Cal player.

When Moen landed, he crashed into an unsuspecting trombone player, Gary Tyrrell. At 5'6" and 148 pounds, Tyrrell was no match for Moen, who was 6'1", 205 pounds and covered in body armor. Moen knocked Tyrrell onto his butt, and then the trombone player did a half-roll, making sure to protect his horn. His hard hat went flying through the end zone. Unhurt but utterly confused, Tyrrell had no idea why a Cal football player had just bowled him over.

Line Judge Riese, dodging band members as he raced behind Moen into the end zone, knew what was happening. He signaled a touchdown, amidst the Stanford band members.

In trampling Tyrrell, Moen felt a thump but didn't know who or what he had hit. But then again, it didn't matter. Stumbling but keeping his feet, Moen then pranced to his left, holding the ball aloft in his right hand.

Moen was jubilant. He had never scored a touchdown for Cal, much less one to decide the Big Game in his final play in a Bear uniform. By the goal post, half a dozen players swarmed him, then, moments later, a dozen more. Mark Weigand pulled the trigger on Tightwad Hill, and the Cal cannon detonated to signify a touchdown. *Boooom!*

Tens of thousands of spectators couldn't believe their eyes. In fact, most did not comprehend what they were seeing. Cal players were celebrating in the south end zone. The Stanford band had improbably been on the field during the play but then dashed to the sideline. Stanford players now stood in shocked wonder, some on the field, most on their sideline. Stanford coaches were screaming that Garner had been down. Penalty flags littered the artificial turf. What exactly had happened? Who had won? Mass confusion engulfed the field. The roar of the stadium gave way to a puzzled quiet.

The Cal players, who had pounded Moen on the helmet and shoulder pads in celebration behind the goal post, turned and began walking onto the playing field, a bounce in their step but uncertain about the outcome. Moen sat down next to the goal post to catch his breath.

"The silence after so many minutes of wild cheering was startlingly abrupt," wrote *Sports Illustrated*'s Ron Fimrite. "The crowd had been transformed into a mute, befuddled giant."

Starkey had become hysterical while describing Moen's run. Now only slightly less frenetic, he captured the uncertainty over the play. "Will it count? The Bears have scored, but the bands are out on the field. There were flags all over the place. Wait and see what happens. We don't know who won the game. There are flags on the field. We have to see whether or not the flags are against Stanford or Cal. The Bears may have made some illegal laterals. It could be that it won't count. The Bears, believe it or not, took it all the way into the end zone. If the penalty is against Stanford, California would win the game. If it is not, the game is over, and Stanford has won. We've heard no decision yet. Everybody is milling around on the field!"

Today, the head official, Charles Moffett, would have gone to the sideline and conferred with NCAA officials elsewhere watching replays of the game. They would have scrutinized video of the play to determine whether

Garner had been down, whether Ford's lateral had been forward, and whether Howell had illegally blocked Grissum. It would have meant a long delay. But replay did not exist in 1982.

So, the six referees convened in a tight circle between the Stanford 35 and 30 to sort it out—the five laterals involving four players, the penalty flags, the Stanford band's bizarre entry onto the field, the Cal player crossing the goal line. The officials would not sort it out alone. Six Cal players, Stanford linebacker Noble, two Cal band members, and a Cal rooter in a tan jacket surrounded them. Moffett, a Pac-10 official for 22 years, took charge. He was flying partly blind, however. The Stanford band had blocked him from seeing Moen run into the end zone. He went around the circle. *Had Garner been down?* The officials' answer was no. Neither Langley nor Wolf had blown a whistle. *Had Ford's lateral been forward?* Riese had not waved it off. But the truth is he didn't know: Riese had taken his eyes off Ford at the moment of the pitch because, as he raced down the right sideline to keep up, he suddenly saw dozens of Stanford band members blocking his path. *The penalty flags?* "I have an unsportsmanlike foul against Stanford for having too many men on the field," Riese said.

"That penalty will be declined?" Moffett asked.

"Yes, it would be," Riese replied.

Gilbert and Sullivan, as in Cal's Gale Gilbert and John Sullivan, had taken several steps onto the field while holding hands during the kickoff, but that was incidental and didn't matter. Members of the Cal band at the north end of the field, far from the action, also had encroached a few steps onto the playing turf. That didn't matter, either.

"Charlie, you know the guy scored?" Riese interjected.

"What?" Moffett replied.

"Yes, the guy scored!" Riese said. "Cal scored a touchdown!"

"Then there's a touchdown!" Moffett shouted, to make sure the others heard him.

The officials heard this—and so did the interlopers surrounding them. The Cal rooter in the tan jacket wheeled around, raised his arms in triumph, and began a victory strut. The Cal players began leaping up and down as they peeled away. Listening in, Cal band bass drummer Mark Stevenson pogoed away from the referees. A roar went up from Cal fans. Moffett turned toward the press box and raised his arms into the air. Touchdown! It was now official!

So many people were congregated on the field that it was hard for spectators to spot Moffett. Weigand, however, had zeroed in on the referee, following his white hat in the crowd. Weigand, seeing Moffett signal the score, detonated the cannon again. *Boooom!* The concussion rippled through the stadium.

Reggie Camp, Cal's fearsome defensive end, had been crying on the bench, thinking the Bears had lost the Big Game, and hadn't seen the kickoff. Now he heard the cannon blast. He stood up. *What the hell?* Camp looked around wildly. Moments later, one of his teammates came by shouting. "We won! We won! We won!"

"What do you mean we won?" Camp asked.

Now he and Cal rooters understood. They had triumphed, even if they didn't quite know how. In the press box, Robert Latin pushed the buttons on a panel in front of him that controlled the scoreboard. After Latin had completed his handiwork, the scoreboard read: California 25, Stanford 20.

Now there could be no doubt. Cal fans poured onto the field. Their roars shook the old stadium like never before.

Exactly three minutes had passed between Harmon's field goal for Stanford and Moffett signaling Cal's touchdown. In that short span, Stanford's fans passed from the proverbial thrill of victory to the agony of defeat—and Cal fans went from feeling absolute heartsick to pure joy.

Upstairs in the broadcast booth, Starkey, the play-by-play announcer, let loose one final outburst of emotion. He sounded almost as unhinged as the manic broadcaster who watched the Hindenburg dirigible blow up in 1937—except that Starkey radiated astonishment, not horror: "AND THE BEARS! THE BEARS HAVE WON! THE BEARS HAVE WON! Oh my God, this is the most amazing, sensational, heart rending, exciting, thrilling finish in the history of college football! I've never seen any game like it in my life…The Stanford band just lost their team that ballgame…This place is like it's never been before! It's indescribable here…I guarantee you, if you watch college football for the rest of your life, you'll never see one like this!"

• CHAPTER 15 •

THE THRILL OF VICTORY AND THE AGONY OF DEFEAT

Referee Charles Moffett briefly stood with the other five officials on the field after declaring a game-winning Cal touchdown on the kickoff return. All hell was breaking loose around them as jubilant Cal fans poured onto the field, joining the players and bandsmen from both schools who were already there. But Moffett was a stickler for the rules. "Get a ball," he said. "We've got to kick the extra point."

"You gotta be crazy," replied James Fogltance, the field judge. "We're not going to get this kick off."

"How are we going to clear the field?" added Gordon Riese, the line judge.

Rod Gilmore, a senior cornerback for Stanford, thrust himself into the conversation. "That guy was down!" he shouted, referring to Cal's Dwight Garner. "You're taking shit away from us! We won that game!"

The improbable scene continued. A Cal tuba player brushed up against Gilmore from behind. The officials side-stepped him and, at Moffett's insistence, ran toward the south end zone for the point-after try. But when they arrived there, Moffett reconsidered. Now he felt like his touchdown signal had, as he said later, "started World War III." His colleagues were right. Attempting the extra point made no sense. They were done.

Umpire Walter Wolf turned to Fogltance. "Fogy, take your whistle off!" Wolf advised. "Let's get out of here! Fans are going to grab for your lanyard and your hat, anything they can get!" They began sprinting to the locker room at the far end of the field, 100 yards away.

Kevin Moen was sitting next to the goal post gulping in air when he heard the cannon detonate to signify Cal had won the game. As he got to his feet, most people, including his teammates, didn't know he was the hero. He ran to the mass of players and Cal fans jumping up and down in the middle of the field, celebrating. One of Moen's roommates saw him and shouted. "I don't know how, but we won!"

"I know!" Moen replied. "I scored the winning touchdown!"

"No way!" screamed the friend and resumed jumping up and down.

Up in the stands, Marsha Moen, Kevin's mom, was no longer crying. Looking down at the pandemonium on the field, she exclaimed, "That was my son!"

Above her, in the press box, Jim Simmons had been on the phone with the chairman of the Hall of Fame Bowl selection committee during the kickoff. Three minutes earlier, they thought Stanford was heading to Birmingham. Now Simmons had to break the news that Cal had lateraled the ball five times, run through the Stanford band, and had scored the winning touchdown. With the loss, Stanford now had five wins and six defeats and would stay home. The selection committee would have to invite another team to play Vanderbilt University.

Dave Newhouse, an *Oakland Tribune* sports columnist, rose from his seat and asked the two men from Birmingham for their reaction. "This happens once in a lifetime," said Simmons' colleague, Coy Collinsworth, shaking his head. "We saw the impossible."

Only three minutes earlier, Stanford president Donald Kennedy had consoled Cal athletic director Dave Maggard after what they both thought was a tough defeat for the Bears. Now Kennedy had no desire to stick around. "Let's get the hell out of here!" he told his daughter Julia, a recent Stanford grad, who had watched the game with him.

John McCasey, Cal's sports information director, had left the press box with several minutes remaining in the game. He had a key task for the athletic department once the game ended—overseeing the awarding of the Player of the Year trophy by a vice president of Home Savings & Loan, a local sponsor of Cal football. Only the Player of the Year hadn't been selected yet. That decision was up to Joe Kapp, and he had told McCasey earlier in the week that he would wait to decide until after the Big Game, the final match of the season.

McCasey was standing in the north tunnel when he watched Mark Harmon's last-second field goal for Stanford sail through the uprights directly in front of him. McCasey had planned to film the presentation in the Cal locker room. But when it looked like the Bears had lost, McCasey decided to move the little ceremony to the north tunnel, away from the dejected players. McCasey turned away from the field during the final kickoff to go upstairs and bring the camera crew and the financial exec down to the new location. When he returned a couple of minutes later, McCasey saw Cal players celebrating while fans streamed onto the field. "What's going on?" he asked.

Bob Orr, the team's trainer, was the first one to reach the north tunnel on the way up to the locker room. "What happened?" McCasey asked.

"We kicked their ass!" Orr said and kept going.

A couple of players ran by. "What happened?" McCasey asked again.

"We scored a touchdown!" they shouted.

McCasey was dumbfounded. A stream of players and coaches passed by. McCasey saw Kapp. "Coach, we won?"

"Yes!" Kapp replied.

"Well, then, who do you want to be the Player of the Year?"

"Whoever scored the touchdown! Whoever scored the touchdown!" Kapp didn't know who it was. Unbelievably, the winning coach didn't know how his team had triumphed. The Stanford band had blocked his view.

McCasey grabbed a passing player. "Who scored the touchdown?" he asked.

"Ford!" the player replied. "Mariet Ford!"

The player was wrong. But McCasey didn't know. He, the camera crew, and the Home Savings & Loan VP went in search of Ford in the locker room to award him the Player of the Year trophy, believing he had scored the winning touchdown.

Max Scheder-Bieschin and Kevin Wells, the two Stanford students locked to the Axe, had retreated to the Cardinal sideline after Moen ran into the end zone. Joining Scheder-Bieschin were two others who had run onto the field just behind them: Helene Leckman, the third Stanford student member of the Axe Committee, and Jon Erickson, the Stanford Axe supervisor. "What's happening?" Leckman asked as the officials met to sort out who had won. "I think we just lost the game," Erickson replied. Moments later, the cannon detonated. "Oh, shit!" Erickson exclaimed.

The four of them stood there in stunned silence. They knew what would happen next.

It seemed like only an instant passed before the half dozen members of the Cal Rally Committee's Axe Guard rushed up to them on the Stanford sideline. "Give me that thing!" demanded one of the Cal students. Erickson knew he had no choice. The Axe had two locks, and he had the keys to both. Erickson stood behind the trophy and tried the first key. No luck! "Get it off! Get it off!" Wells yelled. The seconds ticked by. The Cal students were crowding them. Erickson tried the other key. It worked. "Take it!" he shouted. The Axe Guard members grabbed the trophy and began running with it toward the Cal sideline.

They passed directly in front of John Elway, who was walking onto the field in disbelief at how his last game for Stanford had ended. Where Elway was going and what he might do were not clear. A young Cal rooter jumped into Elway's path. "Face! Face! Face!" the kid taunted Elway. "Face on you!" Elway somehow kept his poise and kept walking.

Cal players normally ran to the locker room immediately after the game. But on this afternoon, many stayed on the field to celebrate as joyous fans hugged them, pounded on their shoulder pads, and offered them beer and shots of liquor. Some players hoisted the Axe aloft. Others were content just to touch it. Tears of joy rolled down the cheeks of wide receiver Wes Howell.

For Cal left defensive end Byron Smith, it was payback time for the richer private school across the bay. "Fuck you!" Smith screamed as he gave the middle finger with both hands while running in front of the Stanford student section. "Fuck you! You motherfuckers ain't shit!"

Phil Neville, Chris Jones, and Steven Hinds, the three Cal fraternity brothers who left immediately after Mark Harmon's field goal, had barely gotten outside the stadium when they heard the cannon boom. "I've been here for four years," Hinds told his friends. "I've never heard the cannon go off unless we scored."

The three broke into a run to re-enter the stadium. Looking down, they saw Cal football players jumping up and down in celebration while fans were swarming onto the field. They looked up at the scoreboard. "We won!" Hinds shouted. "We won!"

The three had entered the side of the stadium where Stanford rooters were sitting. Hinds looked around at them and yelled, "You guys lost! You guys are losers!" The Stanford fans nearby were too dumbfounded to respond.

The Stanford players remained on the field, dazed and unsure what to do next. They had no doubt about what actually happened: Dwight Garner had been down! Cal had committed at least one penalty, if not several! The final lateral was forward! But the referee had signaled a touchdown, the cannon boomed, and the scoreboard registered the final score 25–20.

Paul Wiggin and his assistant coaches told the players to head to the locker room. They would decide their next step while there. The path to the visitors' locker room was unlike that of any other Pac-10 stadium. To get there, the players had to walk down a set of concrete steps near the south end zone, pass through a narrow tunnel underneath the stands, and then take two flights of stairs up. At one point, the players were exposed to the concourse just a few feet away. Cal fans hurled insults.

The players entered the cramped, antiquated locker room and sat down on the wooden benches. Behind them were old-style metal locker doors, the kind you'd see in a high school gym. Players and coaches knew how to react after a win. They knew how to react after a loss. But how do you react when you think you won, but the officials said otherwise?

Wiggin was fighting mad and told his team the result wouldn't stand. But he wasn't sure what to do—until Ray Handley, the associate head coach, drew him aside. As he was taking the elevator down from the press box minutes earlier, Handley overheard a Cal official say he was headed to the TV truck parked just below the concourse to watch a replay of the final kickoff. It was Cal's assistant sports information director, Mike Matthews, and he was going there so he could inform reporters in the press box exactly how the Bears had scored the winning touchdown. It was 1982, and it was years before people inside the stadium could turn to a scoreboard to watch an instant replay of what had just happened on the field.

Handley told Wiggin that they ought to go to the TV truck, too. "Men, keep your pads on," Wiggin told the players. "We'll be back."

Wiggin, Handley, and a couple of other Stanford coaches exited through the back door of the locker room, rushed through the concourse, down a set of steps, and banged on a windowless door on the side of the TV truck. Inside, the technicians had just finished taping the game, which had not been shown live. It would be broadcast at 11:00 PM on a local TV station, and highlight shows for Stanford and Cal would air the following day.

Cal's Matthews was inside the truck, still jotting down who had handled the ball on the final kickoff. The door burst open. "We want to see the play!" said a loud voice. In came Wiggin, followed by several assistants. They took positions just behind two production officials. No coach had ever made a similar request. But Niels Melo, who was in charge, asked a producer to cue up a replay of the final kickoff on one of the TV screens embedded in the side paneling.

"Yep!" said Handley, pounding the counter for emphasis. "He was down! He was down!" He, Wiggin, and the others watched it two more times to be sure before exiting.

On the way out, they picked up Andy Geiger, the athletic director, and Jim Fassel, the offensive coordinator. Wiggin was determined to do something he had never done before, something a coach just didn't do. He and the others pushed through the stadium concourse—where departing Cal fans were whooping it up and Stanford fans were walking out in stunned silence—to the entrance to the north tunnel. They climbed up the steps to the Cal locker room, which by now was in the midst of an uproarious celebration. Wiggin was noted for his calm, fatherly touch. He rarely swore. But if got mad—and it didn't happen often—look out!

And he was hopping mad.

McCasey, Cal's sports information director, was standing amidst the sea of blue and gold in the locker room when he saw several red jackets pushing their way toward him. "Where's the officials' locker room?" Wiggin demanded. Because of a logistical quirk at Memorial Stadium, Wiggin, Geiger, and the others had to cross through the Bears' locker room to reach the officials' quarters.

"Hey, you lost the game!" called out somebody. Wiggin paid no heed. He was on a mission. Led by McCasey, he stormed down a corridor, climbed a short set of blue stairs, and pounded on a door. Inside, the officials were sitting on wooden benches, still in their uniforms, trying to piece together exactly how the game had ended, exactly how many times Cal had lateraled the ball on the final kickoff. One of them stood up to open it. When they saw that it was Wiggin, Geiger, and the others, Moffett jumped to his feet.

Wiggin didn't wait for permission to speak. He told the officials that Garner was down, that Ford's lateral had been forward, that Cal players had encroached onto the field, too. "We need to go back onto the field and kick off again!" Wiggin said. "There's no way this can stand!"

"Coach, I'm listening. I'm listening," Moffett replied.

"Well, then, you need to get us all back on the field and re-kick!" Wiggin said. "That touchdown can't stand!"

"I'm sorry, that can't be done," Moffett said. "The game's over."

"What do you mean it's over!" Wiggin said, his voice rising and a vein sticking out from his forehead. "You got to get it right!"

"Sorry, Coach," Moffett said.

"Sorry, my ass!" Wiggin said, now shouting and turning as red as his jacket. "This is going to cost people their jobs! This is going to cost people their jobs!"

Carver Shannon, the back judge, stood up from the bench. Shannon, who had played defensive back two decades earlier with the Los Angeles Rams, wanted to be ready, just in case things turned physical.

"Coach, you're going to have leave," Moffett said. "You don't belong here."

Wiggin wasn't through, however. "You guys are a bunch of fucking idiots!" he screamed. "How can you do that?"

Now Fassel piped in. "You should have thrown a flag on Cal!" he shouted. "It should have never gone this far!"

Moffett broke in. "Coach, this is the way it is," he said. "I'm going to have to ask you to leave."

Wiggin, Geiger, Fassel, and the others backed down and headed down a corridor toward the weight room, looking for a way out where they didn't have to pass the celebrating Cal players. They saw a door ahead and went through it. Now they were on a balcony overlooking Cal alums whooping it up below. Uh oh! They quickly retreated and headed out of the locker room through a side door. McCasey thought that was symbolic of the coaching staff's ineptitude. "Now we know why John Elway never had a winning season," he said to one of the officials.

Dave Bush, one of the two *San Francisco Chronicle* reporters covering the game, was standing nearby in the Cal locker room, trying to figure out exactly how the Bears had won. He and his colleague, Al Moss, had stayed in the press box long enough to see Harmon kick the apparent winning field goal. Bush and Moss then went to take the elevator down to walk to each team's locker room. Then the ultimate happened. They missed the crazy kickoff, stuck in the elevator.

Kapp met with Bush and a scrum of reporters in the Cal locker room. How had the Bears done it? He mentioned how the players were familiar with the notion of lateraling thanks to *Grabazz*, the game of keep away that Kapp introduced on Sundays to loosen them up after the previous day's game. The Minnesota Vikings played a version of *Grabazz* during Kapp's days there in the late 1960s.

To put it simply, what would soon be known as The Play would not have happened if Kapp wasn't Cal's head coach. It was a maneuver that required the kind of never-say-die attitude and out-of-the-box thinking that epitomized Kapp's career.

In the locker room, the reporters asked about Stanford's complaints. "What's there to dispute?" Kapp asked. "It's a typical Cal–Stanford game, the finest traditional rivalry, 85 years. It's a fitting end to 100 years of Cal football." Kapp paused. "There's only one thing you can say," he said and then referred to his favorite slogan. "The Bear would not quit! The Bear would not die! Sixty minutes!"

As Kapp began to walk away, someone called out, "Coach, they're calling for you!" Kapp made his way to Pappy's Balcony, where Pappy Waldorf, the famed Bears coach during the 1950s, addressed rooters below. Kapp knew what they wanted. "I don't know how to spell it," he joked in an aside, referring to his spelling boo-boo at the bonfire rally the night before. This time Kapp wasn't taking any chances. He wouldn't spell out the entire word. Holding his arms out wide, he exhorted, "Give me a C!"

"CCC!"

"Give me an A!"

"AAA!"

"Give me an L!"

"LLL"

"Go Bears!" Kapp yelled and went back inside.

Reporters were interviewing Moen, now recognized to be the hero. Moen stood in front of his locker, still wearing his shoulder pads and game pants. A reporter asked what he thought, after receiving the final lateral, when he saw the Stanford band between him and the goal line.

"They weren't going to stop me," he said with a smile. "I just tucked it away and got in."

As the reporters drifted away, defensive coordinator Ron Lynn grabbed Moen. "You'll never have to buy a beer in any bar for the rest of your life!" Lynn said. Moen laughed at that idea.

For now, the harder stuff would do. The hero walked into the shower, still wearing his clothes, swigging from a bottle of Jack Daniel's.

J Torchio, the backup quarterback, brought a bottle of champagne to Gale Gilbert, the starter. "It was those Sunday games of *Grabazz* that did it, right?" Torchio asked. Gilbert, his voice now hoarse from yelling, grinned and nodded.

After departing the Cal locker room, Wiggin and the other Stanford coaches pushed their way back through the crush of fans still exiting the concourse and re-entered the Stanford locker room. The players had been waiting for what seemed an eternity. To a man, they believed they had won the game—or at least they should be allowed to kick off again. While cooling their heels, they could hear the triumphant Cal fans just outside, on the concourse. "Go Bears!" they heard over and over again.

And: "Fuck Stanford!"

The players looked up when Wiggin and the other coaches walked in. "Men," he said, "I've met with the officials. It's over. There's nothing we can do. Get undressed and take a shower. We're going home."

"This is bullshit!" one player yelled.

"This isn't right!" shouted another.

Nose guard Terry Jackson, feeling like something had been stolen from him, smashed his helmet against a locker door.

Garin Veris, the huge linebacker who had tormented Gilbert all day, threw a forearm shiver against another locker door.

Sitting nearby, Mike Wyman, a 6'6" defensive tackle, began to boil with rage. Wyman was a backup, but he had made one key stop in the second quarter, tackling a Cal running back for a loss on third and goal. That play forced the Bears to kick a field goal. Now, Wyman thought, the final result was wrong, terribly wrong. He stood up, paused for a second, and then charged a door a few feet away. Wyman hit it once, backed up, and slammed into it a second time, using his hips and butt for leverage. Wyman wasn't done. He charged forward a third time. This time the door tore off the hinges. Wyman held it briefly in his hands and then threw it down flat against the concrete floor. *Crash!* That got everyone's attention. "Your brother has gone berserk!" an assistant coach shouted to Mike's younger brother Dave, a linebacker. "You need to go calm him down!"

"I'm not going anywhere near him, and I recommend that you not do so either," Dave replied. He knew his brother. Mike was a great guy—unless he snapped. If he did, stay away.

Players filed into the shower room. It had six shower heads attached to ancient, exposed pipes overhead, like you might see in an old military barracks. To add to the indignity, the water was cold, and the pressure was so strong that some of the players held up a piece of cardboard to partially deflect the flow.

Reporters were normally allowed to enter the dressing room to interview Wiggin and players about 15 minutes after the game. Stanford officials kept out the press this day. When Wiggin stepped onto a stairwell just outside the locker room to meet with them, he was fighting back tears and chewing gum furiously. "The last play was illegal," he said. "We saw it dead."

Wiggin expressed hope that the Pac-10 office would overturn the result. "I think it's greatly unfair to our kids," he told the reporters. "We simply won the game. I think this is the biggest fiasco of all time. It's tragic that a Stanford–Cal game had to come down to this. In our hearts and our minds, we won the game. We know we won the game."

Elway emerged next. "This was an insult to college football," he told reporters, as he leaned against a wall, his hands stuffed into his blue jeans. "It was just a farce. [The officials] didn't have control of the whole game."

Elway paused and added, "They ruined my last game as a college football player, just like they ruined it for every senior on our team. It's a joke. I'm usually a very positive person, and I don't want to cut people down, but that really burns me up. If one of the officials did call the play dead, all he has to do is stand up and say what happened, that he made a mistake in not telling the other officials. I'm going to be thinking about this one the rest of my life. We got screwed out of it."

A photo shot from the stands during the final kickoff would emerge in a few days and show one official with his arms extended to his side, evidence, Stanford officials believed, that The Play had been blown dead. That official, Jack Langley, would say years later that he extended his arms simply to remind himself to maintain his cool.

Back at Memorial Stadium, reporters took the elevator back up to the press box to write their stories. John Crumpacker of the *San Francisco Examiner*, which had the Bay Area's biggest Sunday circulation, called his editor. They discussed the dramatic ending, and then Crumpacker asked, "How long should my story be?"

"As long as you want," replied the editor.

Hmmm, Crumpacker thought. *They never told me that before.*

One level up in the press box, Ed Gordon was putting the finishing touches on the official play sheet. Gordon, the chief statistician, had kept a running tally of plays throughout the game. Now he typed a shorthand description of how Cal scored the final touchdown. But then he had to explain why Cal hadn't kicked the extra point. "Are you kidding"? he typed. Well, that would do.

Moen's teammates had inadvertently knocked the ball from his grasp when they jumped on him in the end zone after the winning score. No one noticed—except two guys. One was Doug Cohn, the stadium worker who had gone to the south end zone to secure the pad wrapped around the goal post. In fact, Cohn had already rolled the pad up underneath his left arm—and was jumping up and down in celebration at Moen's touchdown—when he saw the ball come loose. Cohn dove onto it a split second before a Cal rooter wearing a cap and a dark jacket also attempted to get it. Cohn held onto the ball for dear life as the rooter tried to grab it from him. Seeing this, a security guard rushed over to their pile. "You won't get away with it!" the guard barked at Cohn.

"I work for Cal!" he cried out. "I got to put it away!"

The guard then pulled the rooter away from Cohn. He and the guard ran to the middle of the field until the mob prompted them to veer to the Cal sideline. There, Cohn saw Sam Gruneisen, the offensive line coach. "This is the ball for the touchdown!" Cohn said as he handed it to Gruneisen. "This is the game ball!"

Robert Stinnett left the stadium a few minutes after the game ended. As a photographer for the *Oakland Tribune*, Stinnett was just glad he had reflexively begun shooting photos as soon as he noticed commotion in front of him during the final kickoff. He was as surprised as the band members to see a blue-and-gold jersey heading toward him in the end zone. Stinnett took one photo of a Cal player leaping into the air just after crossing the goal line and another of the trombone player sprawled onto the turf after taking a hit by the Cal player, a step away from the photographer. Stinnett then snapped several photos of Cal students parading the Axe on the field and left Memorial Stadium to drive to the *Tribune's* office in downtown Oakland.

Taking the elevator to the fourth floor, Stinnett walked through the newsroom and the sports department and pushed open a door to enter the photo department. Inside the darkroom, he went through the laborious steps required to develop his film. After about 30 minutes, he had negatives that he could place against the light table. He printed the photos and dropped them onto the desk of the Sunday sports editor, Leba Hertz. Stinnett was smiling but didn't say much before going his way. Hertz took one look at the photos and knew Stinnett had struck gold. She immediately alerted the weekend editor. Stinnett's photo of Moen leaping in the air would lead the paper the next day and become *the* iconic photo of The Play.

Today, sports fans around the nation would learn immediately about an ending as wild as what happened in Berkeley. Spectators at the game would have loaded video from the final bizarre sequence from their cellphones onto their Facebook and Instagram pages. ESPN would have immediately showed replays and devoted ample airtime to analyzing in granular detail what had happened and what it meant. But the 85ᵗʰ Big Game was not televised live. Fans could only hear a live broadcast on either the Stanford or the Cal radio stations. In retrospect, then, it's not surprising what happened to Curt Wilson, a recent Stanford graduate, just after he left the stadium. A woman walking by asked him who won. "I honestly don't know," Wilson replied.

A San Francisco-based TV station, KPIX, had a cameraman filming the game, so the station was able to broadcast the first images on the 5:00 PM news. "People are saying if they live to be 1,000, they will never see a finish like that," Wayne Walker, the sports director and a former NFL linebacker, told viewers with a smile as he showed another replay of the final kickoff.

*   *   *

After Paul Wiggin, John Elway, and a couple of other players spoke to reporters, the team had no desire to stick around Memorial Stadium. It was like hanging around the scene of a crime. Cal fans taunted Stanford players as they walked to the buses, a block away. The players were given a box lunch as they boarded. The buses did not have tinted windows. One man spotted Elway and began pounding on his window. The quarterback ignored him. He thought about the run by halfback Mike Dotterer during the final minute of the game that set up what appeared to be the winning field goal. If only Dotterer had cut outside, Elway thought, he would have scored the winning touchdown. Like his teammates, Elway couldn't accept the final result. Perhaps, he thought, the league somehow could still give Stanford the victory.

For the visiting team, driving away from Memorial Stadium was always complicated because the buses had to pass through narrow residential streets backed up with post-game traffic. The buses edged onto Prospect Street at the south end of the stadium, on Greek Row. Celebrating students hoisted their beers aloft in mock salute and yelled insults at Stanford as the buses inched past. The players couldn't escape the abuse, even after they traveled a few more blocks onto a four-lane street. They were stopped at a traffic light alongside a van with two teenage Cal rooters inside. One of them slid open their back window. "We kicked your ass!" they sneered. "We kicked your ass!"

Dennis Engel, the right guard, was sitting directly opposite the van. A teammate handed him a can of Coke. Engel vigorously shook the can, leaned out his window, and popped open the top just outside their window. The liquid splattered the boys. It was a small victory. But none of the players said anything or took joy in Engel's testy reaction. They all rode back to Stanford in silence and in deep despair, replaying in their minds what had happened, sure that the officials had robbed them.

When Kevin Moen and Cal players began celebrating in the end zone 45 minutes earlier, members of the Stanford band had finished scattering off the playing field onto the sideline. When referee Charles Moffett signaled a minute later that Cal had scored the game-winning touchdown, many of them realized they had played some role in the heartbreaking defeat—they had been on the field during the touchdown run, after all—but like so many others, they didn't know exactly what had happened. The band members could see Stanford fans on their feet in the stands, trying to comprehend how their team had lost the Big Game. The band had a long-standing tradition of playing a post-game concert for fans, no matter how many remained and no matter the result of the game. Band members took pride in rocking out, even when the team lost. But this afternoon was different. The band was seemingly part of the defeat. Somehow, the band had been in the wrong place at the wrong time.

Still, band director Arthur Barnes cued up the traditional school hymn, "Hail Stanford Hail." Afterward, drum major Disco Ray Gruenewald blew his whistle to play one of the band's favorites, "Livin' in the USA." But band members couldn't muster their usual zest and energy. Besides, Cal students were crowding them, taunting them. Disco Ray shut down the post-game concert after only a few songs.

Band members walked out of Memorial Stadium via the south tunnel, headed to their buses. They immediately ran into the Cal frat boys and sorority girls, drunk and delirious, on Prospect Street. "Thank you, Stanford band!" they heard time and time again. Disco Ray had not run onto the field during the final kickoff and had only a dim understanding of how the game had ended. *What did we do this time?* he wondered.

"You guys are the best band in the world!" sneered a frat boy.

"Hey, thanks for coming to the game!" mocked another.

A Cal rooter proffered a beer to trombone player Lou Casagrande. He declined.

Band bus rides were normally filled with laughter, limericks, and yells made up on the spot. One bus was silent. On the other, Hal Mickelson, a senior attorney for Hewlett-Packard who had spent years as the band's hilarious pregame and halftime announcer, was telling those seated near him that the band was in deep shit, that the band stood to become the scapegoat for the loss. Uncle Hal, as band members knew him, couldn't resist turning to dark humor. "I can see the lead headline in *The Stanford Daily*," he said in his booming voice. "Band Shak burned by students."

Others joined in. "John Hinckley bound to be Stanford band manager"— Hinckley had nearly assassinated President Ronald Reagan the year before.

"Three band members discovered to be in the SLA"—the Symbionese Liberation Army, the domestic terrorist group that had kidnapped newspaper heiress Patty Hearst in 1974.

"Drum major from Stanford band found to have received bribe from Joe Kapp."

Jim Kohn, the saxophone player who had led the charge onto the field, felt safe for the moment on the bus. But he was deathly afraid that his conehead accessory had made him too conspicuous. He had ditched it as soon as he ran off the field, and he tore off the "I heart France" message he had taped to the back of his red jacket. Now, on the bus, Kohn looked out the window and wondered if he might be arrested as soon as they returned to Stanford—or would there be a knock on his dorm room door later from a university official with the news that he had been expelled?

Band manager John Howard, who dealt regularly with the administration, had worked hard that year to keep the band out of trouble and thought his approach had succeeded in winning back favor among students, alums, and his two most important patrons, athletic director Andy Geiger and university president Donald Kennedy. Everything had gone well, until the final four seconds of the final game, Howard reasoned. Asked by someone exactly what had happened, Howard didn't have the full story either. What would Geiger and Kennedy think? Howard, too, thought he might face expulsion.

Back at Stanford, band members slunk off the buses and tossed their uniforms into a pile in the Band Shak. Nobody stuck around for the traditional post-Big Game festivities there. Gary Tyrrell stored his trombone and walked across campus in the dark to his fraternity, Kappa Sigma. Tyrrell thought he was still just an anonymous member of the band. A fraternity brother opened the locked door and offered a hint to Tyrrell that life for him was about to change. "Gary, was that you who got hit?"

Arthur Barnes, the band's director, went to dinner at a restaurant in Berkeley that evening. A group of Stanford fans were toasting the team's victory at the next table. Barnes leaned over and asked, "Did you stay until the end of the game?"

"No," they said.

"Stanford lost the game," Barnes told them.

There was dead silence—for a moment. Then: "What? What? Are you crazy?"

Barnes said Cal ran back the final kickoff, but he couldn't explain all of the details.

Meanwhile, Richey Neuman, Howard, and a group of Stanford band members decided to head to Ramona's, a downtown Palo Alto establishment that served good pizza and cold beer. At least they could drown their sorrows at the restaurant. They were about to enter Ramona's when a boy about 12 years old stopped them. "You guys are in the band," he said.

They nodded, not sure what would come next.

What ensued was a low blow. "You guys lost the game!" the kid sneered. "You guys are fuckers!"

The bandsmen were speechless as they walked into Ramona's. When they sat down, Neuman, a senior who played mellophone, reflected on what had just happened. "If this kid says that," he told the others, "imagine what the rest of the world thinks of us."

Naturally, the worst day ever for the Stanford band had been the best day ever for the Cal band. The pregame show had been flawless, with all band members hitting their marks on the field as they spelled a Capital C, Bears, and a script Cal. They ended the halftime show with a surprise— band members pulled sticks from out of their vests and tapped them while doing a choreographed dance. And then the Stanford band helped cost the Cardinal the game! Cal band members jumped for joy on the field afterward, along with players and students. When they performed their usual post-game concert, the fans wouldn't leave—so they played and played and played. Finally, Robert Briggs, the band's director, signaled for them to march back to the center of campus. They stopped at a couple of fraternity houses along the way, their music drawing raucous crowds. It was a great day to be a Cal Bear.

The band reached Sather Gate and gathered around Briggs. He had joined the band as a freshman in 1947 and had essentially never left, eventually becoming band director in 1971. Now he talked about Big Game day, how the Cal band had done everything right, and the Stanford band had done everything wrong. "I've never been prouder of the Cal band," he said. His voice broke. He couldn't speak any more. The 163 band members were silent for a few seconds. Then a band member spoke up. "Three cheers for Mr. Briggs!" he said.

"Hip hip hooray!" the band members yelled.

"Hip hip hooray!

"Hip hip hooray!"

The band members went off to party late into the evening. So did the football team. Richard Rodgers and John Sullivan, two defensive backs, went to a liquor store to buy a bottle of vodka. While there, they heard an announcer on the TV set behind the counter say, "You'll never believe what happened in the Big Game today," before showing a replay of the final kickoff. It was the first time that Rodgers—who lateraled the ball twice—saw it. He and Sullivan ended up at Memorial Stadium, late that night. They saw a group of fraternity brothers on the field, re-enacting the laterals in a fit of drunken hilarity. Sullivan and Rodgers laughed and laughed.

Many Cal rooters stayed up to watch the taped delay broadcast of the game on Channel 44, beginning at 11:00 PM. After the glorious winning score, they all jumped up and toasted the most improbable of victories. One group of Bears players, partying at McNally's Irish Pub on College Avenue in Oakland, toasted each drink and then threw the glasses into the brick fireplace.

Yes, indeed. It was a great day to be a Cal Bear.

• CHAPTER 16 •

THE CONTROVERSY
CONTINUES

On the day after the game, Joe Kapp's home phone wouldn't stop ringing. Word of Cal's improbable last-second triumph had spread throughout the country the old-fashioned way—through newspaper articles, phone calls, radio news, and some TV broadcasts. Brent Musburger introduced the play to his national audience by showing it twice that Sunday on CBS' top-rated pregame show, *The NFL Today*, which he hosted. Sportswriters, TV producers, radio announcers, former teammates, longtime friends—all called Kapp wanting to hear how Cal had pulled it off. Kapp spoke into one of the bulky, cordless phones from the era that allowed him to roam around the house as long as he didn't stray too far from the phone's base. Because of the calls, he didn't get to bed until late that night.

On Monday morning, two days after the game, a houseguest named Ned Averbuck offered to drive Kapp to the Berkeley campus. Averbuck and Kapp had played basketball together at Cal in the late 1950s and remained close. On the drive over, they talked about the game and the immediate aftermath. "Did you see Elway's comments after the game?" Averbuck asked his friend. "He said that the officials 'ruined' his last college game! What sour grapes!"

Kapp was silent for a few seconds. "Did I say anything to you about the Stanford drive before The Play?" Kapp finally asked.

"No," Averbuck replied.

"I've been telling every journalist to look at that final drive," Kapp said. When they arrived at Cal, Kapp insisted that Averbuck accompany him inside to watch the fourth-and-17 pass completion. An equipment manager wheeled in a little portable TV and cued up the video.

"Watch this," Kapp told Averbuck. He held a remote control in his hand, replaying the video twice. "Watch this pass!" Kapp said. "Watch his feet! Look at the release of the ball! He put the ball where the receiver couldn't drop it!"

Kapp paused as they turned off the TV. "Did you just see that? That is the greatest quarterback of a college football team I have ever seen!" He paused again and added, "They made only one mistake. They celebrated too early. They went against everything we've been taught. I understand the young man's disappointment. I really do. Because what he did was magnificent. I can't take that away from him."

Averbuck asked Kapp whether he voted for Georgia running back Herschel Walker for the Heisman Trophy. "I proudly voted for John Elway," Kapp said.

"You mean you didn't vote for Herschel Walker?" Averbuck asked.

"Ned," Kapp replied, "take Herschel Walker off Georgia, and they're still pretty damn good. You take John Elway off Stanford? We would have beaten them by a lot."

A little later that day, the Axe reappeared in public during a noon rally at Sproul Plaza in the middle of the Berkeley campus. Naturally, Cal students remained ecstatic after Saturday's victory, and members of the Rally Committee's Axe Guard were more than happy to supercharge the celebration by bringing the trophy out of its hiding place. The Cal Straw Hat Band played spirit songs, and everyone reveled in the Big Game triumph. Afterward, the Axe Guard and the band paraded around campus, bursting into lecture halls to display the return of their prize. Students loved it. Even serious professors didn't mind the interruption.

Controversy over whether Cal had scored a legitimate touchdown continued to cast a cloud over the Bears' victory, at least in the eyes of some. John Crumpacker gave credence to Stanford's argument in a story published in the *San Francisco Examiner* on Monday. "Careful inspection of the kickoff on video tape in ultra-slow motion shows that [Dwight] Garner's progress was definitely halted by four Stanford tacklers, and his knee appeared to hit the Astroturf a fraction of a second before he lateraled back to [Richard] Rodgers at the Cal 48," reported Crumpacker, who, as a Cal graduate was no Stanford partisan. "At best, Garner's lateral was simultaneous to his knee hitting the ground. Regardless, the play was not whistled dead."

Crumpacker quoted Paul Wiggin, still angry but calmer than on Saturday. "He was stopped, held, turned back and down on his knees and then lateraled," Wiggin said. "It's too bad the game had to be determined by the officials. I know of no appeal. Andy [Geiger] knows of no appeal, but the damage is done. The bowl game is out, a winning season is out and probably some honors for John Elway are out. It was a very costly play for Stanford's football program."

On Sunday, Geiger appealed the call to the Pac-10. He knew his chances of overturning the result were slim to none, but he still had to try. A retired referee working for the Pac-10 had already backed up the officials in his post-game report. "A very well worked ball game," wrote Chad Reade. The form included a box to indicate the type of game it had been. Reade checked the "routine" box, and added in an enormous understatement, "except for last 4 seconds." Reade wrote that the six officials believed that Garner "was still squirming with the possibility of still going" when he lateraled the ball. Reade did not address whether Mariet Ford's final lateral had been forward.

On Monday, Wiles Hallock, the Pac-10's executive director, did not even address those two issues. His one-page statement only acknowledged that Cal had four players—not the required five—within five yards of the restraining area for the final kickoff. But, Hallock added, the official was supposed to tell Cal to move up a player to get to five. It was not something that would draw a flag and force a re-kick. "The official," who was Jack Langley, "was subject only to human imperfection, imperfection under circumstances even the least charitable might be expected to understand. All officials and those responsible for officiating feel as deeply as the participants affected the impact of their human frailty on the outcome of games."

Hallock added a last word. "This incredible final play of the 1982 Big Game and the scrutiny it has received apart from its uniqueness provide proof…that officiating is an element not to be set apart from but always considered as part of the game," he wrote. "That's one of the reasons why the Pac-10 Conference permits no protests in the sports of football and basketball."

* * *

For almost 20 years, the Stanford band had enjoyed a charmed existence after going on strike in 1963 and becoming a scatter band that played rock 'n' roll. Sure, conservative alums and university officials regularly pined for a traditional outfit, but students and the outside world mostly loved their act. National publications typically wrote reverential reviews of the band. But now they were about to become a punching bag. "Stuff this in yer trombone," read the lead headline in Sunday's *San Jose Mercury News*, above Robert Stinnett's photo showing Kevin Moen's euphoric leap in the end zone. The photo didn't show what happened a split-second later—Moen bowling over trombone player Gary Tyrrell, who remained unknown that Sunday morning as he walked by the university's Tresidder Memorial Student Union after attending Catholic Mass at Memorial Church. *Uh, oh!* Tyrrell thought when he saw the newspaper in the vending machine. He put in six quarters to buy two copies and then hurried back to his fraternity. Tyrrell figured he'd better lay low. Besides, as an industrial engineering major, he had plenty of homework. He hid out in the library for the rest of the day. Afterward, Tyrrell learned that reporters had been calling the Band Shak looking for him. He didn't return any calls. He wanted the whole mess to blow over.

Fans, however, were having fun at the band's expense. "That was the first time I ever saw a tuba player leading the interference on a touchdown—or on any other play," a rooter told the *San Francisco Chronicle*. "It appeared to me that the weakest part of Stanford's defense was the woodwinds."

But others took the outcome as an opportunity to blast the band. "Over the seasons the Stanford band has offered more than a modicum of originality," wrote Art Spander, the lead sports columnist for the *San Francisco Examiner*. "The solo trumpet version of the national anthem was special.

Many of the halftime shows were clever. Against USC a couple of seasons back, one musician carried an oversized report card depicting the subject matter and grades for the 'typical' Trojan football player. Good, clean fun is what they used to call it. Now, seemingly every stunt has a double entendre. They've become the 'Animal House' of music. At one game several members dropped their britches. One of the administrators should have given them a good spanking. Or the word that this sort of behavior is not only juvenile but stupid."

Kevin Starr, a noted historian who had obtained a doctorate from Harvard and a master's afterward from Cal, wrote a weekly column for the *Examiner*. To him, the Cal and Stanford bands represented a larger dynamic in society, with his view clearly reflecting his own up-from-the-bootstraps rise out of poverty. "The University of California at Berkeley marching band emanates an atmosphere of standards, seriousness, and respect for its audience," Starr wrote. "Attired in traditional uniforms, the Cal band executes a series of musical and marching maneuvers that are the result of long hours of patient practice. In every way possible—the precision of its maneuvers, the selection and performance of its music, the demeanor of its membership, its high standards of conducting—the Cal band says to its audiences: we are university students who respect ourselves, respect Cal and the opportunities this great university offers, and most importantly we respect you, the people of California, whose taxes make this great university possible.

"The Stanford band, by contrast, each time its spells out an obscene word on the field with a certain disturbing pre-pubescent adolescent preoccupation, each time it performs music in a slipshod manner, each time, in short (to use a '50s term) it RFs the public, communicates the exact opposite sort of message. The Stanford band says, in effect, we are the sons and daughters of Privilege, or at least we are aspiring to become the sons and daughters of Privilege, and we will therefore conduct ourselves as we think that the spoiled children of Privilege conduct themselves, with what we consider amusing brattiness."

But not everyone turned on the band. Art Rosenbaum, the longtime sports editor of the *San Francisco Chronicle* and a columnist, wrote that he missed the final five-lateral extravaganza because he had set out for the Stanford locker room, sure they had won the game. "I empathize with the Stanford band," Rosenbaum wrote. "I thought the game should have been over, too."

That was Andy Geiger's view as well. "Everybody thought the game was over except the officials," said Stanford's athletic director. "Hell, both teams were on the field; the Cal band was on the field, too. Why should our band be singled out? They showed an honest and exuberant excitement. Unfortunately, they had a premature celebration."

That premature celebration, of course, was followed by a deep letdown, the lowest of lows at Stanford. And not just among the bandsmen. Members of the football team remained in the dumps on the day after the game. Two backups, Ken Orvick and Jim Clymer, were trying to ease their pain by downing cans of Coors Light at the Delta Tau Delta fraternity where they, Elway, and other football and baseball players lived. Orvick and Clymer agreed that the referees had robbed them of victory the day before. They had to do something spectacular in return. As they washed down the suds, Orvick and Clymer hatched a plan. They would grab a couple of teammates, drive across the bay, sneak into Memorial Stadium, and cut the script *Cal* out of the Astroturf. They would drop it on the front porch at Paul Wiggin's home as a form of war booty. They thought it was a brilliant plan. Now all they needed were the necessary tools. Orvick, Clymer, and the two teammates stopped at a Shell gas station on the Stanford campus and convinced the friendly attendant to lend them what they needed—knives, pliers, and a saw. They set off for Berkeley. It was about 8:00 PM, or a bit more than 24 hours after the defeat the day before.

The four parked near Memorial Stadium. One of the teammates stayed with the car. He would be the getaway driver. Orvick, Clymer, and Tom Nye, a backup guard, walked around the stadium. It was cold, dark, and rainy, and it seemed deserted. Perfect. They found a good spot and climbed over an eight-foot fence. So far, so good. The three walked into the stadium and looked around. No one was in sight. Approaching the Cal logo at midfield, they pulled out the knives, only to discover that the Astroturf had been glued to the slab of concrete underneath. Cutting through the turf was a bit like trying to cut through shoe leather with a butter knife. After a difficult half hour, they concluded that they couldn't do it at all.

Well, the three hadn't driven all the way to Berkeley to come away empty-handed. What could they do instead? Someone suggested they cut down the goal posts. Yeah, someone else agreed, that would be good revenge! They grabbed the tools, ran 50 yards, and began sawing the goal post. They had cut in only one-eighth of an inch when the saw broke. *Damn! What now?* Still determined to do something, they climbed the stadium stairs to the press box. Maybe they could claim a souvenir from there. The door was locked. The hapless vandals were getting nowhere.

Then Orvick, Clymer, and Nye heard a police walkie talkie in the stadium concourse below. They had been spotted! Lying flat under the bleachers, they saw a police car drive onto the field. They were wet and cold—and now their escapade seemed more hare-brained than brilliant. Plus, they faced the real possibility they'd be caught. But after a while, the coast seemed clear. They crept out of the stands, onto the concourse, and ran out an open gate to their car, high-tailing it out of Berkeley. They wouldn't be able to deliver the Cal logo to Coach Wiggin on his front porch after all.

As for the coach, the loss left him heartsick. More than anything else, Wiggin felt badly for his players. But he couldn't do anything else. On the Wednesday after the game, he and his family flew east. His wife Carolynn was glad they had made plans to leave town for the Thanksgiving break. *The change in scenery would do her husband good,* she thought. Their destination was Williamsburg, Virginia, home to Colonial Williamsburg, a historic district and living-history museum where actors in period costume depicted daily Colonial life. The Wiggins wanted to show a corner of American history to their daughters and a Spanish exchange student staying with them. The family was standing in line to enter a museum exhibit when the coach felt a tap on his broad shoulder. Wiggin turned around and saw a short man standing with his wife and two kids. "Are you the guy who coached the team that was beaten by that play?" he asked.

"Yes, I am," Wiggin said, ever polite.

"I thought so!" said the man, turning to his family.

Wiggin turned back to Carolynn and muttered, "We can't even come to a place like Williamsburg and get away from it."

• CHAPTER 17 •

THE FINAL ACT

In a long-standing tradition, Stanford students ended the school week at Memorial Auditorium, the largest indoor performance space on campus, watching a movie no longer screening at theaters. It was called Sunday Night Flicks, with shows at 7:00 PM and 9:30 PM. The cost: $1.50.

A junior economics major named Adams Berns attended the 7:00 PM showing on November 21, 1982, the night after the Big Game. Like a number of other Stanford students, Berns brought a sheaf of paper and took a seat in the balcony. Berns was one of the students who, before the movie began, carefully folded sheets into paper airplanes that he let fly in hopes they would reach the stage down below. It was such a popular ritual that hundreds of students typically arrived well before the movie began to cheer those who landed their airplanes on the stage. It was a moment of glory for those students.

That night, however, Berns had other things on his mind than just making paper airplanes. He was co-editor of *Cardinal Today*, a football game-day supplement published by *The Stanford Daily*. That role had landed Berns in the press box for the Big Game the day before. Were it not for the unwritten rule that forbade cheering in the press box, Berns would have whooped up during Stanford's amazing last-minute drive, highlighted by John Elway's fourth-and-17 completion for a first down and the apparent winning field goal that followed.

Like other Stanford rooters, Berns was convinced that Dwight Garner's knee had been down on the final kickoff and that the final lateral by Mariet Ford had been forward, making it illegal. But, observing protocol, Berns didn't dare voice his thoughts there in the press box. "They'll never allow the play," he said to himself immediately afterward. Like other Stanford rooters, he was dumbfounded by the referees' decision a minute later to allow the kickoff return and rule it the game-winning touchdown.

The movie began at Memorial Auditorium, but Berns could not stop thinking about how the referees had stolen the game from Stanford. He wanted to do something about it. But what?

Then Berns remembered an old front page tacked to the wall inside *The Daily's* newsroom. He had seen it a million times. It was the front page of a special edition of *The Daily Californian*, published on November 21, 1975, the day before that year's Big Game. "NCAA Nixes Rose Bowl; Bears Back on Probation," screamed the lead headline.

"'What a crazy decision,'" Cal coach Mike White was quoted as saying, "his voice cracking with emotion. 'The team is ready to call it quits right now. But we'll come back. I have faith in my guys.'"

The newspaper was actually a fake produced by *The Stanford Daily* staffers.

Watching the Sunday night flick, Berns wondered whether the current *Daily* staff could pull off a similar stunt. By the time the movie ended, he had made up his mind: *By hook or by crook, I'm going to get this done. This will be so funny. It will be a way to get some revenge over Cal.*

Berns called his best friend, a sophomore named Mark Zeigler, who was *The Daily's* features editor. Zeigler had attended the game with his dorm mates and also believed that the referees had jobbed Stanford. They agreed to meet the following day at *The Daily*.

On Monday, sitting in the sports department's office, in the rear of the newsroom, Berns outlined his plan to Zeigler. They would produce a special four-page edition of *The Daily Californian* that they would distribute Wednesday morning on the Berkeley campus. The spoof newspaper would report the NCAA had awarded the victory to Stanford. "We got to do this," Berns implored Zeigler.

Zeigler demurred. He had a couple of tests coming up and a term paper due. "Do you know how much work it would require?" he asked Berns.

"Look, 30 years from now, when we're sitting on my yacht in the Greek Islands, we won't remember the midterms we failed," Berns rejoined. "But we will remember *The Daily Cal* we produced."

Zeigler relented. "Okay, I'm in," he said. "I'm sold."

Berns needed the approval of *The Daily's* editor, a senior named Richard Klingler. He was a by-the-books sort, not one prone to pushing the envelope. Klingler would have never fit in with the Stanford band. He would, however, go on to be a Rhodes scholar at Oxford and serve as a White House counsel to president George W. Bush.

Klingler expressed his doubts to Berns. Publishing a fake newspaper was contrary to *The Daily's* core mission to publish accurate and meaningful information, Klingler remarked. "Are we perpetrating fraud on readers?" he asked. Klingler also wondered whether Berns and the paper could pull it off since it was late in the school year, a time of high stress, and on the eve of the Thanksgiving break.

Another person joined the conversation. He was an adult, which gave him gravitas. Tom Mulvoy, 40, was a deputy managing editor at *The Boston Globe* who was spending the year on a journalism fellowship at Stanford. But Mulvoy was the kind of newsman who couldn't stay away from the newsroom, so he dropped in at *The Daily's* offices from time to time to impart ideas and advice to the young staffers. Mulvoy had gone to *The Daily* on the Monday after the Big Game in 1982 to write a story for *The Globe* about the incredible ending that he had witnessed.

Now a hesitant Klingler asked Mulvoy if the staff should proceed with the parody. "Go for it," Mulvoy advised him. "If you don't, you'll kick yourself in 20 years." Klingler thought he had a good point.

The Daily operated independently of the university, so Klingler didn't need the approval of administration officials. But what about the potential legal ramifications? Klingler called Hal Mickelson, best known as the Stanford band's announcer, but also a member of *The Daily's* corporate board of directors and a respected attorney. "I won't tell you not to do it," Mickelson responded.

That was enough for Klingler. He greenlighted the project.

Klingler and Berns decided they should produce the hoax in secret, even keeping it from the newspaper staff. Berns' main conspirators would be Zeigler and Tony Kelly, the paper's entertainment editor. "You are not to tell anybody—friends or family," Berns stressed.

Berns sat at the sports editor's desk while Zeigler sat in a chair facing him as they riffed various ideas. Kelly, who was sitting in his cubicle several feet away, repeatedly heard the two break into laughter. Berns and Zeigler stayed up most of Monday night to write the spoof.

The Boston Globe's Mulvoy wrote the lead front-page story, using every sports cliché in the book. The article would be headlined, "NCAA awards Big Game to Stanford." A subhead would read: "Three days later, it's 20–19."

A page four article would say the NCAA had overturned Saturday's result because of Rule 65, Section C of the group's amended bylaws. Mulvoy helpfully invented those bylaws, which were also printed on page four of the phony edition and said the NCAA's "Oversight Committee on Athletics" could reverse an outcome if officials "have reason to believe that an injustice has been done to a member institution by virtue of official negligence, incompetence or inadvertence."

It was a nice touch.

Zeigler penned a front-page story headlined, "Decision stuns Joe Kapp."

Zeigler began the story with these words: "The phone rang a dozen times before a weary Joe Kapp answered it." The Cal coach was awakened with the news of the NCAA ruling, the article reported. "All the shocked Kapp could muster was a slow, shocked 'Oh my God, oh my God.'"

Kelly contributed an editorial headlined, "Bears 25, Snots 20." Impersonating an outraged staffer from *The Daily Californian*, he wrote, "We were robbed, pure and simple, and we shouldn't feel sorry about saying so."

Berns wrote three letters to the editor and signed them with the names of three of the Big Game referees.

The photo editor doctored a real photograph, which showed Stanford band members trying to get off the field as Kevin Moen and Cal players raced by on their way to the end zone. The editor spliced in a photo of a referee signaling the play was over.

Berns and Zeigler added authenticity by including the bylines of *The Daily Californian* staffers, but they changed a letter or two to make sure no one could accuse them of going too far. Sports editor Bill Kunz became "Bill Kuns." Editor Daniel Woo became "Dan Wo." Publisher Mandalit del Barco became "Mandalit Embargo."

In the smallest possible font at the bottom of page two, a "Fictitious Business Name Statement" revealed it was "a prank."

Given their proximity to leading tech companies, *The Stanford Daily* had a sophisticated computer system for the era. This allowed them to easily produce the typeface of *The Daily Californian* and mimic their masthead, headline type, and volume number.

At one point on Tuesday, Kelly realized they had a hole in the newspaper's layout. They came up with a phony ad that purported to be from the student association. It called for an "ALL CAMPUS RALLY" to "protest the NCAA's Big Game decision," at noon in Sproul Plaza.

It was another nice touch.

Berns, Zeigler, Klingler, Kelly, and a half dozen others were gathered at *The Daily* at about 4:30 AM on Wednesday when the fake newspaper came back from the printer. They admired their handiwork in the predawn hour and drove to Cal. There, they set off in teams to place the "extra" edition on the front porches of fraternities and sororities on Greek Row and in *The Daily Californian's* blue newspaper bins scattered around campus and downtown Berkeley.

Berns and Zeigler, the lead conspirators, were anxious. What happened if they got caught just as they were getting started, and all their work went for naught? They also wondered: *would Cal's students even be able to find the spoof amidst that day's edition of* The Daily Californian?

Here the hoaxers got lucky. *The Daily Californian* was publishing a special Thanksgiving-eve edition packed with 36 pages and featuring color photos on the front page. All of this required extra work, so the newspaper was printed late and hadn't yet been distributed when the Stanford students placed 7,000 bogus editions in the blue bins.

The Stanford Daily staffers stuck around to see the reaction to their ruse.

Cal students began showing up on their way to class at 8:00 AM. Sitting on a bench at Sproul Plaza, Zeigler repeatedly saw students grab the newspaper, stop short in their tracks, and then look around blankly. *The NCAA had overturned Cal's amazing victory!??!*

One student put her hand to her mouth in disbelief. Two others began crying. A male student expressed outrage and wrung his hands. "This is bullshit!" he said.

"They can't do this!" shouted backup running back Scott Smith as he scanned a copy. "They can't take away this win!"

"Oh, my God!" said defensive tackle Rich Stachowski when he read the lead headline.

"There's no way this can stand!" an outraged Tim Smith, the long snapper, told a couple of buddies. "They can't do this!"

One of Gary Plummer's roommates picked up a copy, found a pay phone, and called him at their apartment with the news. "There's no way!" shouted Plummer, the starting nose guard. "That can't be real!"

"It's clearly real!" the roommate told him. Plummer felt crushed.

Dennis Cohen, the Cal band's student manager, took several copies to the band's rehearsal hall underneath Sproul Plaza. "We were robbed!" one angry band member exclaimed.

Another tried to calm him down. "It's just a game," she said.

Outside linebacker Ron Rivera grabbed a newspaper in Sproul Plaza. "I can't believe they've done this!" he said to himself. "What the hell?" He headed to the athletic department in a half-trot, wanting answers.

Dwight Garner's heart dropped when he saw the newspaper. Garner had mostly sat on the bench during Saturday's game. But he had been at the center of the most controversial play when a gang of Stanford defenders tackled him on the final kickoff. Thinking he was down and that they now had won, Stanford players and band members began racing onto the field to celebrate—only no referee blew the play dead, and Garner lateraled the ball away. Seconds later, Kevin Moen raced through the Stanford band, scored the winning touchdown, and flattened trombone player Gary Tyrrell. Or so it seemed.

Had the NCAA now overturned the result? Garner rushed to the athletic department to find out what happened.

There, he found Coach Kapp. He set Garner and the other players straight. "I recognized it for what it was—good college humor," Kapp later told the *Oakland Tribune*.

One person who knew the edition was fake right away was Marty Rabkin, general manager of *The Daily Californian*. He grabbed an armful of the phony papers and told a reporter from the *Peninsula Times Tribune*, "I think it's in real bad taste, but the timing is particularly good for a jack-assed stunt like this."

But even as Rabkin was holding onto the stack of prank papers, students came up to him to snatch a copy.

Staffers for *The Daily Californian* were dispatched to collect the remaining bogus newspapers. By then, *The Stanford Daily* staffers, feeling triumphant, were driving back to campus. Word quickly spread of their exploit. Stanford students rushed to *The Daily* to obtain a copy. The newspaper helped alleviate the mood of despair on campus.

Stanford president Donald Kennedy called the newsroom and asked to speak to the person behind the prank. Berns grew anxious when he got on the line with the university president. Not to worry. Kennedy said he loved the parody and congratulated Berns.

The spoof became big news in the Bay Area. The *Oakland Tribune* called it "a masterful hoax." The *San Francisco Chronicle* published a front-page article on it the following day.

The fake newspaper, the *Chronicle* reported, gave Stanford "a soothing last laugh."

No doubt.

But the bigger laugh would always remain with their Bay Area rival. Stanford players, students, and alums could say what they might, and they said plenty. Within weeks after the 1982 game, Stanford's sentiments were reflected in what appeared in the glass case where the Axe resided at the university's Tresidder Union. In the empty space, Stanford placed a giant screw.

In the following years, whenever Stanford possessed the Axe, the people in charge of the Axe would change the little plaque that gave the score for the 1982 game. The altered version would read: Stanford 20, Cal 19.

But none of that changed the final result. As the inimitable Kapp proclaimed, "The Bear would not quit. The Bear would not die." The California Bears won the 1982 Big Game 25–20—and so the last laugh, which is always the best laugh, went to UC Berkeley.

EPILOGUE

Kevin Moen caught the final lateral and stormed through the Stanford band at Cal's Memorial Stadium. Only one thing stood between him and a clear path through the end zone: a red-jacketed band member toting a trombone and armed for battle with a white hard hat. "Oh, no, here we go again," Gary Tyrrell exclaimed.

It was a humorous reenactment 39 years later, starring Moen and Tyrrell on an ESPN program hosted by Eli Manning, the former NFL quarterback. This time, Manning spared Tyrrell from a bruising hit by Moen. Wearing a Stanford bandsman's uniform and shouting, "I can't watch this," Manning shoved Tyrrell aside with one hand without dropping the baritone he held with the other.

A moment later, viewers saw Manning flat on the ground, as if he had taken the brunt of the Cal man's charge. "Sorry, Eli," Moen said as he extended a hand to lift up the faux bandsman. "When I see brass, I go into beast mode."

Tyrrell stood to the side, looking relieved. "I'm just glad I wasn't on the receiving end this time," he said with a smile.

In his program, Manning called The Play "the most fantastic finish in the history of college football." I describe it a little differently. I call it the wildest finish ever to a college football game. What tops it? Doug Flutie's Hail Mary touchdown to beat the University of Miami in 1984? Auburn's Kick-Six game-winning return of a missed Alabama field goal in 2013? No. Those were extraordinary and memorable plays. But the dozens of former football players and coaches I interviewed for this book all agree that The

Play remains the wildest ending or, as Manning put it, "the most fantastic finish."

It was so wild and fantastic that one thing can be said confidently: it will never ever be repeated.

Tens of thousands of words have been written about the zany ending of the 85th Big Game in Berkeley on November 20, 1982. A couple of thoughts come to mind for me. The Play serves as a reminder that in sports, as in life, there are no guarantees. The Play also shows that in sports, as in life, almost anything is possible, no matter how improbable. It *can* happen.

Today, you can look back in wonder at one thing: in 1982, it took The Play a day or two to become famous the old-fashioned way—through newspapers, TV news, radio reports, and word of mouth. Now, of course, an unbelievable football finale would go viral within seconds thanks to digital media.

Back then, Cal fans immortalized The Play on T-shirts and posters, and anyone fortunate enough to have been at the game relishes telling their memories of that day even decades later. The Play remains a bright, shining moment in the history of Cal football, especially because the team has enjoyed so few of those moments over the past 60 years. The Bears still haven't returned to the Rose Bowl since Joe Kapp quarterbacked them there for the 1959 game.

For Stanford, it was arguably the most ignominious defeat in the university's sports history. For decades afterward, Stanford players and fans continued to blame the referees for the loss, insisting that Dwight Garner's knee was down and that Mariet Ford's final lateral was forward. Most of the Stanford players on the field during the final kickoff have yet to come to terms with the final result four decades later.

Tom Briehl, a backup linebacker, was L-1 on Stanford's kickoff team, just to the left of the kicker. After graduation, he went on to sell pacemakers and defibrillators for Boston Scientific in Scottsdale, Arizona. "It's still a devastating loss," said Briehl, one of several Stanford players who tackled Ford. "It's still a hard pill to swallow, even though you're part of history. I don't talk about it often. My manager includes that as part of my introduction to others. It's still a bitter taste in my mouth. No, I don't joke about it. Other guys might have done better than me in moving past it. I have not."

Kevin Lamar, a backup nose guard who was L-2, just to the left of Briehl, became a senior executive for sports fitness and consumer packaging companies in Boulder, Colorado. He remains convinced that he had stopped Garner. "It was such a pinnacle moment," Lamar told me. "Then we had the rug ripped out from under us. How could the referees not take control back of the game?

"When someone learns that I went to Stanford, it will inevitably come up," Lamar added. "They'll ask, 'Did you ever see that play?' I'll say, 'I'll do you one better. I was *part* of The Play.' But it's this gnawing feeling like you let your teammates down."

Kevin Baird, a starting cornerback for Stanford who was L-5, forced Cal's Richard Rodgers to make his second lateral to Ford. Baird went on to become an attorney in England. "Most people don't understand, even my wife," he said. "They think it must have been cool. There's no glory to that. I'm still somewhat on the bitter side. It doesn't make me proud of who I am. I am not glad I was part of that play."

Dave Wyman was a backup linebacker who was R-3 on Stanford's kickoff team. He went on to play in the NFL for the Seattle Seahawks and Denver Broncos and became a popular sports talk radio broadcaster and color radio analyst for Seahawks football games. "It wasn't a cool event in my life," said Wyman, who also tackled Garner. "It's not like it stings, but it's not something I like to joke about."

Barry Cromer, a backup safety who was R-4 on the kickoff team, went on to become an orthopedic surgeon in Las Cruces, New Mexico. "With replay, The Play never would have stood," said Cromer, who forced Rodgers to make his first lateral to Garner. "At first, I was angry and bitter. I've gotten over that. When the topic comes up now, there's always a twinge of pain and bitterness. But that historic aspect, I guess I'm grateful for it. It was a special event. I just happened to be in the right place at the right time. It was my 15 minutes of fame. All 22 of us who were on the field have something in common."

Steve Lemon, a backup safety who was L-4 for Stanford, tried to grab Rodgers the first time he had the ball and was one of three Stanford players who, seconds later, converged to tackle Ford just after he lateraled the ball to Moen. During the Christmas break a month later, Lemon was watching a bowl game on TV with his dad at home in Portland when The Play flashed on the screen. "You should have made the tackle," Lemon's dad told him. Lemon bolted from the room and started crying. His father wasn't trying to be hurtful, but Lemon felt the weight of what had happened. It was like re-opening a wound.

That scar has now healed. "There are so many more important things in life—your kids, your job, how you interact with others, people you love," said Lemon, who became a bond trader in Portland. "I'm not thrilled with the result, although people say you were part of history. It's mind-boggling that it happened. We have to own up to it as a team. We screwed up. They took advantage of it. We screwed up, and the refs did, too."

Mark Harmon kicked the apparent winning field goal for Stanford and then squibbed the final kickoff. He went on to handle claims for Liberty Mutual in his native state of Oregon. "I didn't like talking about it for a while," he said. "But it doesn't hurt my feelings to talk about it anymore."

Vincent White, the running back who scored both of Stanford's touchdowns in the 1982 Big Game, has also gotten over his disappointment and bitterness. "My kids bring it up to me when it's on TV. They say, 'Dad, dad, that play's on.' I don't even want to look at it," said White, who went to become a high school and college football coach. "We didn't like the outcome at the time, but now it's pretty exciting. It's kind of funny."

Cal fans still believe that John Elway sounded like a crybaby when he angrily blamed the referees for the defeat immediately after the game. Here's what Elway said: "They ruined my last game as a college football player, just like they ruined it for every senior on our team. It's a joke. I'm usually a very positive person, and I don't want to cut people down, but that really burns me up...I'm going to be thinking about this one the rest of my life. We got screwed out of it."

Decades later, Elway explained his thinking to me: "After you have that great drive and you go down and kick what you think is the winning field goal, it gives you the chance to extend your college career, play with your college buddies for one more game, go to a bowl game—and then it's taken away with one play, one of those historic plays. It's disappointing. I always look back and say there's a reason for that. I've been fortunate enough to play in more Super Bowls than most. I guess it all evens out."

Five months after The Play, Elway was the first pick in the 1983 NFL Draft. He starred for the Broncos during 16 seasons, becoming the first quarterback to lead his team to the Super Bowl five times. Denver lost the first three badly but won the last two during Elway's final two years. He retired on top and went on to open a chain of restaurants and own several successful car dealerships. Elway was also the Broncos' general manager when they won the Super Bowl again in 2016.

In time, Elway could joke about the wild ending to the 1982 Big Game. "Each year it gets a little funnier," he acknowledged when he was inducted into the College Football Hall of Fame. Then he added: "We just wish we had the band come out for some tackling practice."

Blamed by some students and alums for the devastating loss, Stanford band members were mortified after The Play. That didn't last long, however. The band's compulsion for irreverent fun returned in time for the 1983 Big Game when the band spoofed the crazy defeat one year earlier. During the pregame show, band members spelled out SORRY and took the blame for…the decline of the Roman Empire and California earthquakes. In the next formation, the band spelled BUT, while the announcer explained the band *wasn't* taking the blame for The Play.

During the halftime show, the band identified the culprit by forming an arrow that pointed at Tyrrell, who had been pushed onto the field in a wheelchair. Tyrrell, wearing a neck brace as if he had been injured, was identified as "the official scapegoat of the 1982 Big Game." During another formation, band members dressed as Cal football players lateraled the ball as they ran down the field. As the faux Cal players neared Tyrrell, he leaped out of the wheelchair, grabbed the football, and ran the length of the field for a touchdown. Stanford students in the stands went nuts, chanting, "Gary! Gary! Gary!"

In later years, the band's mischievous antics got it banned from several venues, including the state of Oregon, the University of Notre Dame, and Disneyland.

Days after the 1982 Big Game, the Stanford employees who oversaw the Axe hung a giant screw in the otherwise empty trophy case to signify the university's feelings about The Play. They also placed a small typewritten piece of paper underneath the screw with a saying attributed to Admiral Yamamoto after the Japanese attack on Pearl Harbor on December 7, 1941: "I fear all we have done is to awaken a sleeping giant."

In fact, Stanford's football team went 1–10 in 1983, its worst season in 23 years. The biggest factor for the downturn was the graduation of Elway and several other key starters, but many players and coaches told me the team had never fully recovered from The Play.

Stanford coach Paul Wiggin was fired, even as he remained widely admired and liked as a stand-up guy. Two years later, the Minnesota Vikings hired him as their defensive line coach.

Decades later, Wiggin no longer remained bitter about The Play. "Father Time has a way of healing," he said.

Here's the balm: Wiggin spent more than 30 seasons working for the Vikings and is still a team consultant, while coaching friends bounced from team to team or were forced out of football earlier than they would have wished. "I got to live a life that was happy with family," Wiggin said. "[The Play] was absolutely a blessing in disguise."

When they look back, football players typically express a strong connection with their former teammates—the shared experience of competing against each other during practice, traveling to and from games, engaging in hand-to-hand combat as they try to defeat the other team. But the bonds of Cal's 1982 football team seem especially close thanks to The Play. "How many teams have won on the final play with five laterals and running through the band? None," explained Ron Lynn, the defensive coordinator, who spent 50 years in football.

After Harmon's field goal put Stanford ahead 20–19, with four seconds left for the final kickoff, "If you were a gambler, you would have bet your house that Stanford would win," Lynn said. "We ended up going from being downtrodden to complete ecstasy over a few seconds. The post-game locker room is something you can never forget."

Lynn ended up forging an especially close relationship with his players even as he worked for a series of teams in the NFL and college football, including nearly a decade at Stanford. Four decades after the 1982 Big Game, Lynn was part of a group text with 20 Bears players.

His relationship with Gary Plummer has been especially intriguing. As related in chapter seven, Plummer was determined during his first practice at Cal as a junior walk-on to show naysayers that he was big enough to play in the Pac-10. In his first drill, Plummer exploded out of his stance and bowled over the center opposite him. "Oooooo!" his teammates murmured in admiration. Two days later, Lynn named him as the starting nose guard but did not award him a scholarship. The slight infuriated Plummer. He had more than pride at stake. Dollars were stretched thin in his household, and he would have a tough time staying in school without the financial aid.

Plummer barged into Lynn's office and demanded the scholarship that he said Lynn had promised him if he became a starter. Lynn replied that he had never made such a pledge. "I was incensed," Plummer remembered years later. "I began screaming and poking my finger in his chest. I was ready to choke him to death. I remember this like it was yesterday."

Another Cal coach came into the office and pulled Plummer away. He played that fall without a scholarship and ran out of money when the quarter ended. Plummer then received his scholarship.

After playing as an undersized nose tackle in his senior year, Plummer was deemed too small to play in the NFL. Lynn, however, wanted him to play in the new United States Football League for the Oakland Invaders, where Lynn had become the defensive coordinator. There, Lynn helped Plummer become a star linebacker. When the league folded after three years, Lynn became the defensive coordinator for the San Diego Chargers and convinced the head coach to give Plummer a chance. The team did, and he ended up starting 106 of 119 games during eight seasons there. Plummer called himself a "flesh bomb," taking pride at how he launched himself into ball carriers full throttle. "Most coordinators didn't think players could absorb an understanding of the plays," Plummer told me. "Ron wanted you to learn. He'd tell us why we were playing the coverages we were playing and the weaknesses and what to expect the offense to audibilize to. It was nice to be treated as someone who wasn't just a dumb jock. He spent extra time to help me understand what was happening on the field."

Plummer left the Chargers and signed with the San Francisco 49ers in 1994. Their coach? George Seifert, who had told Plummer 15 years earlier that he wasn't big enough to play at Stanford. Plummer starred for the 49ers and won a Super Bowl championship with them in 1995.

Still, Plummer didn't forget about Lynn. One day about 15 years later, Lynn was coaching at Stanford (of all places) when he received a heads-up call from Plummer that he was sending something to Lynn's office. It was a framed jersey signed by Plummer. "There never would have been a jersey without Ron Lynn and his belief in me," he told me.

Of course, the oversized personality on Cal's 1982 team was Kapp. After the Bears' 7–4 season that year, he lasted four more seasons as the team's head coach. But he never had another winning season. The critics who had questioned hiring someone who had never previously coached were right: the game had passed him by, and he never caught up. Kapp finished with a 20–34–1 record at Cal. Nonetheless, Kapp's oversized love and respect for the university never dimmed.

Kapp's bravado and machismo also continued to burn bright. In 2011, he made headlines after exchanging punches with an old Canadian Football League adversary, Angelo Mosca, at a luncheon. Kapp greeted Mosca that day by reviving an old accusation that Mosca had deliberately injured one of Kapp's teammates during the 1963 Grey Cup. Mosca responded at the luncheon by hitting Kapp on the head with his cane. Kapp knocked him down with a punch.

Ron Rivera became the most famous member of Cal's 1982 team. A linebacker, he played nine years for the Chicago Bears—including on the squad that won the Super Bowl in 1985—and went on to serve as the head coach of the Carolina Panthers and then the Washington Commanders. For Rivera, The Play instilled the notion that "it's not over until it's over. It's been a constant reminder."

Gale Gilbert, Cal's starting quarterback in 1982, lasted 10 years in the NFL as a backup quarterback. But he has the unenviable distinction of having played for five losing Super Bowl teams in a row, the first four with the Buffalo Bills, then with San Diego in 1995. After his career ended, Gilbert lived in Austin where he ran a trucking company. One of his sons, Garrett, also bounced around the NFL as a backup quarterback.

Reggie Camp, the defensive end who repeatedly stymied Elway and Stanford in the 1982 Big Game, played six years in the NFL. He would remember ruefully that he was on the wrong end of two back-and-forth playoff games with the Cleveland Browns against Elway's Broncos, one known as "The Drive" and the other as "The Fumble." "I'm 1–2 against him," Camp recalled with a pained smile.

More importantly, Camp took great pride in learning to control his anger from the rejection of his biological father. Here's the most telling example of this: in practice one day at Cal, he had erupted in rage against an offensive lineman named Brian Hillesland and knocked him unconscious. In time, the two became friends, vacationing together as adults, and Camp was in Hillesland's wedding party.

Camp also fulfilled a promise to his mother that he would graduate from Cal and became the doting husband and father that he wished his father had been. Camp also became a role model in Stockton, California, as the head coach of a high school football team.

John Tuggle, who gained 97 yards on 28 rushes in the 1982 Big Game for Cal, was chosen by the New York Giants as the last player taken in the 1983 draft. That won him the title "Mr. Irrelevant." But Tuggle won respect and admiration by making the team that fall and becoming a standout on special teams. Three years later, however, he was dead of cancer. The Giants honored him by wearing a sticker with his number, 38, on their helmets during the 1986 season when they won the Super Bowl.

Joe Starkey, who made The Play's famous radio call, continued broad-casting Cal football games, a job he had begun in 1975, through at least 2022. He also broadcast San Francisco 49ers games from 1989 to 2008.

The four Cal players who lateraled the ball on the final kickoff seemed destined to be a band of brothers, linked with other great multi-player sports legends, such as baseball's Tinker-to-Evers-to-Chance. But a dark cloud now hovers over Moen-to-Rodgers-to-Garner-to-Rodgers-to-Ford-to-Moen. Ford was arrested and charged with homicide for the brutal killings of his pregnant 31-year-old wife Tess and their three-year-old son Mariet Jr. at their home in Elk Grove, California, on January 16, 1997.

At the time, Ford was a 35-year-old sales rep for a company that installed voicemail systems. He had entered the working world after playing briefly for three teams in the Canadian Football League and getting cut by the NFL's Atlanta Falcons near the end of training camp.

Circumstantial evidence convinced a jury to convict Ford on April 22, 1998. Ford has always maintained his innocence, pointing to the lack of physical evidence tying him to the crime. Mark Curry, the chief prosecu-tor, wrote a book on the murder, investigation, and trial. He called it *The Final Play* to remind Ford "of the truth and to prevent him from forgetting."

Ford's teammates remain shocked that he could have committed such a heinous crime. "It was not the Mariet we ever knew," said Rich Stachowski, a Cal defensive lineman, in a remark echoed by teammates.

Ford has made several attempts to overturn his 45-year sentence, but none have succeeded. His role in the final kickoff seems to be a fond, recur-ring memory as he spends year after year at a maximum security prison. "When I get very depressed, I think back to that game," Ford told the *San Francisco Chronicle* in 2002. "It brings me joy. I have a place I can always go [mentally]. That one moment of time keeps me going."

Ford was the only one of the 22 players on the field for The Play that I didn't interview. He didn't respond to any of the three letters I sent to him at Folsom State Prison.

Garner provided the pivot point of The Play. It was when he was stopped that Stanford players and band members raced onto the field, thinking

Stanford had just won the Big Game. "I still smile when I see it," Garner said about The Play. "I'm still proud to have been a part of it. I'm humbled that I was a part of history, and it's a testament to never give up, to the proverbial last second." Garner became a risk manager for a health company in Coral Springs, Florida.

Rodgers, the special teams captain for Cal known as "The Rock," inspired his teammates to keep the ball alive during the final kickoff. After he graduated from Cal, he signed with the Oakland Raiders and survived until the last cut. After a month of playing in Canada, he spent five years in the Arena Football League.

The Play, Rodgers said years later, "brought me out of my shell about what I could do. It gave me more reason to become a coach." What better example of your ability to motivate others than the way his teammates made history by listening to his admonition not to fall on the football? "When I stand in front of anybody, I know now I have the ability to lead and encourage them," he said.

Rodgers began as an assistant at Diablo Valley Community College, near Berkeley, in 1989, and then slowly worked his way up the coaching ladder. Rivera gave him his first NFL job with the Panthers in 2012 and then brought Rodgers with him after he was fired by Carolina and hired by Washington.

Rodgers' son Richard became a tight end in the NFL. In 2015, Richard II caught a Hail Mary pass from Aaron Rodgers, who starred at Cal, to stun the Detroit Lions. News stories couldn't help but note the connection to his father and the outcome of the 1982 Big Game.

Moen fielded Harmon's kickoff in the 1982 Big Game, lateraled the ball when he saw he couldn't advance, collected the fifth and final lateral seconds later, and then improbably became the most famous football player in the history of Cal football. In the coming weeks and months, Moen was toasted at alumni events, and he and several of his teammates threw out the opening pitch at an Oakland A's baseball game in 1983. After graduation, he taught history for several years before becoming a real estate investor back home in the southern part of Los Angeles County. Among his mementos:

the Wilson football, given to him in the locker room after the 1982 Big Game, that brought him immortality.

Reminders of The Play would die down over time but not completely. At the 2018 Big Game, fans received a bobblehead doll of Moen. "I run into people all the time who have a tale about the game or leaving early or not being there," Moen told me. "It's fun getting people's perspective of that moment. I know where I was."

Indeed he does, and so do the rest of us.

Moen's parents taught him to be humble, not to call attention to himself, and that comes through when I asked him how he looks back on The Play years later. "What that play has done is connected that team to a special event," he said. "The highlight is being able to share memories about a special moment."

Moen went on to call it "a highlight of my life." But, he added, "it never really changed my life. It wasn't a defining moment. It was something I was a part of, but it's not who I am."

The cover photograph of this book shows Moen celebrating his touchdown, mid-leap. A saxophone on the turf just behind him belonged to Scott DeBarger, a sophomore bandsman. Just as Moen crossed into the end zone, he clipped DeBarger, knocking the tenor sax out of his hands. Amidst the mayhem, DeBarger thought Moen was being a sore loser, running with the ball even though the game had ended. Minutes later, after Cal's Victory Cannon had sounded and it became clear Moen had actually scored the winning touchdown, DeBarger thought, *Uh, oh. We'd better get out of here.* He remembered it as "the quietest bus ride I was ever on with the Stanford band." DeBarger, an engineer, now oversees large construction projects for the Stanford Linear Accelerator, better known as SLAC.

Standing just to the right of Moen in the photo was Dwayne Virnau, a junior trombone player. Virnau was looking toward the field because he thought all of the commotion there signified Cal fans had encroached onto the turf. That meant he might be at risk. Virnau and his bandmates were in enemy territory at Memorial Stadium, after all. They were wearing hard hats to protect themselves from the Cal students throwing fruit from the stands.

As with DeBarger, Virnau knew something had gone terribly wrong when he heard the cannon's explosion. Time has allowed Virnau, now retired in his native Texas after working for Stanford's information technology department, to put The Play into perspective. "There's a certain amount of pride of having been there," he said. "I was part of history."

Racing to get away from Moen to the left was Jamison Smeltz, a freshman alto sax player. "We headed to the field for the end of the game," Smeltz recalled. "It looked like we were going to win. In band mode, you wait for the whistle and run. If you don't hear the whistle and everyone starts running, you run anyway. You follow the herd. I was at the back of the end zone and took off running. I then saw there was still activity. I turned around and started to run away. Kevin just missed me. I was thinking, *Oh, man. We screwed up big time. There will be some consequences.*" Smeltz went on to become a band teacher in, of all places, Berkeley. He took delight in showing the photo as an icebreaker.

The bandsman cowering in the photograph was Stu Weiss. "I wandered into the end zone," he said. "The next thing I know, I saw a Cal football player running toward me. I turned to get the hell out of the way. He weighed 230 pounds and was wearing body armor. I probably weighed 170 pounds." Weiss had graduated from Stanford the preceding June but returned to play that day, a not uncommon practice. "It was about 20 years later before I realized it was me in the photo," he said. Weiss, who obtained a PhD from Stanford in biological sciences, is the chief scientist for Creekside Center for Earth Observation, based in Menlo Park, next to Stanford. He seeks ways to conserve endangered butterfly populations and other endangered species. "Now I use that photo a lot when I give presentations, especially at Berkeley," Weiss said. "People just crack up."

When Moen crashed into Tyrrell in the end zone, he only felt a thump. He didn't know what or who he had hit as he celebrated the winning score. Moen and Tyrrell first met each other about a month later when a TV variety show invited both to a taping in Los Angeles. Tyrrell wore his band uniform and appeared with a broken-down trombone. Moen pulled

$500 out of the trombone's bell and told Tyrrell he could use it to buy a new instrument.

In reality, Tyrrell's trombone suffered no damage when Moen bowled him over because Tyrrell artfully kept his instrument from hitting the ground as he landed on his butt and rolled to his side. He later donated the trombone to the College Football Hall of Fame, where it is on display.

Tyrrell had a second trombone while at Stanford. Shortly after the 1982 Big Game, his fraternity threw a party. Tyrrell returned to his room later that night to find an open window and one thing missing from his room—the second trombone. It was only the latest prank theft by students at one university or the other over the years. Tyrrell, who became a chief financial officer in Silicon Valley, learned from me later that a Cal alum had it and viewed it as war booty.

Tyrrell didn't mind. By then, he had appeared at countless Cal events marking one anniversary or another of the 1982 Big Game. A good sport, he became a favorite of Cal grads.

Tyrrell and Moen even became friends after appearing at so many events together. "We converse and talk about family, work, and sports," Tyrrell told me. "We're compatible, and there was no animosity at all on my end."

Their routine became so familiar that "It's almost like we can finish each other's lines with the questions," Tyrrell said.

Their camaraderie is evident whenever Moen good-naturedly quips, "If you're out there, you better be ready to play!" Tyrrell ripostes that Moen ought to be prepared to give him his best shot.

The two men at a young age were on the opposite side of the wildest finish ever to a college football game. Four decades later, Moen appreciates that they've gotten to know each other. "It's a good respectful relationship of two guys from rival schools.

"He was in the wrong place at the wrong time," Moen added. "But he has never complained about getting hit."

ACKNOWLEDGMENTS

The idea for this book began in the most improbable of places—a big out-door jacuzzi at the Northstar resort near Lake Tahoe. My daughter, Luciana, and I were enjoying the soothing hot jets there in December 2016 after a day of skiing when another family joined us. I began talking to the other dad. He introduced himself as Kris Van Gieson, and he soon learned that I graduated from Stanford. Kris, a 1987 Cal grad, immediately began giving me crap about the 1982 Big Game—the Stanford band, the unbelievable ending, John Elway's post-game lament. Luciana, 14, looked on, uncompre-hending. Of course, I riposted with Kris by noting how Cal hadn't played in the Rose Bowl since 1959 and that Stanford won the title for the most successful athletic department year after year. We thrust and parried for a few more minutes, smiling throughout. Cal and Stanford are good-natured rivals off the field, after all. Kris and I parted on friendly terms.

Back at the condo where Luciana and I were staying, I pulled out my laptop. I had to show her what Kris and I had talked about. Midway through watching The Play, with Joe Starkey screaming, "And the band is out on the field!", tears welled in my eyes. What happened that day was such a touchstone for me—I grew up in Palo Alto attending Stanford football games and then played trombone for four years in the Stanford band, before my graduation in June 1982. I knew most of the band members on the field that day, including the immortal Gary Tyrrell. I listened to a radio feed of the game while in Washington, D.C., at an event for Stanford and Cal alums. When Stanford kicked the "winning" field goal, my buddies and I gave a "Give 'em the Axe" yell and went off to celebrate the last-minute victory. I didn't know Cal had actually won until I picked up *The Washington Post* the next morning.

I remembered all of this at the condo as I closed my laptop. I smiled and thought: *I have to write a book on that game!*

So, Kris, here's a big thanks to you for inspiring me.

In all, I interviewed about 375 people for the book, and some of the interviews lasted four hours. Why such an effort? Besides wanting to know the story, I kept looking for better and better anecdotes and behind-the-scenes details. With the same thinking, I copied articles from nine different newspapers on the 1982 seasons for Cal and Stanford, more than 1,500 articles in all. That was step one, I learned. Step two was turning each article, now a PDF, into a searchable Word file. How could I do that? My friend David Siegel came to the rescue by running an optical character recognition (OCR) program on my laptop that converted each PDF into a Word file. Still, it took me more than a year to complete step three: getting a clean Word document by comparing each PDF original with each newly-created Word file to eliminate the garble created during the OCR process. Boy, was I happy when I had completed that chore.

Among the long list of people I want to thank, I'll begin with John Elway. Over Zoom one day in 2021, he narrated Stanford's final drive as we watched the game video together, and he also talked about his Stanford days, including the 1981 game against San Jose State and his father Jack. John and I talked again in preparation for his foreword, and I thank him for agreeing to write it.

I also want to thank Ron Rivera for answering my questions for two hours one morning in 2021 during my research phase and also for writing his foreword.

I sought to interview all 22 players who made history by being on the field during The Play. I interviewed 21 of them. For Stanford: Mark Andrew, Kevin Baird, Tom Briehl, Barry Cromer, Jack Gilmete, Darrell Grissum, Mark Harmon, Kevin Lamar, Steve Lemon, Mike Noble, and Dave Wyman. For Cal: Steve Dunn, Dwight Garner, Wes Howell, David Lewis, Tim Lucas, Kevin Moen, Richard Rodgers, Scott Smith, Ron Story, and Garey Williams. The only player I missed was Cal's Mariet Ford. He didn't respond to the three letters I sent him at Folsom State Prison.

I also sought to interview all of the 13 Stanford players who played at some point during the Cardinal's last-minute drive and all 11 Cal defenders. From Stanford: Jeff Deaton, Mike Dotterer, Chris Dressel, John Elway, Dennis Engel, Emile Harry, Matt Moran, Eric Mullins, Chris Rose, Mike Teeuws (he later changed his last name to Tevis), Mike Tolliver, and Vincent White. I missed one player: Stanford fullback Greg Hooper died in 2016, before I could interview him. From Cal: Ahmad Anderson, Reggie Camp, Gary Plummer, Richard Rodgers, Byron Smith, Rich Stachowski, Jimmy Stewart, John Sullivan, Eddie Walsh, and Fred Williams. I missed one Cal player: Clemont Williams did not respond to repeated phone calls.

Other players on Stanford's 1982 team I interviewed: Steve Aimonetti, Shaun Avant, Kevin Bates, Jim Clymer, Steve Cottrell, Rod Gilmore, Charles Hutchings, Terry Jackson, Pat Mitchell, Rob Moore, Ken Orvick, Billy Reed, Garin Veris, Gary Wimmer, and Mike Wyman.

Other players on Cal's 1982 team: Mike Ahr, Andy Bark, Gregg Beagle, Kevin Brown, Joe Cooper, Gale Gilbert, Matt Grimes, Brian Hillesland, Rance McDougald, Steve Pas, Harvey Salem, Tim Smith, and J Torchio.

Paul Wiggin graciously allowed me to interview him for 10 hours at his home outside of Minneapolis during one weekend in 2019. Now I know firsthand why everyone thinks he's such a terrific person. Tom Wiggin, a younger brother, and Jerry Angove, a Stanford teammate, provided perspective on Paul Wiggin for me. Thanks to other Stanford coaches I interviewed: Jim Anderson, Jim Fassel (three months before he died in June 2021), Ray Handley, Pete Mangurian, Mike Nolan, Dave Ottmar, Steve Schulz, and Fred von Appen.

Other Stanford athletic department officials from 1982: Stuart Epstein (student manager), Andy Geiger (athletic director), Michael Go (who had just stepped down as head trainer), Steve Raczynski (assistant sports information director), Meryl Robertson (equipment manager), and Bob Rose (sports information director).

Joe Kapp's health did not permit me to interview him. But thanks to his 1982 coaches: Al Borges, Bill Cooper, Ed Hall, Ron Lynn (who deserves extra thanks), and Nate Wright.

Other people associated with Cal football in 1982: Mike Arellano (equipment manager), Gordon Barr (stadium worker), Doug Cohn (stadium worker), Howard Comrie (stadium worker), Ed Gordon (play-by-play typist for the stat crew in the press box), Ross Hering (a student who was assistant senior manager), Robert Latin (scoreboard operator), Shawn Linder (stadium worker), Dave Maggard (athletic director), Mike Matthews (assistant sports information director), John McCasey (sports information director), Paul Mohler (assistant athletic trainer), Michael Moss (assistant athletic director), Eric Naftaly (statistician for defensive plays in the press box), Steve Oldenbourg (a 14-year-old water boy), Bob Orr (head athletic trainer), Kevin Reneau (assistant sports director), Blake Rothfuss (a student who was senior manager), Ron Salvemini (assistant equipment manager), Dave Stenger (assistant athletic trainer), and Cyril "Bulldog" Turner (security for the football team). Orr and Turner have since passed on.

The Play has kept its renown at least in part because of the legendary call by Starkey, Cal's veteran play-by-play announcer. Thanks to Joe for our two lengthy interviews and also to Len Shapiro, his statistician, and Mickey Luckoff, then the general manager at KGO-AM, which broadcast the Bears' games.

Thanks to Jim Grundberg and Joe Mitchner, who called the game for KZSU, Stanford's student-run radio station. Thanks also to four people involved with the production of the Stanford TV highlights show: Gary Cavalli, the executive producer; Niels Melo, who oversaw the production and editing; Gordy Ceresino, the color announcer; and Bob Reynolds, a switcher in the TV truck.

Thanks to Terry Shuchat, the videographer of Stanford's football team, and Kevin Reid, who processed the video.

Thanks to Brad Williams, a hero for Stanford at the 1974 Big Game, for not only recalling how he impersonated George C. Scott's opening monologue from *Patton* after a Stanford practice before the 1982 Big Game, but also reenacting it for me as well.

I interviewed all five surviving referees from the 1982 Big Game. They are Ron Blum, the alternate official; Jim Fogltance, the field judge; Jack Langley, the head linesman; Gordon Riese, line judge; and Walt Wolf, the umpire.

I interviewed a number of journalists who were at the game: Michael Bryant, *San Jose Mercury News* photographer; David Bush, *San Francisco Chronicle* sportswriter; John Crumpacker, *San Francisco Examiner* sportswriter; Dan Hruby, *San Jose Mercury News* sports columnist; Kristin Huckshorn, *San Jose Mercury News* sportswriter; Jim Mendenhall, *San Jose Mercury News* photographer; Dave Newhouse, *Oakland Tribune* columnist; and Sid Spaeth, *The Stanford Daily* co-sports editor.

Jim Stinnett shared memories of his father, Robert, who shot the game's most famous photograph for the *Oakland Tribune*, one that graces the book's cover. To recount his dad's activities that day, I also interviewed five journalists who worked then for the *Oakland Tribune*: Leba Hertz, Sunday sports editor; Dave LoVecchio, assistant sports editor; Ron Riesterer, photographer; Jack Rux, sports copy editor; John Simmonds, assistant sports editor.

Thanks to Coy Collinsworth and Jim Simmons, the two Hall of Fame Bowl representatives who offered their recollections.

Thanks to Cal and Stanford fans in the stands who reminisced about that memorable day: Jim Branson (Cal), Jean Greaves (Stanford), Steven Hinds (Cal), Julia Kennedy (who watched the game in the press box with her father, Stanford president Donald Kennedy), Chuck Machlin (Stanford), Donne Moen (Kevin's father), Marsha Moen (Kevin's mother), Pete Neville (Cal), Jim Rutter (Stanford—and thanks also to Jim for sharing his extensive 1982 memorabilia), Jim Smith (Cal), and Curt Wilson (Stanford).

Thanks to two buddies of Elway's from the baseball team for describing how they ended up on the field during The Play: Mike Aldrete and Vince Sakowski.

Thanks to five of Elway's teammates at Granada Hills High School for offering their reminisces. They are Paul Bergmann, Nick Macias, Scott Marshall, Paul Scheper, and Chris Sutton.

My thanks to members of the Stanford band in 1982 begin with Tyrrell. Besides Gary: Lynn Baker, Arthur Barnes (the band director), the late Robby Beyers (the band photographer), Lou Casagrande, Scott DeBarger, Scott Gode, Disco Ray Gruenewald (the drum major), John Howard (the band manager), Jim Kohn, Ben Langlotz, Bill Martin, Hal Mickelson (the band announcer), Richey Neuman, Jamison Smeltz, Simon Streets, Dwayne Virnau, and Stu Weiss.

I conducted a fun Zoom interview with the four surviving Dollies from 1982: Gina Moreno, Sue Cameron, Melinda Myers, and Betsy DePalma. I'm identifying them by their maiden names.

I researched the history of the transformation of the Stanford band from being a near-clone to the Cal band in 1962 to becoming just the opposite. So thanks to Ron Bannerman (band member on the 1970 trip to Arkansas), Sam Boot (band member on the 1970 trip to Arkansas), Rich Brown (1962 band manager), Charlie Carrera (1968 and 1969 band manager), Phillip Cline, 1987 grad who served as the band's unofficial historian and archivist), Chuck Donnelley (1966 band manager), Linda Haines (late 1960s band member), Alex Jardetzky (1978 band manager), Geordie Lawry (1969 and 1970 drum major), Bernie Mayer (1964 band manager), Andy Paul (1968 drum major), Bob Pearce (1964 drum major), Ken Peterson (1970 band manager), Steve Ritchie (1975 drum major), Doug Rosene (1967 band manager), Frank Robertson (band member in the 1960s and the 1990s), Roy Stehle (1960 and 1961 band manager), Eric Strandberg (band member in the mid-1970s), Bob Tiffany (band member in the mid-1970s), Gary Wilson (1963 solo trumpet player), and Si Yates (1965 band manager).

It was a pleasure to interview a number of Cal band members from 1982: Pete Alvarez (the assistant band director), Dave Bowen, Gary Bowen, Dennis Cohen (senior band manager), John Gibson, Betty Kaufman, Ron Keimach (the point of the wedge during the pregame opening formation), Leslie Louie, Steve McClaine, Jamie Rawson, Rob Rawson, Mark Stevenson, Bob Willis (drum major), and Lisa Willis. Michael Markowitz not only talked about the Cal band but provided special insight into the Big Week chemistry lecture tradition by his father Samuel.

To understand the role of the Axe at the 1982 Big Game and the history of the Axe, I turned repeatedly to Jon Erickson, a Stanford grad and longtime university employee. Thanks to the three Stanford students attached to the Axe at the '82 game: Kevin Wells, Max Scheder-Bieschin, and Helene Leckman; and to four Stanford grads, besides Erickson, who provided adult supervision that day: Steve Hansen, Barry Hennings, Keith Light, and Rick Miller.

Thanks to members of the Cal Rally Committee in 1982: Debbie Choate, Bob Hernandez, Gail Hoffmann, Karen Lingel, Leslie McNeill, Ken Raust, Tim Sheridon, Karen Toth, and Mark Weigand. Tom Edwards and Jamie Sutton, two Cal grads from the 1960s, described their performances at the Greek Theatre on the night before the 1982 Big Game.

To profile Kapp, I interviewed four of his Cal football teammates from the late 1950s (Tom Bates, Pete Domoto, Bob Gonzales, and Hank Olguin), one of his basketball teammates (Ned Averbuck), a UCLA tight end who scored three touchdowns against Kapp while playing defense in a 1955 freshman game (Craig Chudy), and a student assistant in the Cal athletic department news bureau in the late 1950s (Bob Steiner). I also interviewed Kapp's oldest son, J.J., and two of his teammates with the Minnesota Vikings (Dave Osborn and Gene Washington). Thanks to Chad Osterlund for putting me in touch with them.

It was fun talking to Jack Burgett about how he helped shape two key Cal players, Reggie Camp and Richard Rodgers, at Jefferson High School in Daly City.

To write about the hiring of Kapp and what happened during Cal's subsequent 1982 season, I had to understand the downfall of head coach Roger Theder in 1981. Thanks to three Cal coaches from that season: Al Saunders, Darrel "Mouse" Davis, and Rollie Morshead.

Chapter One tells the story of the climactic play of the 1980 Big Game. Besides Elway and Moen, I interviewed three Cal defenders (Steve Cacciari, Ron Coccimiglio, and Kirk Karacozoff) and three players on Stanford's offense (Jeff Haile, John Macaulay, and Andre Tyler).

To get background on Walsh, I interviewed Guy Benjamin and Steve Dils, his starting quarterbacks during Walsh's two years at Stanford. That was especially fun because I had watched them play at Stanford.

To write about Jack Elway, Bob Hiegert and Sam Winningham talked about him at Cal State Northridge, and Mike Price talked about their time together at Washington State.

To write about the 1981 Stanford–San Jose State game, John Elway's worst at Stanford, I interviewed Dave Baldwin, Tom Beckett, Rick Cook, Dennis Erickson, Claude Gilbert, Greg McMackin, and Jimmy Walsh from San Jose State's coaching staff and athletic department. I also interviewed two San Jose State players: Gill Byrd and Bob Overly. Dave Arslanian gave me insight into Overly from coaching him earlier at Snow College.

I interviewed eight of the 20 or so Stanford students and recent alums who concocted an elaborate plan to steal the Axe from Cal in 1981: Mark Breier, T.J. Heyman, Shauna Lehv, Doug Mitchell, Bob Moog, Terri Oppelt, Shaun Pickering, Eddie Poplawski.

Thanks to Tim Conway and David Suliteanu for sharing the incredible tale of how they stole the Axe from Cal at Ming's restaurant in 1973. I interviewed two of their Theta Delt fraternity brothers as well—Daniel Broderick and Steve Shupe—and two members of the football team who returned the Axe to Cal at the pregame coin toss: Mike Boryla and Randy Poltl. Thanks as well to James Atkinson for being willing to share his memories of being among the Cal students who lost the Axe at Ming's.

Thanks to two Cal grads for sharing their history of the Axe: Bart White and John Larissou. And to Claudia Temby for sharing her story as a Stanford student responsible for Axe security at the 1974 Big Game.

Special thanks to John Welborne for detailing how he stole the Axe from Stanford's Tresidder Memorial Union in 1967, and to his getaway driver, Pat Gilligan; to Michael Drewes for his role when the Axe resurfaced; and to Jay Miller, who chaired the Cal Rally Committee in 1967. I interviewed five members of Cal's 1967 football team for their memories on the Axe being brought to the locker room on the day before the Big Game. They were Barry Bronk, Eric Kastner, Mike McCaffrey, John McGaffie, and

Wayne Stewart. I interviewed a number of Stanford students who lived at the Stanford firehouse, just behind Tresidder, in 1967 or before: Barney Adler, Frank Bates, Bill Boller, Carl Boller, Doug Brubaker, Geoffrey Clarke, Phil Henderson, Ray Masson, David Pugh, Eric Rex, and Ross Smith.

Thanks to the three Cal students whom I called for information on the 1964 Treaty of Castle Lanes, which attempted to settle the theft of university totems: Chris Conrad, Robert Iding, and Mike Leite.

A number of Cal professors, university officials, and boosters lent a hand. They are Maya Goehring-Harris, Donna Houser, Pat Joseph, Nadesan Permaul, Bob Price, and Reza Sirafinejad.

For help finding old newspaper articles: Mike Hiserman, *Los Angeles Times*; Eric Sondheimer, *Los Angeles Times*; Shane Curtin, San Jose Public Library; Rosemary Van Lare, San Jose Public Library; Sarah Mallory, Central Arkansas Library System; Dean Smith, Bancroft Library at Cal; and Kathryn Neal, associate university archivist at Bancroft.

Thanks to Herb Benenson, Cal's sports information director, and Jonrie Davila at Stanford's office of development, for helping put me in touch with alums from their universities. Thanks to Steve Kroner from the *San Francisco Chronicle* for connecting me with several people early in my reporting.

I interviewed the main actors for my chapter on the fake newspaper version of *The Daily Cal*: Adam Berns, *The Stanford Daily* sports editor of the Card Today section; Wayne Brandt, *The Stanford Daily* production manager; Tony Kelly, *The Stanford Daily* entertainment editor; Richard Klingler, *The Stanford Daily* editor; Allen Matthews, *The Daily Cal* reporter; Tom Mulvoy, Knight Fellow at Stanford who wrote the lead story; Tom Nelson, advertising manager for *The Stanford Daily*; Anita Seline, student representative to *The Daily Cal* editorial board; Dan Woo, editor in chief of *The Daily Cal*; and Mark Zeigler, *The Stanford Daily* sports editor of the Cardinal Today section.

For photos, thanks to Jim Stinnett, Andrea Geyling, Chuck Machlin, Herb Benenson, Art Streiber, Josh Schneider, the university archivist at Stanford, and Bill Beyers, the executor of Robby Beyers' estate. Robby, the

Stanford band photographer for decades, left us too early, after heroically battling ALS.

I owe a huge thanks to my Stanford buddy Glenn Sorensen, and to Kevin Kearney, a brother-in-law, for reading the entire manuscript and offering edits and comments. They improved it immeasurably. I want to extend to Kevin the same offer I gave to Glenn with an earlier book: free sushi for life! And for Glenn: more free sushi for life! Special thanks to Michael Fitzgerald, my Nieman Fellowship friend, for editing Chapter 12, the first chapter I wrote. Thanks also to a Stanford classmate, Pete Frost, for reading a number of chapters, and to Bruce Heiman and John Mannion, both former band managers, for reading the section on the Stanford band.

Lots of love and thanks to Nayana Abeysinghe for putting up with my need to spend so many nights and weekends working on the manuscript.

I hit the lottery when Kathleen Hall Jamieson emailed me one day in 2020 to ask if I wanted a writing fellowship that fall at the University of Pennsylvania's Annenberg Public Policy Center. Kathleen and I had become acquainted when we were Shorenstein Fellows at Harvard University during the fall of 2017, and she wanted to tap into my experience from having covered David Duke and the far right as her team surveyed voters in the run-up to the polarized 2020 presidential election. Covid, alas, scrubbed that plan. But Kathleen was kind enough to offer me the same fellowship a year later. This gave me an uninterrupted opportunity to write the manuscript. I'm grateful that Kathleen's husband Bob stopped by my office from time to time to offer support and reveal his astonishing knowledge of local history.

Thanks to Jonathan Eig, Jason Cole, and Ivan Maisel (all top-notch writers) for helping me prepare my book proposal.

Many, many thanks to Doug Grad, a terrific agent. He offers good advice, plenty of encouragement, and a willingness to stand up for his authors.

Thanks to Jeff Fedotin at Triumph Books for his careful editing and overseeing the numerous details required to turn a completed manuscript into a book. Thanks to Clarissa Young and Noah Amstadter at Triumph for seeing my vision.

Author Tyler Bridges performs with the Stanford band in 1980.
(Robby Beyers)

Sources

Books

100 Years of Blue & Gold, by Nick Peters

The Big Game, by John Sullivan

Blitzed by Blessings, by Bill Glass

Bud: The Other Side of the Glacier, by Bill McGrane

Elway: A Relentless Life, by Jason Cole

The Final Play, by Mark Curry

The Genius: How Bill Walsh Reinvented Football and Created an NFL Dynasty,
    by David Harris

Golden Bears, by Ron Fimrite, with new material by Peter Fimrite and
    David Bush

I Did It My Way: A Remarkable Journey to the Hall of Fame, by Bud Grant
    and Jim Bruton

The Toughest Chicano, by Joe Kapp, with J.J. Kapp, Robert G. Phelps, and
    Ned Averbuck

Pokey: The Good Fight, by Pokey Allen and Bob Evancho

The Stanford Axe, by R.G. O'Neil and J.F. van der Kamp

Who Let the Mexicans Play in the Rose Bowl?, by Hank Olguin

Documentaries

The Play, by Peter J. Vogt

Newspapers

Arkansas Democrat Gazette

Arkansas Gazette

Berkeley Daily Gazette

Chicago Tribune

Contra Costa Times

East Bay Times

Los Angeles Times

Oakland Tribune

Palo Alto Times

Portland State Vanguard

Rocky Mountain News

Salinas Californian

San Francisco Chronicle

San Francisco Examiner

San Jose Mercury News

San Mateo Times

Spartan Daily

The Boston Globe

The Christian Science Monitor

The Daily Californian

The Denver Post

The Modesto Bee

The New York Times

The Oklahoman

The Oregonian

The Peninsula Times Tribune

The Sacramento Bee

The (San Fernando) Valley News

The Stanford Daily

Magazines

California
Oui
Rolling Stone
Sports Illustrated
Stanford
The Sporting News
TRUE

University Resources

NCAA play-by-play summary and scoring summary for all Stanford games
    in 1982
NCAA play-by-play summary and scoring summary for the 1982 Big Game
1982 Big Game program
1982 Stanford Media Guide
1982 Cal Media Guide
1983 Stanford Media Guide
1983 Cal Media Guide
Stanford yearbooks
Stanford Band Handbooks

Websites

berkeley.edu
saecalbeta.org
espn.com
gettyimages.com
marietford.blogspot.com
musictimes.com
paloaltoonline.com
ruleoftree.com
sanfrancisco.cbslocal.com
stanford.edu

thesixfifty.com
youtube.com

Wire Services
Associated Press
United Press International